The Fight in the Clouds

The Fight in the Clouds

The Extraordinary Combat
Experience of P-51 Mustang Pilots
During World War II

James P. Busha

ZENITH PRESS

First published in 2014 by Zenith Press, a member of Quayside Publishing Group, 400 First Avenue North, Suite 400, Minneapolis, MN 55401 USA

© 2014 Zenith Press
Text © 2014 James P. Busha

All photographs are from Jack Cook unless noted otherwise.

Zenith Press titles are also available at discounts in bulk quantity for industrial or sales-promotional use. For details write to Special Sales Manager at Quayside Publishing Company, 400 First Avenue North, Suite 400, Minneapolis, MN 55401 USA.

To find out more about our books, join us online at www.zenithpress.com.

Library of Congress Cataloging-in-Publication Data
Busha, James P.
     The fight in the clouds : the extraordinary combat experience of
P-51 Mustang pilots during World War II / James P. Busha.
        pages cm
     ISBN 978-0-7603-4518-4 (hardcover)
     1. World War, 1939–1945—Aerial operations, American. 2. World War, 1939–1945—Personal narratives, American. 3. World War, 1939–1945—Campaigns. 4. Fighter pilots—United States—Biography. 5. Mustang (Fighter plane) I. Title.
     D790.B86 2014
     940.54'49730922—dc23
                2013043115

Editorial Director: Erik Gilg
Design Manager: James Kegley
Layout: Helena Shimizu
Cover Design: Andrew Brozyna

On the front cover: First Lieutenant Bob Eckfeldt in P-51B "Bald Eagle" leads a flight of four 376th FS P-51s over Germany in 1944.

Printed in the United States of America
10 9 8 7 6 5 4 3 2 1

To the Greatest Generation—For the heroes who didn't make it back.

Contents

Acknowledgments

PERSONAL ACKNOWLEDGMENTS

To my best friend, my moral navigator—my wife Jean. And to my daughter Caitlin, sons Charlie, Riley, and Benjamin: Without your love, unselfish understanding, and support, none of what I have written would have been possible. You are my most precious joy.

And to Doug Schultz, who gave me my first ride in a P-51 Mustang so many years ago, and taught me to take no day for granted. I think of you often and wish you were still with us. I miss you, my friend

ACKNOWLEDGMENTS

I blame many wonderful people in my life for encouraging me to write *The Fight in the Clouds*. Some were kind in lending a helping hand while I pursued this project to preserve history by capturing the words of these brave men who flew and fought for our country's freedoms and democracy. Others shoved me forward, never allowing me to quit.

I guess I blame my fellow L-bird flying buddy, award-winning Warbird aircraft restorer Sam Taber, the most. Sam was the first to shove a pen and a legal pad in my hand, and he introduced me to the unsung heroes of World War II. From that very first interview I was hooked and vowed to interview as many wartime pilots as I could find. Fifteen years later, with hundreds of interviews completed, the conversations have begun to slow to a trickle. It's not from the lack of trying; it is, unfortunately, because we are losing this great generation at a rapid rate. As they pass, so too do their remarkable experiences.

I blame others, such as my great friend John Dibbs, who has been a true inspiration and a constant source of encouragement. We have teamed up countless times together in the past. His stunning photographs make the veteran's stories come to life. I owe a debt of gratitude to another wonderful comrade, world-renowned aviation author and editor Budd Davisson. His constant drive for perfection and his passion for aviation history are second to none. And although he has been relentless with deadlines and caused many sleepless nights, Budd is truly a rare breed of man who will not settle for second best—all in the name of preserving historical accuracy.

My wonderful friends at Stallion 51—Lee, Angela, KT, Candy, Peter, Richard, Bill, and all the rest who keep the Mustangs flying—must also take some culpability. Because of their tireless efforts and stringent adherence to safety procedures, the P-51 Mustang soldiers on, so that a future generation can experience firsthand the plane's magnificence.

And finally, I cannot give enough thanks to all the veterans who have graced me with their time and experiences. I am not ashamed to call them my heroes, these great men—such as Bud Anderson, Don Strait, Ted Lines, Don Bryan, Ken Helfrecht, Clyde East, Jerry Yellin, Robert Butler, Clinton Burdick, Bob Goebel, Charlie Waddell, Kelly Gross, Jim Starnes, and the countless others you will read about—all asked me the same thing: "Why do you want to talk to me? I was just doing my job and didn't do anything special. The real heroes are the guys who didn't make it back."

After you read *The Fight in the Clouds*, I hope you disagree with them, as I did, and realize they all did very remarkable things at the controls of a P-51 Mustang, during some of the world's darkest days. In my humble opinion they are all heroes.

Blue Skies!
Jim

Foreword

Maj. Gen. Donald J. Strait, USAF (Ret.)

The presentation of hair-raising accounts of P-51 Mustang combat stories found in Jim Busha's *The Fight in the Clouds* not only covers operational missions flown by Allied fighter pilots in all theaters of World War II, but it also gives the reader a true taste of what it was like to be in combat at the controls of the legendary P-51 fighter plane. From tight-turning Lufbery circles with a determined Luftwaffe pilot on your tail, to long-range bomber escorts over enemy territory and endless wide open oceans, to hard-hitting dogfights and treetop combat, *The Fight in the Clouds* will give the reader an authentic glimpse into history, and into what it took to fly and fight as a fighter pilot at the controls of the various P 51 Mustangs in combat.

From the early days of the Allison-powered P-51A Mustang and A-36 Apache dive bomber, the Mustang held the line for the Allies until more advanced models entered service. When bomber crew loss was at an all time high and morale at an all time low, prayers were answered when the P-51B, with its Rolls-Royce Merlin engine, entered the war and effectively helped turn the tide, quickly establishing air superiority. With the introduction of the P-51D and its signature "teardrop" canopy, the ultimate fighter was born.

What makes this book even more enjoyable is the fact that these tales of day to-day aerial combat are written in an "as told to fashion," as

Jim Busha has captured firsthand accounts through detailed interviews with the men who flew and fought with the Mustang in World War II. I am honored to have this unique opportunity to write the foreword for *The Fight in the Clouds*, especially since I became quite familiar and rather fond of the P-51 Mustang during my combat tours while assigned to the Eighth Air Force during World War II.

When I graduated from pilot training in January 1943, I was assigned to Westover Field in Massachusetts, where I was to be checked out in the P-47 Thunderbolt. After completing the transition training program in March, I was assigned to the 361st Fighter Squadron of the 356th Fighter Group, where I obtained advanced fighter training prior to deployment to the Eighth Air Force in England. Our group arrived in Liverpool in early September 1943, and was eventually located at Martlesham Heath RAF station for combat operations.

By August 1944, I had completed eighty-seven combat missions and notched three victories while flying the P-47. But by the fall of 1944, as the Allied air forces advanced farther and farther into Germany, it became necessary for our group to convert to the P-51 Mustang. We soon found out that the Mustang had "long legs" when we increased our fuel capacity with external drop tanks. We could not only stay with the bombers all the way in, but after escorting them out of harm's way, we could drop down to the deck and look for targets of opportunity. But by far the Mustang's greatest attribute was its superior dogfighting abilities over the Axis aircraft. There was nothing else that could compare to the Mustang. In my mind, the P-51 Mustang was the ultimate fighter of World War II.

Ever since earning my wings, I had dreamed of becoming an "ace" (a military pilot credited with shooting down five or more enemy aircraft). My dream finally came true while flying the P-51 Mustang on a B-17 escort mission to Berlin in early December 1944. As the bombers turned west after dropping their bombs, my squadron observed forty-plus Fw 190s approaching from the southeast. I initiated an attack on one and observed strikes in the cockpit area. The Fw 190 did a snap roll and went straight down, out of control. Pulling away from that engagement, I bounced another 190 in a turn, firing at thirty degrees deflection using the K-14 gyroscopic gun sight from four hundred yards away. I observed hits in the cockpit and fuselage as the 190 did a violent snap roll before diving sharply. The pilot bailed out before his aircraft crashed. Those two kills gave me a total of six, which more than qualified me for ace status. Before the war ended, I more than doubled my score and became the leading ace of the 365th Fighter Group with 13½ victories. I flew more than thirty five combat missions in the Mustang.

But as you will see in this book, I was not alone. I am honored and humbled to be associated with fellow Mustang aces such as George Preddy, Don Blakeslee, Bud Anderson, Bob Goebel, and countless others who proved that the P-51 Mustang was a fighter that had no equal and that in the hands of a skilled pilot it was a force to be reckoned with. It not only had excellent firepower, with the later models carrying six .50-caliber machine guns, but it was the only fighter with sufficient long-range capabilities to take the fight to the enemy. With the introduction of the P-51, Allied bomber casualty rates were reduced by 75 percent when being escorted by the Mustang.

Although World War II is now a distant memory for most of us, the mere mention of the P-51, along with the sights and sounds of a restored example, stirs up vivid details that until now were seldom shared with the general public. Climb aboard with me as you take a historic journey back in time while at the controls of the P-51 Mustang. I hope you agree with me that *The Fight in the Clouds* is next best thing to actually being there.

Telling Stories

Lee Lauderback

Stories are treasures that have had significant impact on human history. Without stories, history is lost. Stories involve real people, their exploits, their failures, and their accomplishments. Storytelling has existed since primitive man. Paintings on the walls of caves that date back thirty-five thousand years tell of life-changing events that were shared with others.

In September 1940, the first P-51 took to the skies, and a storybook of epic proportions followed. But now, nearly seventy-five years later, the chapter on these courageous men who flew this magnificent fighter in combat is rapidly closing.

I have been privileged to fly the P-51 Mustang almost every day for the past twenty-five years, but the real blessing has been to share the Mustang once again with some of the warriors who flew the aircraft for real, and listen to their stories.

Men such as Irving Reedy, whose last combat mission was in March 1944, a fateful day when he was shot down by enemy ground fire and became a prisoner of war. Nearly fifty-six years later, we flew the Mustang together one last time. It was a special flight, but even more special was to listen to his stories of flying the P-51 in combat. The facts had little if any emotion, while his stories make his history very real.

Or the legendary Robin Olds, the "Break glass in case of war" leader who flew the P-51 in combat and quickly became an ace. I had the privilege to requalify Robin almost twenty years ago in *Scat VII*, a TF-51 Mustang. We had an awesome time, but even more special was the chance to hear some of his stories of flying the Mustang; to hear how he precisely maneuvered his nimble Mustang to defeat enemy aircraft; to hear how the Mustang always brought him back from combat; to hear how *Scat* became the name on all his combat aircraft.

Or the very best stick and rudder man ever to fly, R. A. "Bob" Hoover, the "pilot's pilot." Over the years I've had the privilege to fly with Bob many times, and each was an adventure. However, the real treasure was an exclusive invite to drink gin and vodka while listening to Bob and Tex Hill tell stories on each other. If I'd only had a recorder!

Jim Brooks, Buck and Bill Patttillo, Bud Anderson, Joe Peterburs, Bruce Carr, and many others have unique stories that have been shared with me over the years. These are stories that I have never written down or really even shared with others, but were permanently carved in my memory. Special times, special places, special pilots, special people!

These are my stories, but there are other incredible stories to be told, and *The Fight in the Clouds* collects extraordinary accounts of other warriors and their missions in different models of the P-51 Mustang. These are accurate stories, well researched and unembellished, that take you into combat with these brave young fighter pilots.

Mark Twain once said, "I do not claim that I can tell a story as it ought to be told. I only claim to know how a story ought to be told." My good friend Jim Busha must have taken notes from Mr. Twain.

So find your most comfortable chair, pour your favorite beverage, and share the cockpit with some of the pilots who made the P-51 Mustang a legendary fighter.

Mustangs forever,
Lee Lauderback

Lee Lauderback is president and CEO of Stallion 51 Corporation, located at the Kissimmee Gateway Airport, Florida. Stallion 51's innovative and comprehensive curriculums have instructed thousands of pilots on the correct and safe methods of flying both the legendary P-51 Mustang and the historic T-6 Texan for the past twenty-five years.

Lee has been the chief flight instructor since Stallion 51's inception, amassing over 20,000 flight hours in all types of aircraft, including over 8,700 hours in the P-51 Mustang. Lee is the world's highest-time P-51 Mustang pilot.

Stallion 51
www.stallion51.com

Stallion 51 P-51 Photographs

Introduction

Creation of a Thoroughbred

Legend has it that the initial depiction of the P-51 Mustang was drawn on a napkin. The fact of the matter was that the British RAF was in desperate need of fighters during the early days of World War II, and didn't care if the design had been drawn on tissue paper. The RAF's need for fighters was so great that RAF command contacted Inglewood, California's North American Aviation, Inc. (NAA) to ask if the company would be interested in manufacturing license-built P-40 Tomahawks to assist in repelling the Luftwaffe. Instead of tooling up their plant in California for P-40s, the movers and shakers at NAA promised a better, all-around fighter, one that could be designed, built, and delivered in about 120 days. NAA came very close to meeting the deadline and rolled out its new beauty on borrowed AT-6 wheels. The plane was given the name NA-73 and became the grandfather of all P-51 Mustangs.

The RAF liked the new single-seat fighter, and the potent, 1,150-horsepower Allison engine, and placed an initial order for more than three hundred, renaming the new arrivals the Mustang Mark I. The Mk I carried an assortment of .50-caliber and .30-caliber machine guns in the wings and embedded in the nose. The distinctive belly scoop was enlarged for better airflow. Most of the British Mustangs were thrown into the ground attack and photo recon roles, due in part to their labored performance above twenty thousand feet and their exceptional performance down low. The U.S. Army finally took notice of the Mustang in early 1942 and placed its own orders for the down-and-dirty little scrapper. North American Aviation knew they had a winner on their hands; they just needed to convince the Army Air Force power brokers before they were forced to shut down all production.

CONFIDENTIAL
North American Aviation Inc.

SUBJECT: PRODUCTION OF THE NORTH AMERICAN P-51
           MUSTANG FIGHTER AIRPLANES
TO: ASST. CHIEF, MATERIAL DIVISION,
         A. C. WRIGHT FIELD, DAYTON, OHIO
THROUGH: AIR CORPS RESIDENT REPRESENTATIVE

The subject aircraft were originally contracted for by the British in May 1940, without prototype, and a total of 620 were ordered at this time and in subsequent orders. Under the Defense Aid program, 150 additional were ordered by the army, making a total of 770 aircraft.

Approximately 220 have been delivered and the production rate is now 78 per month. Stating about March 1, the production rate will be 104 per month in conjunction with the Inglewood production of 104 B-25 bombers per month. At this rate the fighters will all be delivered by August 1942, and no additional orders have been indicated.

As a quick review, the Mustang is powered with an Allison engine of 12,000-foot critical altitude with a maximum speed of 386 mph at 15,000 feet without backfire screens (allowing for ram), and is armed with four (4) .50-caliber and four (4) .30-caliber machine guns. The last one hundred and fifty (150) will be armed with four (4) 20mm Hispano-Suiza cannons. The airplane has been tested with a new blower raising the engine rating from 1,150 hp at 12,000 feet to 1,125 hp at 15,000 feet. The actual speed in military trim was increased to 395 mph at 18,000 feet. The Allison Company is preparing to bring out a two-speed engine which can be mounted upon the same engine mount, which will increase the speed substantially more than 400 mph at at least 21,000 feet. Current studies are at hand indicating that a 300-pound bomb rack may be provided on each wing and that dive flaps can be installed. Extra fuel tanks can also be carried increasing the present maximum range from about 1,350 miles to 1,700 miles without difficulty.

This airplane has been thoroughly tested by the British and most of the information available is in the hands of the British representatives and military pilots. However, two airplanes have been turned over to the Air Corps in accordance with our original contract. Based on all available information and comment, this Company believes that this airplane is the best combat fighter and ground support plane currently in production in this country, all points considered. It is certainly the most adaptable to production and easiest to maintain in service. It is fitted with substantially all the features desired by the British representatives.

Consequently it is felt the within a few months there will be a great demand for additional quantities of these airplanes, particularly after actual combat experience is obtained. The flying characteristics and maneuverability are reported to be exceptionally good. Admittedly, this is only our point of view and it does not take all factors into account. However, it is our duty to so inform you and to point out that the time has come, if not actually past, when continuity of production of this model can be maintained. If additional airplanes are ordered at once, the new features can be engineered and incorporated and comparatively little loss of production will result. If such an order is not forthcoming, arrangements will be made to dismantle and store the tools and the plant will be re-arranged to produce only B-25 airplanes. Your immediate comment is urgently requested.

North American Aviation, Inc.
J. H. Kindelberger,
President

MUSTANG MODEL DEVELOPMENT

Beginning with the original 1940 prototype, called the NA-73X, through some twenty-five variants that concluded with the postwar P-51H in 1945, North American Aviation's P-51 Mustang was relentlessly polished, tweaked, and refined. Here is the development sequence of the basic models:

A-36 APACHE

The air corps realized the Mustang's positive attributes. The A-36 Apache (as the air corps called its version of the Mustang) was born out of necessity. The U.S. Army desperately needed a dive-bomber/ground-attack platform to assist its ground troops. The Apache retained many of the features of the Mustang Mk I, including the guns in the nose and wings. It was powered by a 1,325-horsepower Allison inline engine. The major difference with the A-36 was that it employed large dive brakes on both the top and bottom of the wings, enabling it to place its ordnance on target while in a controlled dive. At pull-up, the brakes slid back into place while the Apache zoomed away. The army was impressed with this hot new fighter and asked for a bomber-escort version. In all, five hundred A-36s were built.

P-51A

The P-51A utilized the 1,200-horsepower Allison and retained the three-bladed propeller. The two nose guns were removed, leaving just the four .50-caliber machine guns in the wings. Fewer guns meant less weight, which allowed the A model to sling a pair of 150-gallon drop tanks under its wings, for greatly increased range when performing escort duty. The A model was also supplied to the British, who called it the Mk II Mustang. In all, 310 P-51A/Mk IIs were built by NAA. But it wasn't until the British experimented with one of their Rolls-Royce Merlin two-stage, two-speed, supercharged engines that the Mustang's potential began to be realized.

P-51B/C

The P-51B/C model was powered by a Packard-built version of the Rolls-Royce Merlin that produced 1,450 horsepower. The B/C model used a four-bladed propeller instead of three, but retained the four-gun setup found on earlier models. The B was built at NAA's Inglewood plant, with a Hamilton Standard propeller, while the C was built in Dallas. Other than unique engine serial numbers, there were really no differences between the Inglewood and Dallas aircraft. The B existed because of a production need; the California plant couldn't produce the P-51s fast enough! Both models retained a larger air scoop that was installed in the belly, giving the Mustang its signature appearance. Although the plane retained its razorback canopy configuration, in the field it borrowed the Malcolm hood design from the British (designating these models the Mustang III), which afforded the pilot all-around better visibility. But the greatest asset was its long legs, which finally gave the Mustang the ability to fly and fight at high altitudes while staying with the bombers all the way to the target area and back. With external fuel tanks, the P-51 could easily roam more than two thousand miles nonstop. Later tweaks, including the addition of a tail fin and a clear-top canopy, soon turned the Mustang into what many aviation connoisseurs refer to as the ultimate fighter of World War II.

P-51D

The P-51D was by all accounts one of the greatest fighters ever produced. To offset and correct some directional stability issues, a small fin fillet that extended the vertical fin was added. This addition to the dorsal fin, along with the addition of two more machine guns in the wings (bringing the total to six .50 calibers), made the Mustang an ultimate killing machine. But one of the biggest refinements of the D model was the total redesign of the canopy area. The "French windows" found on the B/C were replaced with a bubbletop canopy. This gave the pilots an almost unrestricted view, which assisted them greatly during bomber escorts and dogfights. By war's end, the Mustang enjoyed a five-to-one kill ratio over its enemies, and shot down 4,950 enemy airplanes during its service. Over eight thousand P-51D Mustangs were built by NAA. A total of 281 pilots achieved ace status while at the controls of the P-51 during World War II.

P-51H

Originally designed to be lighter and faster than its older brother, the P-51D, the P-51H had similar looks—but that was about it. The H model was a complete redesign, weighing some six hundred pounds less than the D, with no interchangeable parts whatsoever. The fuselage was shortened, the tail made taller, and the teardrop canopy redesigned. Because of these modifications, the H model became the fastest Mustang of the bunch, reaching speeds of 487 miles an hour at twenty-five thousand feet. Although the H model came out in the latter part of the war, it never saw combat. Over 555 H models were built; many of these were stationed stateside, with National Guard units.

MUSTANG NEMESES

MESSERSCHMITT BF 109

The Bf 109 first flew in 1935 and had its baptism of fire during the Spanish Civil War a few years later. Later war 109s were powered by a liquid-cooled Daimler-Benz inverted V-12 engine with speeds approaching 400 miles per hour depending on the powerplant. Able to cruise comfortably above 30,000 feet, the 109s were a constant threat to the Allied bomber stream. Armed with both 20mm cannon and 7.9mm machine guns, the 109 was a lethal threat to bomber and fighter pilots alike. Over 30,000 109s were manufactured during the war, accounting for almost 60 percent of all Luftwaffe fighters.

P-51 MUSTANG SPECS

Model	P-51A	P-51B/C-1	P-51B/C	P-51D/K	P-51H
Numbers built	310	650	3738	9,600	555
Length	32.25	32.25	32.25	32.25	33.33
Height	12.2	13.67	13.67	13.67	13.67
Wingspan	37	37.04	37.04	37.04	37.04
Fuel load (gal.)	180	180	269	269	255
w/ drop tanks	330	330	419	489	475
Empty weight (lb.)	6,433	6,840	6,985	7,635	7,040
Takeoff weight	9,000	9,200	9,800	10,100	9,500
Max weight	10,600	11,200	11,800	12,100	11,500
Powerplant	Allison	Rolls-Royce	RRM*	RRM*	RRM*
Max speed	390	430	439	437	487
Horsepower	1,200	1,380	1,490	1,490	1,380
Ceiling	31,350	41,500	41,900	41,900	41,600
Combat range (no drop tanks)	750	755	1,180	1,155	755
Armament machine guns	4 .50-cal	4 .50-cal	4 .50-cal	6 .50-cal	6 .50-cal
Bombs (lb.)	2 x 500	2 x 1,000	2 x 1,000	2 x 1,000	2 x 1,000
Rockets	—	—	—	10	10

Combat record, all Mustangs: 4,950 air kills, 4,131 ground kills, 230 V-1 kills

*RRM: Rolls-Royce Merlin with engines built by Packard.

FOCKE-WULF FW 190

The Fw 190 entered the war in late 1941 and quickly established itself as an all-around heavy-hitting fighter. Able to carry a variety of ordnance, the 190 could operate down low as a fighter-bomber or a ground attack platform, and quickly transition into a air-to-air adversary role. The Fw 190 did not share the same high-altitude capabilities of the Bf 109, but nonetheless could hold its own against most Allied fighters. Like the Bf 109, the Fw 190 carried a combination of both machine guns and cannons. There were two variants of the Fw 190—one powered by a radial engine and the other late war examples powered by a liquid-cooled inline engine. Speeds ranged from over 400 miles per hour with the radial engine variant to over 440 miles per hour with the inline models.

MESSERSCHMITT ME 262

Dubbed the "Swallow," the Me 262 was a game changer for the Allied pilots during World War II when it arrived in combat in mid-1944. As the world's first operational jet fighter, the twin jet engine Me 262 could pounce on bomber formations at will and zoom away from their startled escort fighters. But a 262 could easily stand and fight even the mighty Mustang as long as the pilot kept his speed up. Armed with four 30mm cannons in the nose, the Me 262 dealt a death blow to most any airplane that got within its reach. But the 262 had one major Achilles' heel—its range and time aloft was very limited due to the lack of a large fuel load. Many Allied fighter pilots gave up chasing the 262s and instead formed their own "wolf packs" and became Swallow catchers, flying high over 262 bases and waiting for them to either take off or land before pouncing on them.

THE ULTIMATE SACRIFICE
REQUIEM FOR A HERO

Western Union

AUA152 44 GOVT=WUX WASHINGTON DC 28 1242P 1944 DEC 29

JOHN DESJARDINS=
868 HUBBARD ST GBAY=

THE SECRETARY OF WAR DESIRES ME TO EXPRESS HIS DEEP REGRET
THAT YOUR SON SECOND LIEUTENANT JAMES A DESJARDINS HAS
BEEN REPORTED MISSING IN ACTION SINCE TWENTY FIVE NOVEMBER
OVER GERMANY IF FURTHER DETAILS OR OTHER INFORMATION ARE
RECEIVED YOU WILL BE PROMPTLY NOTIFIED.
 DUNLOP ACTING THE ADJUTANT GENERAL.

The dreaded words "Missing in Action" contained in the Western Union telegram above were unfortunately a commonplace experience for many families during World War II. In those years, over 78,750 U.S. servicemen were listed as MIA. Many families that received similar telegrams held out hope that their loved one was either evading enemy capture or had became a prisoner of war. It was the same hope that John and Nettie Des Jardins of Green Bay, Wisconsin, held for their son James, a P-51 Mustang fighter pilot with the 356th Fighter Group, 360th Fighter Squadron, based at Martlesham Heath, England.

James A. Des Jardins was born on November 14, 1923, the second of three boys in the Des Jardins family. His father John had been part of the U.S. Army Signal Corps in World War I. When John returned home, he became an original member of the Green Bay Packers football team before settling down to start a family with his sweetheart, Nettie. As a boy, James was fascinated with aviation. Like many other young men of that era, he built model airplanes. After high school,

James enrolled in Ripon College with hopes of becoming a dentist. But his hopes and dreams, like those of other young American men and women, had to be placed on the backburner when the Japanese attacked the American naval base at Pearl Harbor on December 7, 1941. Following in the footsteps of his older brother Earl, who enlisted in the Army Air Corps in August 1942, James signed up in December 1942 and became part of Class 44-D.

James quickly transitioned from primary trainers, where he was taught fundamental airmanship, to basic flight training, where he learned how to fly in formation, perform aerobatics, and do cross-country work at the controls of a BT-13 Vultee Vibrator. Moving onto advanced training, James was introduced to the North American AT-6 trainer and became proficient in gunnery, instrument flying, and dogfighting—all in preparation for his assignment to a fighter squadron. After his checkout and advanced fighter tactics training in the P-47 Thunderbolt, James was finally deemed combat ready. Although James had yearned to "do his part by battling the Axis scourge," he received the following "combat reality" letter from his brother Earl, a B-24 Liberator pilot stationed in Italy:

ENCOUNTER REPORT: JULY 30, 1944
ITALY

Dear James,

Combat is rough and don't let anyone tell you different. If I were you I wouldn't be in any great hurry to get over here. That's a lot of shit when they tell you all the good flying stuff is in combat. My last mission was the Standard Oil plant at Ploesti [Romania] and it was a little rough. We stopped quite a bit of flak over the target. Our hydraulic system was shot out, number one turbo ran away, number two prop ran away and I had to cut that one on the way home. That left me way behind the rest of the formation. On approach numbers three and four ran out of gas. We landed okay. I checked the gas in number one and two and we had 15 gallons all together.

Enough for now brother. We got to practice formation in the morning; they don't even let you rest on a day off!

Earl

Christened with a set of silver wings and given the rank of Air Corps second lieutenant, twenty-year-old James Des Jardins, five feet six and a half inches, 150 pounds with brown eyes and matching brown hair, was sent to England. In November 1944, he was assigned to the 356th Fighter Group as a replacement fighter pilot. Unfortunately, James was unaware for some time that his brother Earl had been killed on the night of September 12, 1944, when his black B-24 slammed into the side of a mountain in the Roya Valley, France, during a mission to supply underground Resistance fighters with ammunition and weapons.

By the time James turned twenty-one on November 14, he was pilot in command of a P-47 Thunderbolt, flying combat over Occupied Europe and earning standard fighter pilot pay of $268.50 a month. His time in the Thunderbolt was short-lived, however, as the 356th Fighter Group, like most Eighth Air Force groups stationed in England, switched to the P-51 Mustang. The 356th FG flew its last P-47 mission on November 21, 1944.

ENCOUNTER REPORT: NOVEMBER 25, 1944
Eighth Air Force
356th Group, 360th Squadron
Mission #300
Missing Air Crew Report #10472

Capt. Strait led "A" Group (the 360th and 361st) and Capt. Tarbutton led "B" (the 359th) on a bomber support from 0959 to 1532. Landfall came at 1036 near Ostend and R/V followed at 1057 southeast of Namur. The 361st swept east and south, with two flights strafing Zwickau Airfield for claims of 5-7 planes. Lt. Hooker also strafed a marshalling yard near Zwickau, claiming 2-0 locos [locomotives] and 0-10 vehicles which were loaded on railcars. Meanwhile the 359th strafed in the Fulda area; two Ju 88s were damaged near Ettinghausen, and Lt. Brown and Lt. Carr shot up a downed B-17. A marshalling yard near Fulda was heavily strafed with claims of 7-7 lococs, 2-23 railcars, and 0-4 vehicles. A 360th flight flew with the 359th and one of its pilots was lost.

ENCOUNTER REPORT: NOVEMBER 25, 1944

Time 1300 hrs
Aircraft: P-51D-15; AAF Serial number 44-15133
Number of persons aboard aircraft: Crew 1; Total 1
Pilot: Des Jardins, James A. 2nd Lt. O-83Q187   KIA
Subject: Eyewitness Statements Re: 2nd Lt. James A Des Jardins
To: War department, HQ, Army Air Force, Washington D.C.

On 25 November 1944, I was leading Bucket Purple Flight when all Bucket section went down to strafe trains about 40 miles N-NW of Schweinfurt. Our flight strafed four trains and then we made a pass at a small Marshalling Yard. We were flying in string at the time and I made the first pass without getting any flak. I then pulled up and watched Lt. Des Jardins make his pass. While he was firing, I saw flame shoot out of the right side of his plane and I saw him pull up to about 300 feet burning and then the plane slowly fell off on a wing and crashed. I did not see any chute and think it is very impossible that he could have survived the crash. Lt. Hildebrand, who was following Lt. Des Jardins, got some light flak so we think it was a lucky hit by one machine gun which got Lt. Des Jardins.

Edward M. Nebinger
1st Lt. Air Corps
Pilot

As a fellow 360th Squadron pilot summarized, "Flying a fighter in combat was a deadly game—and that's the way it was! Those were the days when you could tell who the good guys were and who were the bad. But we felt that our cause was just and noble. I know it seems a high price to pay for a few trains, but that was part of our job."

James Des Jardins, like the more than 405,000 other U.S. servicemen killed during the war, had died while doing his job for our country. Regrettably, his hopes, dreams, and wishes vanished while he was at the controls of P-51D Mustang on a cold November day in 1944.

This book is written, in part, for all those heroes, such as 2nd Lt. James Des Jardins, who paid the ultimate sacrifice for our country as they laid their lives on the line to ensure that future generations would enjoy the freedoms and liberties that have been bestowed upon us.

1

Have Guns, Will Travel: Early Mustang Combat Memories

The Mustang was a beautiful and sophisticated airplane that brought enormous capabilities into combat. Its success as a fighter in both theaters of World War II may be unmatched. Little wonder, then, that the P-51 Mustang burns brightly in the memories of the men who flew them.

RHUBARBS AND RECCES
FLYING TACTICAL RECON WITH
RCAF 414 SQUADRON
P/O Clyde East, RCAF

EARNING MY WINGS
I was faced with a dilemma back in 1940—I wanted to become a fighter pilot, but the Army Air Corps wanted me to get a college education first. Thankfully, a rather simple situation presented itself to me in June 1941. The Royal Canadian Air Force (RCAF) was looking for a "few good men." With my mind made up and ten bucks in my pocket, I set out with a buddy, hitchhiking from our home state of Virginia to the Canadian border near Hamilton, Ontario. The RCAF welcomed us with

open arms, along with the other five thousand American men that beat us to Canada, all itching to fly and fight.

Although I joined the RCAF in the summer of 1941, I wasn't able to sit inside a cockpit until later that winter; there were more pilots than there were airplanes. By the time I took my first flight, I had the distinct "pleasure" of flying around the Quebec area in subzero temperatures! It was cold and miserable—but I couldn't have been happier. I was also part of the first cadet group that flew the de Havilland Tiger Moth biplane on skis. A year later, I was commissioned as an RCAF officer and selected to become a fighter pilot. I was sent on to England and was given a choice of the fighters I wanted to fly in combat.

If I had chosen the Supermarine Spitfire, I would have been assigned to a group that was responsible for protecting the air space over England. The Hawker Hurricane was another fighter I could have jumped into; I would have been assigned to the big action in North Africa, chasing Rommel around in the sand. But when I laid eyes on my third available choice, the North American Mk I Mustang (P-51A), there was no doubt in my mind: I had made the right decision.

The thing that impressed me about the Mk I was the fact that it was an American-built fighter. I could tell it would be a real up and comer during the war, and in that respect I was right. The Mk I was built for the British RAF and carried more guns than any other fighter during that time of the war. It had two .50-caliber machine guns housed in the lower nose, one .50-caliber in each wing along with two additional .30-caliber machine guns in each wing as well. The Mk I's only drawback was the Allison V-1710-81 inline engine. The Mustang was a very, very honest airplane and could outrun just about any other aircraft at low altitude. But when you took the Mk I above ten thousand feet, the plane began to get tired—it only had a single-stage supercharger.

Unfortunately, the Luftwaffe's Messerschmitt Bf 109 and Focke Wulf 190 fighters typically operated well into the twenty-five-thousand- to thirty-thousand-foot range, and could sit up there all day long, pouncing on us at will. But as a recce (reconnaissance) pilot, I rarely operated above five thousand feet anyway, and typically flew at five hundred feet or below—the lower you got the easier it was to sneak up on the enemy! I was quite satisfied with the Mustang's performance down low. It became the premier fighter of the war when the Rolls-Royce Merlin was mated to it—but that would come later.

I soon found out that most of my flying would be down low, *real* low.

RHUBARB RECCE

In July 1943, I was assigned to the RCAF 414 Tactical Reconnaissance (TAC Recon) Squadron and would fly with them for the next five months. Our job was to fly our camera-equipped Mustangs in pairs, at low level, over Occupied France, Belgium, and Holland on "rhubarbs"—harassment flights against German ground targets. When we weren't taking photos, we strafed trucks, barges, troops, and power lines—anything to interrupt German activity. But my favorite targets were the trains.

We would wander all over France at low level, driving up and down the railroad tracks looking for locomotives. When we found one, we would make quick work of disabling the engine, especially with all the firepower we carried on the Mustang. The Mk I was an excellent strafer and it only took a burst of a couple seconds to stop a train dead in its tracks. Although shooting at trains was exciting, I really wanted to tangle with the Luftwaffe.

Because the British realized the Mustang's altitude shortcomings, they switched the plane's role to exploit its strengths down on the deck. Primarily assigned to the RAF Army Cooperation Command squadrons in a tactical reconnaissance role, our Mustangs carried out a variety of missions. Our main job was to cause the Germans as much confusion, havoc, and disturbance as we could. The British war planners wanted to know what was going on with the Germans on the other side of the English Channel, so there was always something to shoot at and plenty of photos to take. The Mustang's .50s could punch holes in most trains and the early German armor; unfortunately the .30s barely chipped the German paint so we didn't fool with them very much. The

Mk I's deadliest weapon was the F24 aerial camera carried in the rear window, mounted obliquely just behind the pilot and shooting across the wing. Our main task was to gather intelligence by taking photos of German troop buildups and infrastructure. Shooting with a camera was okay, but shooting at targets of opportunity was more my cup of tea.

Most of the twenty-six tac/recon rhubarb missions I flew with 414 Squadron were over France, Belgium, and Holland. This called for two Mustangs to go out as a pair from our forward bases in England and hunt for targets of opportunity, such as stray airplanes, barge traffic, light armor, communication wires, and trains—especially trains. Driving up and down railroads, it was easy for us to spot the large plumes of smoke coming from the engines as they roared across France. When we were able to get our gun sights properly set on a train, we could normally knock out the engine with a burst of just a couple seconds. When we pounded the engine with our .50 calibers, it would stop in its tracks, and we'd make one more run to beat up the train again before departing to look for another one nearby. Now, one pass was dangerous enough for us; two was more of a death sentence, especially if the train had flak guns mounted on it.

As tac/recon pilots, we had always been encouraged to mix it up with the Luftwaffe, but due to our limitations of altitude, it was almost impossible for us to tangle with them. The whole time I was with the Canadians I saw only a couple of Fw 190s, and never got the opportunity to tangle with them—they were flying their way and we were going our way. My flight leader chose to let them go, determining that it wasn't his day to fight. One of my squadron predecessors, however, Hollis "Holly" Hills, was able to fight them down low, where the early Mustangs held the advantage. Although he had left the squadron just prior to my arrival and joined the U.S. Navy, he was held in very high esteem by the other squadron pilots. I ended up meeting Holly after the war and enjoyed listening to his account of his August 19, 1942, mission over Dieppe, France, in support of a failed Canadian/British amphibious landing. But during the fight in the sky, Holly became the first Mustang pilot to carn an aerial victory.

FIRST BLOOD
Flt. Lt. Fred Clarke and P/O Hollis Hills, RCAF
as told to Christopher C. Clarke

The aerial encounter above the French port of Dieppe on August 19, 1942, was one of the largest and most ferocious single air battles of the war between the Allies and the Luftwaffe. The sky that day was filled with RAF squadrons of Spitfires, Hurricanes, and Mk I Mustangs, all flying as top cover for the invading Allied troops below. For the men of RCAF 414 Squadron, the mission was simple: seek out and destroy the advancing German amour.

P/O (Pilot Officer) Hollis "Holly" Hills, originally hailing from Los Angeles California, and Flt. Lt. Fred "Freddie" Clark had flown 414 Squadron's first sortie of the day at 4:45 during the morning of the Dieppe Raid. Clarke flew low on a photo reconnaissance mission looking for German armor while Hills stayed high above him, acting as a "weaver" to cover his leader. Unfortunately, the two of them became separated in the predawn darkness and each returned to England alone. Later that morning, the pair volunteered to go up again on a second sortie at 10:25 a.m. This mission was a tactical reconnaissance south of the town of Dieppe. Holly was up on his perch, flying cover for Freddie, who was to do a low-level visual check of the road from Abbeville to Dieppe. The squadron pilots had been briefed about landing near the Dieppe racetrack if they were damaged or disabled. A Canadian corps was supposed to have secured this site during the morning hours for just such an event, but by midday it had become all too clear that the raid was going badly.

Without the cover of night, it was particularly important that the relationship between the observer and his cover be maintained at all points during the mission. Observing radio silence according to standing orders, they had no way of knowing that Flight Lieutenant Clarke's radio/telephone had failed him once again, as it had in an earlier mission with the Mustang. As they neared the coast west of Dieppe, Hills spotted a flight of four Fw 190s to the right at 1,500 feet, on a course that would take them directly overhead of the two RCAF Mustangs as they crossed the beach. Hills broke radio silence and called Clark twice, but it was to no avail; his radio was dead again. Not realizing the looming threat behind him, Clarke turned left toward the Amiens road, looking for German armor below. Unfortunately, he gave the German fighters an ideal bounce advantage as they formed up for an easy kill. Realizing that he would need to take extraordinary action, Pilot Officer Hills swung his Mustang wide to Clark's left in order to cut off the attackers. Hills recalls:

> This put me right over the town as I was down low dusting chimney tops! I believe the 190s had lost sight of me as I stayed under them. My plan was to cut off the lead 190 before he could open fire on Freddie. My timing all went to pot when a crashing Spitfire forced me into a sharp left turn to avoid a collision with it. That gave the Fw 190 pilot time to get into a firing position and hit Freddie's Mustang hard with his first burst. Glycol was streaming from the radiator, but there was no fire. I was able to get a long shot at the leader but had to break hard right as the number-two man was having a go at me. He missed and made a big mistake sliding by my left side. It was an easy shot and I hit him hard. I knew that he was a goner.

Clarke was oblivious to the action that was unfolding above his head until the first shells slammed into the oil cooler of his Mustang's Allison engine. Clarke remembered:

> The next thing I know is "all Hell and corruption's going by." I had been hit! The radiator was shot up; my instruments on either side of me were gone. The amour plating saved me. I jettisoned the hood, hoping that it hadn't been jammed with the shots I took. Thankfully, it wasn't. And I thought, They're right, it's nice—not windy in here at all.

Clarke instinctively he twisted his aircraft into a hard climbing right-hand turn: "I went from the treetop level to about eight hundred feet before the engine seized. That's all she'd get."

Without his radiator and the life blood of glycol that flowed through it, Clarke knew it was only a matter of time before his Mustang's engine seized up completely. Although the pilots of 414 Squadron had been offered the inland racetrack as a potential crash or emergency landing site, Clark had no intention of risking capture or, worse yet, potentially handing his Mk I Mustang over to the Germans. Fred Clarke preferred instead to take his chances with a summer swim in the English Channel. Clarke would never have made it to the channel, however, had it not been for the timely return of his wingman, Holly Hills, who showed up to find another Fw 190 trailing the stricken Mustang. Although the 190 slid in behind Clarke's Mustang for what looked like an easy kill, Hills believed the German was hoping to capture the Mustang intact. He recalled, "I had to try and stop him so I gave a short high-deflection burst at him. I was hoping to get his attention and it worked—he broke hard left into my attack."

As Hills attempted to mix it up with the Germans (proving that the Mustang could at least out-turn the Fw 190), Clarke continued his struggle to reach the safety of the channel. It was a perilous moment, however, considering that no one had been known to successfully "ditch" a Mustang and survive. The principal reason was that the large air scoop under the Mustang's belly acted like a rudder that would direct the long, slender nose to the bottom of the channel. Fortunately, this did not happen in Clarke's case. Clarke's memory has survived to include the moment ten feet above the water, and an airspeed indicator showing ninety miles an hour—and then he woke up soaking wet in the bottom of a landing craft:

I limped out over the water. Just as I crossed the coast, that prop seized as solid as a . . .

There I am downwind, across the trough, everything's ag'in ya! Using my trim to keep my tail down, the last thing I remember is about ninety miles an hour on the clock, trying to get that tail down. I wanted the tail to hit first to kill the speed before she flopped in, because it would just go in if you hit the air scoop. The next thing I remember I came to in a landing craft. I hit the gun site I think. The Perspex [acrylic glass] was coming out of my forehead up until ten or fifteen years ago! They later told me a young army guy hit the water with his arms going and swam over and got me out of the aircraft. I would give anything to have known who he was.

Clarke was transferred with the other wounded to the destroyer HMS *Calpe*, which was itself under extremely heavy attack for most of the morning and early afternoon, while she tried to retrieve as many retreating soldiers as she could. Up in the air, Holly Hills had his own problems to deal with as he continued to play cat and mouse with the pursuing Fw 190. Turning and turning, the Fw 190 took a desperate shot at Holly's Mustang before finally breaking off and heading for home. Flight Officer Hills did the same and returned to England minus his flight leader.

After being treated for the wound to his head, Clarke finally returned to Purley, Surrey, where he and Holly were billeted in a requisitioned house. Hills said:

> About 5:00 the next morning, my door burst open. I was grabbed in a bear hug by what smelled like a huge clump of seaweed. It was Freddie Clarke, rescued by the amphibious forces, as I had told the squadron [about him] on my return from the mission. His head sported a huge bandage covering the severe cuts he had received in the ditching. We had been warned that ditching a Mustang could be hazardous to your health!

Flight Lieutenant Clarke was the only pilot to ditch a Mustang during the war and survive to tell about it—at least what he was able to remember. On his return to the squadron on the morning of August 20, Clarke confirmed witnessing an Fw 190 crash into the ground from a steep dive. This was determined to be the same Fw 190 that Flight Officer Hills had first fired on, making him the first Allied pilot to score a victory with the Mustang. Freddie Clarke also shared in the accolades, having the dubious honor of being the pilot of the first Mustang to be shot down by the Luftwaffe.

Clarke flew a few more sorties over France until May 1943. At that time, the extent of his injuries became apparent and he was given ten days' sick leave due to severe migraine headaches and partial black-outs. When the commanding officer became aware of these afflictions after Clarke returned to duty, Clarke was grounded permanently. In late 1943, he became 414 Squadron's operations officer through their time in Holland and Belgium.

Freddie Clarke, my father, was the last surviving member of the original 414 pilots who formed the Squadron on August 7, 1941. He passed away in Calgary, Alberta, Canada, in May 2005.

Hollis H. Hills had attempted to join the USAAF 4th Fighter Group soon after the Dieppe air battle but was informed he would be assigned to a P-38 squadron instead. Not wanting to fly a twin engine fighter, he opted instead to fly for the U.S. Navy, where he flew the F6F Hellcat and scored another four victories. Not only did he become an ace, but he was one of two Allied pilots who had victories over both Japanese and German aircraft. Hollis Hills passed away on October 31, 2009, and was buried in Arlington National Cemetery with full military honors.

HIGH DIVER: FLYING THE A-36 APACHE IN COMBAT
Maj. Charles "Charlie" E. Waddell, USAF (Ret.)
27th Fighter Bomber Group, Twelfth Air Force

LEARNING TO FLY
When I joined the service in early December 1941, right around the time Japan attacked Pearl Harbor, I was already considered an old man at twenty-one. I was born in 1918, and grew up in Brooklyn, New

York, where I tried to join the Air Corps in late 1938. But they didn't really want anybody because the country was just coming out of the Great Depression and the government was flat broke. Back then, with no war going on, they were a lot choosier about who they would take. December 7, 1941 changed all of that.

I spent almost a year waiting for my cadet appointment. Finally, in September 1942, I was assigned to flight training school. I started out in low-wing Fairchild PT-19s, then went on to BT-13s and then into the AT-6. I was selected to become a fighter pilot and was shoved into an old P-40 Warhawk—honestly, I thought the P-40 stunk! They were greatly overrated and the ones we had at the Army Air Force base in Eagle Pass, Texas, were complete dogs!

The very first time I was up in a P-40 the whole electrical system went out. I had no electric pitch trim, and I couldn't lower my landing gear, so I had to pump it down by hand. For an "old guy," it became quite exhausting! The flaps had to be lowered by pumping them as well. It wasn't until after I landed that I was reminded of a bypass switch that would have solved all these problems, and helped me avoid using the "Armstrong" method! There was so much to learn as "green fighter pilot" when checking out in a new airplane! But thankfully, the very next one I was assigned to I absolutely fell in love with.

I first laid eyes on the P-51A at Hillsborough Field, near Tampa, Florida. The Mustang was a hot fighter at the time—in my opinion, the very best we had. We got to fly them for three months before we were shipped out for combat, and they were a true delight—except for one small item. The cockpit cooling system didn't work at all. We were soaking wet in that hot Florida sun when we came down from flying, and that was just during the morning flight! But truthfully, I wouldn't have changed it for the world. Heck, going from an AT-6 into a Mustang was like jumping out of your father's truck into a souped-up hot rod! The P-51A models had Allison engines. Down low the planes were great, but above twelve thousand feet they got really tired in a hurry and had their tongues hanging out. By way of comparison,

I got a chance to fly P-51B Mustangs while in tactical flying school. They were real beauties—powerful and yet graceful. Although their Rolls-Royce Merlin engines liked to buck and bang on startup, they really made up for it as they zoomed well past twelve thousand feet and kept on going. But going up high was not the reason I was in Florida. I was there to learn the tricks and traits of the A-36 Apache dive bomber.

DIVE-BOMBER SCHOOL

Checking out in the early Mustangs meant only one thing: dive bombing. Most of the early Air Corps dive bombers had been A-24 variants of the Navy's venerable Dauntless SBD (Slow But Deadly), along with a behemoth known as the Vultee A-31 Vengeance. The SBD was a well-proven airplane in the Pacific, but it was slow. We needed something that could get in and out quickly. The A-36 Apache, a variant of the Mustang P-51A, was specifically designed for swift, in-and-out dive bombing. North American Aviation redesigned and strengthened the laminar flow wings, added bomb racks to carry a five-hundred–pound bomb under each wing, loaded it up with six .50-caliber machine guns, including two in each wing and two more in the nose. Down low, it was fast, and it cruised at around 260 miles an hour; wide open it could hit 365. But by far the greatest attribute of the Apache was its dive brakes.

Embedded in the wings, the dive brakes were aluminum-grated slats that popped out ninety degrees like clam shells on the top surface and the bottom. They were activated by a small control knob located on the pilot's left. When deployed in a dive, they allowed us to hold our dive steady and keep the gun sight's pipper right on the target. In fact, as A-36 dive-bomber pilots, we would often brag that we could put a five-hundred–pound bomb in a pickle barrel from two thousand feet! Of course, there would be nothing left of the barrel to prove our accuracy, but I think you get the point.

In training and later in combat, we would normally operate in flights of eight, twelve, and sometimes sixteen A-36s. We climbed to ten thousand to twelve thousand feet and waited for the leader's signal to dive. When he "fishtailed" his Apache, he wanted all of us to fall in behind him, no more than ten feet behind the tail of the A-36 in front, as if we were on an invisible string. It must have looked like a Broadway show from the ground, as we waited for the leader to roll over on his back and dive almost vertically for the target below. Before pushing over, though, we deployed the dive brakes to ensure that we'd be able to control our vertical speeds. We were told this was an "incline" dive and that no other Air Force fighter could really do what we were doing—basically, dive straight down without tearing our wings off. During those steep dives, the brakes allowed us to hold our airspeed steady down to around 220 miles per hour. We would release our dummy bombs at 2,000 to 2,500 feet, close the dive brakes, and then zoom away as fast as we could. The training was continuous and at times strenuous, but I had a lot of fun. About the only thing missing was the flak and ground fire—something I would experience firsthand over the skies of Italy.

JOINING THE FIGHT

I took a long, slow boat ride across the Atlantic Ocean and arrived in Casablanca, French Morocco, on Christmas Day 1943. From there we were loaded in World War I–era boxcars called "40 in 8" because each one could hold up to forty men or eight horses—thankfully, not at the same time. Five days later I arrived in Libya, where I was shoved into the bombardier's station in the nose of a B-17 Flying Fortress and took off for Italy. The B-17 pilot must have been a frustrated fighter pilot because he never really got much higher than the wave tops as we zipped over the water, across the war-torn countryside of Sicily, and on to our base near Naples, Italy.

I was part of the 27th Fighter Bomber Group (FBG) and joined them at an old commercial airfield called Pomingliano d'Arco field. We shared our turf with our sister Apache squadron, the 86th FBG, along with some bomber outfits. We were only thirty miles from the front lines, and to add to the excitement of war, Mount Vesuvius decided to blow its top and send rocks as big as cars into the air! My initial combat hops were more or less familiarization flights with "old hands" that had been in combat for a while. My indoctrination lasted only about two hours. In that time I absorbed every word the old timers said because it was the only way to stay alive.

Shortly before I arrived, the big January 1944 battle at Anzio had erupted. On my first combat hop, I was assigned to fly on the squadron commander's wing. His job was twofold: to lead the mission and to keep me out of trouble. We found plenty of trouble that day as flak and small-arms fire filled the sky. The Germans threw everything they had at us. So what was it like to fly my first combat mission? In a nutshell, scary as shit! It took just twenty minutes to cross the bomb line and then we were on a fighter sweep, looking for targets of opportunity. The formation we flew was what we called line abreast. It was hard for the Germans to hit us as we kept close to one another—only fifty feet away from the other A-36s. While we made our runs on the targets, we constantly changed our altitude and directions, turning and jinking the stick the whole time.

I will never forget my first target: a German ambulance. It sat in a parking area with a bunch of other vehicles around, so I didn't know if anybody was in it. Trouble was, there were a bunch of Germans standing near it and they were of course firing back at us. And they were very, very good at it, getting great accuracy with their 20mm and 88mm guns. They knew how use them and they filled our planes with holes.

My Apache took three hits in the tail, but it kept on going as if it had only had its paint scratched. It would have been a lot different had the hits swapped ends and I took them in the engine or the coolant system. Had that happened, I am sure I would have had to bail out and become a guest of the Germans for the remainder of the war. Thankfully, the A-36 kept on ticking and I made it out alive. Our missions increased during that time, and sometimes we flew multiple ones each day. We rarely encountered German fighters, though, and most times had top cover from British or American Spitfire fighter squadrons.

Some of the A-36s in our squadron were armed with two 20mm cannons in the nose instead of machine guns. The cannons packed a punch, firing straight ahead up to a thousand yards, but they didn't converge into a cone of fire like our machine guns did. As a strafing machine, the A-36 was fearsome, but in its primary role as a dive bomber, it was deadly.

Most of our missions began with the squadron commander standing before us in the briefing room, where he'd pull back the curtain back to reveal a large wall map of Italy. We would be given our targets and routes and, on some occasions, photographs of our targets. All of our A-36s were painted in the same flat, olive drab scheme with just a number or letter signifying individual planes. We wrote all the numbers on the back of our hands so we knew who was next to us and what A-36 they were in, and who was who in what position. As we strapped inside the A-36, we were struck by the sight of identically colored Apaches warming their Allison engines, dust flying as airplanes rocketed down the runway.

With our target photos strapped to our legs, we struggled to get to twelve thousand feet with a five-hundred–pound bomb slung beneath each wing. Although I could feel the prop wash from the guy ten feet in front of me, I got used to it after awhile. We kept our eyes peeled for German fighters, and hoped the Spitfires would latch onto them before they spotted us. Our targets were command posts, dams, bridges, airfields, and troop concentrations. We usually avoided bombing the German airfields because they were heavily defended by antiaircraft guns—but we sure strafed the hell out of them when we came zooming in at treetop level, all of us line abreast with our machine guns shooting up the whole damn place!

Saying Goodbye to an Old Friend

But just as soon as I got comfortable in the A-36 and felt like it was an extension of my body, the planes were ripped away from us. North American Aviation built only five hundred of them. Some stayed back in the States and others went to the Far East Theater of Operations. In

Italy, there was nothing else around that could do what we were doing. But our numbers were dwindling quickly because of operational losses. The Army Air Force could no longer keep two A-36 groups going so they had to decide between us and the 86th. We did it the old-fashioned way and flipped a coin. Unfortunately for me, the 86th got to keep flying the Apache. Our 27th FBG was promised the new P-51 Mustang, but like everything else in the army, nothing ever goes as planned. Instead of Mustangs, we ended up with war-weary P-40F Warhawks that had been cast off by the RAF. As far as we were concerned, we were stepping backwards, but orders were orders and we made do with what we had. The A-36 was designed perfectly for its dive-bombing role; why the Air Corps gave them up was a mystery to me!

The P-40F could only do around 240 miles per hour on the deck compared to the 300 miles per hour plus in the A-36. We should have learned that gambling only gets you further in debt! Bottom line is the A-36 was designed for one very important and particular task: dive bombing. When the Corps tried to replace it with a new airplane, they fell short. We later got P-47 Thunderbolt "Jugs" as replacements for the P-40 dogs. But diving in a P-47 was a tough deal. You couldn't come diving straight down because that behemoth picked up speed so rapidly you had to think ten thousand feet ahead of it in order to pull out safely. We developed a glide-bombing technique. That helped, and it must be said that the P-47 had one advantage over the Apache: it could carry twice the load—two thousand-pound bombs. I think that that capacity was the deciding factor for the powers that be.

I think our dive-bombing accuracy dropped in the P-47. One big reason was that you couldn't see over the Jug's goddamn nose. As a consequence, we *had* to glide bomb. There was no way we could direct a bomb into a pickle barrel (the fabled claim of radar-guided bombing enthusiasts)—or even close!

How did I keep going as a fighter pilot, and avoid stewing about whether today was my day to cash in? Truthfully, I never gave it a thought. I was scared to death every day, but I always thought it was going to be the other guys that would get hit—never me. There was one big reason I felt this way. I knew I had an excellent airplane strapped to me. The A-36 Apache was my good luck charm!

Charlie Waddell wound up flying 120 combat missions in the A-36, P-40, and P-47. Of the twenty-six men he went into combat with as part of the 27th FBG, only nine survived the war and returned home.

THE FLYING MISADVENTURES OF A JOURNEYMAN APACHE PILOT
Lt. Col. Robert J. Hahlen, USAAF (Ret.)

In March 1941, with two years of college under my belt and a devil-may-care attitude, I joined the Army Air Corps Cadets. I was a fat, dumb, and happy Wisconsin farm boy. Just a kid, really, not knowing how close this country was to war. I graduated from cadet class on October 31, 1941, flying PT-19s and BT-14 trainers in primary and basic, and then moving up to AT-6s and BC-1s in advanced training at Kelly Field, Texas. Eventually, I was sent over to England, where I flew C-47 transports and Cessna Bobcats—a small, twin-engine transport. Without a doubt, I was a "frustrated fighter pilot in a transport pilot's body!"

My luck changed while on detached service in England, when I wandered into a repair depot that was overhauling and repairing badly damaged P-47 Thunderbolts. As I stood there looking at all these beautiful "Jugs" lined up with no one flying them, it almost brought a tear to my eye. I walked up to one of the mechanics servicing the P-47s and said, "How's about letting me fly one of these on a test hop?" The mechanic looked at me and said very matter-of-factly, "Well, somebody has to fly them. Have you ever flown one?" I replied, "Nope, never have." And the mechanic said, "Okay, climb in."

I jumped into that cockpit as fast as I could while the mechanic sat on the wing and gave me a systems and cockpit checkout. He told me to make my final turn at 120 miles per hour, make my "final prayers" at 105 miles per hour, and come over the fence at 100 miles per hour— and that was it. I had never flown a fighter before, but the P-47 was just as smooth as silk. It felt like flying a large barrel with that big Pratt & Whitney engine out in front and the large four-blade propeller pulling me along at breakneck speed. This was a helluva nice-flying airplane! I flew around the English countryside for about an hour, making climbs and descents and a few "tight" turns, pretending I was a hotshot fighter pilot. With eight .50-caliber machine guns at my disposal, I was ready to take on the entire Luftwaffe! I returned to the base and did what the mechanic told me and made a nice three-point landing. I made two or three more "test" hops in the P-47 and then we were moved to France right after the D-Day invasion.

While in France, I wound up being stationed in Lyon. Also stationed on the field was a P-47 fighter group. I got to know a major in this Thunderbolt group, and he told me he had "acquired" an A-36 Apache. The A-36 was the dive-bomber version of the P-51 Mustang. It had the Allison engine but no supercharger. It did, however, have dive brakes, and had served well in Africa and Italy early in the war. This major had acquired the A-36 in Italy and flew it up to our base in Lyon. The guns had been removed and the plane had no paperwork whatsoever. The major flew the A-36 whenever he could but always complained that it was constantly overheating on him. Lucky for me, the P-47 group shortly got orders to move and the major had to leave "his" A-36 behind.

Once the P-47 group left, I had our mechanics pull the Apache over to our hangar and try to find out why the thing always heated up. After a very short once-over, they found a piece of berry bush in the coolant tank, probably from some low-level mission! They took out the bush, drained and replaced all the coolant fluid, and cranked up the engine. It ran fine! I stood there and thought, *Well, I don't have my Cessna Bobcat anymore, but I got this Apache here, so I might as well fly her.* I had flown the P-47 two or three times before and thought that flying the Apache would be no big deal, but I did ask one of the fighter pilots still stationed on our field to come over and test fly the Apache for me and give me a checkout.

That fighter pilot came over and looked at the A-36, which was a ratty-looking airplane, a molted olive drab and covered in dust and dirt. Obviously, it had seen a lot of combat without any maintenance for a long time, if ever. The pilot looked at me and looked at the A-36, its paint peeling and fading, dings and nicks all over the leading edges, and fluid dripping from unknown locations. He said, "Nope, no way. I've been flying P-47s in combat for too long. I am not going to kill myself in this rat trap." Then he turned and walked away. So I decided right then and there, if I'm going to fly it, then I'm going to fly it. I never said I was smart.

I climbed in, cranked it up, taxied to the end of the runway, and tried to make myself ready for the ride of my life. In the P-47s that I flew, you had a mark on the trim tab to adjust for torque on takeoff. But this A-36 had nothing like this. And if it did, and it had been there, it had been worn off or broken off long ago. So being the "hotshot" pilot that I was, I jammed that throttle forward to wide open and it took me across the runway like a cat on a razorblade! I was so far behind the curve that by the time I finally got the beast straightened out, I looked back and I swear I was fifteen miles off the field! When I finally settled my nerves down, I found myself in one of the most magnificent airplanes I have ever flown.

The A-36 was light on the controls, very nimble. If you thought "roll," it would roll and keep on rolling. Strapped into that cockpit, I felt like I was an extension of this awesome aircraft. Flying around the French countryside made me forget there was still a war going on. Lucky for me, there were no stray Fw 190s or Bf 109s flying nearby, or my "dream" may have been shot out from underneath me. This plane was a real lady in the air. But landings, however, were almost always eye-popping, high-hopping experiences. It wasn't as easy to land as the P-47. The Thunderbolt was a lot heavier and the gear a lot wider. To land a P-47, you just came over the runway and cut the power, and it would just set right in. With the Apache, the gear was quite narrow and the plane a lot lighter. It made landing a "religious" experience for me every time.

The other problem I had with the A-36 was that the compass either didn't work or worked only when it wanted to. One day we got orders to move again so I flew the A-36 on ahead of our unit to check out our new base. I set my compass course and took off. I was flying for a while and thought I should be coming up on the base pretty soon. I finally took out my map and couldn't find anything that looked familiar. I flew around, running low on gas, and finally admitted to myself I was lost. I flew over a field that the Germans had scraped off to make a runway, and noticed three P-47s already on the ground. I landed on this strip of mud and learned I was up near Paris. I figured that damn compass was way off. I also found that the three P-47 pilots had gotten lost, too. I staggered out of that mud field the next day and I held my thumb on the map all the way back to my new base. I knew better than to trust that damn compass.

I flew the Apache two or three more times, but the war was becoming busy again for me. I decided that if I couldn't fly the A-36 anymore to become familiar with it, then I would just let it sit. About that time, the major who was the original owner of the Apache found out I had his pet Mustang, and he wanted it back. He called our base at least a half dozen times looking for me, and each time he called, I had my sergeant tell him I was out flying. My sergeant was catching a lot of flak from this major so finally I told him that if he wants his plane back, then come and get it himself!

The major arrived at our base and took his Apache with him. Before he left, though, he was told that the erratic compass shouldn't be trusted. The major said he had a girlfriend in Marseilles, and that he could find his way just fine. He never made it. We later found out that he got caught in some weather and flew the A-36 into a mountain. War is hell.

2

Killer Bs: P-51B/C Mustangs over Europe

American bombers carried staggering loads of ordnance to enemy targets, but the planes were large, clumsy, and slow. B-17s, B-24s, and others bristled with guns, but without fighter-plane escort, the bombers were easy meat for enemy fighters. This was proved in the early part of the Allied bombing campaign over Europe, when issues of fuel capacity restricted U.S. fighters to only partial escort duty. After a point, the fighters had to turn back for home, leaving the bombers to fend for themselves. Later, when auxiliary drop tanks were added to P-38s, P-47s, and P-51s, fighter range was greatly extended. By then, P-51s—the longest-range fighter planes of World War II—could accompany bombers all the way to the targets, and all the way back home. And on those return trips, if no enemy fighters were in sight, the P-51s were free to drop to the deck and look for targets of opportunity that might be strafed and destroyed.

LIVE BAIT!
FLYING AND FIGHTING WITH THE PIONEER MUSTANG GROUP
Capt. Clayton "Kelly" Gross, USSAC (Ret.)
354th Fighter Group, 355th Fighter Squadron

I remember the day I became infected very clearly. As a kid growing up in Washington State, my dad shelled out fifteen hard-earned bucks for me to take a ride in a Ford Tri-motor in 1928. Although I was only seven years old at the time, I knew right then and there that I would be a pilot someday. Boy, oh boy, I was hooked! I had been bit hard by the flying bug, and rarely a day passed by where I didn't think of flying. While going to college at Gonzaga University, I heard of a new government program called the Civilian Pilot Training program (CPT). I quickly became one of the first to sign up. I enlisted in the army in 1940 and was told that they would contact me when they were ready. By March 1941 I had soloed in a small airplane, and eventually became a private pilot. The day after the Japanese attacked Pearl Harbor, the army was now good and ready for me. I earned my silver wings and became a commissioned fighter pilot.

I started out with tricycle-geared P-39 Airacobras near San Francisco, California, and found them to be very nice flying machines. They were agile and responsive, a fact I proved more than once when I found myself engaged in "mock dogfights" with Navy F4F Wildcats. After a bunch of tight turns that left them unable to shake me, they wagged their wings in defeat as they headed back to their base to lick their wounds. The tactics I learned while flying the P-39, including gunnery, dogfighting, formation spreads, and bombing and strafing, really prepared me for combat.

Joining the Pioneer Mustang Group
Because of the war, new fighter groups were forming at a rapid pace. With sixty-five hours of P-39 time under my belt, I was assigned to the

Ninth Air Force's newly formed 354th Fighter Group and became a flight commander with the 355th Fighter Squadron. We continued to train in the P-39 until we received orders to ship out and head to England, where we would join the fight. Although we flew Airacobras, we were told we would not be flying them in combat, but instead would fly a "new fighter" that was just coming on line. We arrived in England in early November 1943, and that's where I met the airplane of my dreams— the P-51 Mustang! Actually, the first model I checked out in was the dive-bomber version called the A-36 Apache. This early model used the Allison engine, had only three propeller blades, and had machine guns in the nose and wings. Dive brakes were embedded in both the upper and lower surfaces. It looked fast just sitting on the ground!

After spending two days going over a very through cockpit checkout and some last minute commands from my instructor to "leave the dive brakes alone," I was sent on my way to check out this new thorough-bred. The Apache was definitely no P-39! I guess I had become spoiled with tricycle-gear airplanes and had to go back to my early tail-dragger days to taxi the Apache without hitting something. The A-36 had a long slender nose and you couldn't see out the front end. We had to S-turn from side to side until ready for takeoff. I felt the power to be similar to the P-39's, especially with the familiar Allison engine (in front of me instead of behind, as in the Airacobra). But once airborne, the Apache was a quite different aircraft. I could tell right away that it was much more responsive and lighter on the ailerons. After two flights in the A-36, I was deemed ready to check out the rest of the squadron pilots. We continued to train, and this time it was in the P-51A Mustang, the same as the A-36 but without dive brakes. We spent just a couple of hours on the A model before the more powerful P-51Bs arrived in mid-November 1943. From then on, the 354th FG would be known as the Pioneer Mustang Group—the first U.S. Army Air Force group to take the Mustang into combat.

I'd done my time in the Apache and the P-51A, but the P-51B was an entirely different animal. It was powered by the well-built and reliable

Rolls-Royce Merlin engine, which, instead of getting tired above twelve thousand feet, only became stronger as it literally took us to new heights. The B model had four propeller blades instead of three but carried only four .50-caliber guns instead of six. With less weight, we were able to carry more gas; now we could escort the bombers to and from the target area. With the entire group checked out and equipped with P-51Bs, we were moved to our first airfield, Boxted, which was located near Colchester. Before we went on our first combat mission, we were visited and instructed by the commanding officer of the 4th Fighter Group, Col. Don Blakeslee. Colonel Blakeslee was already considered an "old hand," as he'd been fighting early on as part of the volunteer-American Eagle Squadron during the Battle of Britain. The thing I remember most was that he emphasized to us that during a head-on attack, the guy who broke first would be at a disadvantage. I silently thought it would be more of a disadvantage if we rammed into one another!

BAPTISM OF FIRE

On December 11, 1943, I flew my first combat mission: a B-17 bomber escort over Germany. Some of the guys in the squadron already had nose art on their Mustangs, and at first I was going to put my wife's nickname, "Lil Pigeon," on it. The problem was that the name had a history of bringing bad luck. I had given my first P-39 that name and someone made a wheels-up landing in it. The second P-39 suffered a worse fate when the pilot cartwheeled it. The third time was not the charm because another pilot crashed that one as well. I agonized over it until just the right name came to me on one of my missions.

We had been out on an escort and I became separated from the group. I was able to latch onto another Mustang flown by Bob Stephens, and the two of us turned for home. Bob suddenly called me over the R/T [receiver/transmitter] and said, "You stay where you're at and I'll climb above you into the sun and then hopefully we can draw some action." Although I relished the thought of tangling with the Luftwaffe, I wasn't too thrilled about being the lure. I replied to Bob, "What the heck do you think I am, live bait?" He just said yes, and because he outranked me that's how we did it. My neck was never the same after turning my head from side to side looking for an attacking German! When we got back, I had my crew chief paint the name *Live Bait* on the side of the Mustang.

I continued to fly a lot of escort missions without getting to slug it out with the Luftwaffe. I finally came face to face with the enemy in April 1944. Our group had escorted the bombers to Schweinfurt and was able to latch onto a lone Me 109 that was in a turn. I liked to get in close before firing; I guess I wanted to be sure I was going to hit him without warning him. And being in close also meant I would have extra ammo when we went down and strafed targets of opportunity on the way home. I closed in on the 109, and as I looked behind me, I noticed two red-nose P-47s of the 56th Fighter Group coming up fast and covering my tail. As I eased in for the kill on the 109, I opened up from less than a hundred yards out and noticed strikes on his left wing and fuselage area. That's when my world exploded around me.

It felt as though my neck had been hit by a brick. My canopy was gone, the armor plate behind my head was all chewed up, and my Mustang went into a very violent snap roll and then into a spin. Those P-47s had mistaken me for the enemy and just clobbered me! I lost a few thousand feet as I spun earthward, but finally was able to get the Mustang back under control. Man, it was cold up there with no canopy. As my two "attackers" slid up next to me, I rocked my wings so that they could tell I was not the enemy. They gave me a once-over and then quickly peeled away for fear of me turning my guns on them. All alone over enemy territory in a shot-up Mustang was no place to be. I noticed a box of B-17 bombers above me. Thankfully, my radio still worked and I called them. I arrived at their altitude and was assured that their gunners would hold their fire. So we switched roles, as the protector became the protected. The problem was, they were headed for the target area and I didn't think I stood much of a chance staying with them. I was finally able to get hold of a fellow squadron mate who stayed on my wing as I nursed the Mustang back to England.

First Kill

On the afternoon of May 11, 1944, we were escorting B-17s to Saarbrücken, Germany. I was leading my flight of four Mustangs as we weaved back and forth over the bomber stream, looking for trouble. The trouble came from above as I called out a large number of bandits a thousand feet above and off to our right. I told the rest of the flight, "I'll go get them," as my wingman, Billy D. "Bucky" Harris, and I peeled off and went after them, climbing under power from underneath. As we got closer, we could see they were Me 109s. I counted over thirty-five of them before I checked my six o'clock (tail) and noticed the other group of bandits following behind. The second group was even larger, over forty Me 109s coming up quickly to join the first. Bucky and I held our Mustangs down so the enemy wouldn't spot us. We let them go by over the top of us.

Satisfied that the "Me 109 train," which had now grown to over seventy-five, had passed, we pulled up even to their altitude and began our stalk from the rear, closing to less than fifty yards. I motioned for Bucky to slide over to the right as we lined up our prey in front of us. I opened fire and my four .50s sent bullets tearing into the first 109. All I saw was smoke and flame as he winged over in a twisting turn that became tighter and tighter. I tried for a second 109, but all hell broke loose as the whole flock of them scattered like chickens. How they didn't run into each another was anybody's guess!

Bucky got another one, but because we were outnumbered thirty to one, it was time to go while the getting was good! Both of us rolled over and headed earthward before the tables were turned on us.

We leveled off at around five thousand feet and went looking for other targets. It didn't take long: I spotted a lone Me 109 in front of me, heading the other way below us. Bucky and I did a quick reverse turn and dropped in behind this guy. With just a short pull of my trigger, my rounds found their mark. His canopy came off, and when the pilot saw two Mustangs behind him, he decided to jump, knowing full well he could get into another fighter once he touched down. Bucky and I headed for home. As I came roaring over our field at Boxted, I couldn't resist doing a couple of victory rolls for my buddies below. Unfortunately, my CO, George Bickell, was waiting for us when we taxied in. He congratulated me on my two victories, then smiled and fined me ten bucks for my little air show routine. I didn't care. I finally had some victories to my name. I later learned that George put Bucky and me in for an award for breaking up the German gaggle before they could attack the bombers. Things were really getting busy during the spring of 1944.

WORK UP TO THE BIG DAY!
Our group continued to fly escort missions during the entire month of May 1944. You could tell something was in the works as more and more ships were seen in and around the harbors of England, and countless supplies choked the docks. Most of my time was spent over Germany at places such as Berlin, Frankfurt, and Magdeburg, as the bombers continued to pound the Axis hard. Of course, the Germans didn't lie down and take our attacks lightly. On May 28 the Luftwaffe thickened the skies over Germany as swarms of fighters, like fireflies on hot summer night, came roaring into our bomber formations.

I picked out an Fw 190 and almost got him before I had to disengage for fear of ramming another fighter that crossed closely in front of me. Separated from my flight, I latched onto another Mustang to set a course for home. On our way out, our flight of two encountered a stricken B-17 that was having engine troubles, probably due to all the cannon and machine gun rounds it absorbed from the earlier Luftwaffe attacks. Suddenly, an Me 109 came in fast from the bomber's six o'clock, hell-bent on finishing him off. I rolled the Mustang over and shoved my throttle forward. I was still over two hundred yards away when I saw the 109 let loose with his cannon and machine guns. I responded with my own machine guns and saw them tear into his wing root and cockpit area; he snapped over and dived straight down before crashing.

I flew two missions on D-Day, and although we didn't encounter any German airplanes, the scene below on the beaches of Normandy was surreal. There were ships of every shape and size out in the channel with landing craft zigzagging back and forth. Intense ground fire and flak were everywhere, and we did what we could to help the guys on the ground. We continued to fly in support of our advancing troops, sometimes three missions a day as they pushed inland and pushed the Germans back.

On the 14th of June we were escorting some B-26 Marauder medium bombers over France when the Luftwaffe finally showed up again. We had a heck of a fight, and I tacked onto a 109. Closing fast, I let him have it at less than a hundred yards. He turned over slowly as flames shot out from beneath his engine cowling. I saw no parachute as he went down and finally crashed. I was one away from becoming an ace. By the end of June, the Pioneer Mustang Group had already shot down 370 enemy aircraft. And we weren't done yet! With over two hundred combat hours under my belt, I was sent home for thirty days of rest and relaxation. There would be plenty of war left when I returned.

ANOTHER TOUR

I arrived back in the fight in mid-October 1944. The Pioneer Mustang Group was no longer based in the comfortable surroundings of England but was instead somewhere in the French countryside, trying to keep up with General Patton's ground advance. Our missions began to change slightly as we became more of a tactical air unit that supported our advancing troops. I was given a brand-new P-51C Mustang and quickly had the same nose art applied. The only real difference between the B and C models was a modification to the propellers, and a clear Malcolm Hood canopy instead of the old style that used bars to support the glass. The Malcolm offered the pilot greater visibility and could even be slid backwards.

On October 26 we were sent up on dive-bombing missions to help soften up some German resistance. After we released our bombs, I found myself all alone except for two P-51s cruising below me, just above the cloud line. As I pointed the Mustang's nose in their direction and tried to catch up to them, I noticed an Me 109 rise from the clouds and get hot on their tails. The two Mustangs never saw him and the 109 never noticed me as he focused on the P-51s in front of him. For whatever reason, the 109 was closing too quickly, and he suddenly dropped his landing gear to slow himself down. I eased up behind him and hit him hard. He rolled over and went down, straight through the clouds. I was so determined to claim my fifth kill that I followed him through the cloud deck. I had no idea if there were mountains below or flatlands or other German fighters waiting below—I was determined to become an ace!

I popped out with a thousand feet of altitude left and found the 109 burning in a smoking hole below. Officially I was now an ace, and by the end of October our group surpassed the six hundred airplanes–destroyed mark. Unfortunately, November 1944 would bring its own set of problems for me and my beloved P-51 Mustang.

Lucky Shot

On November 18 I was leading a search and destroy mission of eight Mustangs. We weren't having much luck as we droned around so I decided to split up the flight. I sent four planes in one direction as I took the other three and went hunting. My flight eventually found what we were looking for: six German trucks on a narrow road. With just a quick turn, we began our firing pass. The trucks saw us coming and stopped in their tracks as we let loose. As I zoomed by, I turned to look back and saw three of the trucks burning. I decided to bring the flight back around and do it all over again. Unfortunately, one of my wingmen who was brand new to combat got a little excited and got ahead of me.

We were barely ten feet off the ground as we approached the trucks. I couldn't turn right because my wingman was in front of me. Turning left meant I would have driven the "Tail-end-Charlie" Mustang into the ground. My only option was to hold it down while we came across the field. That's when I saw the surprise waiting for me—the field was full of German soldiers and each of them had a rifle pointed skyward! I was able to call the Mustang in front just as the hail of bullets hit our flight. Regaining the lead position, I took our flight skyward to get some air under our wings. Then I started counting bullet holes in my Mustang. I saw eight hits in total, most of them in the wings, but the one that concerned me the most had gone through my Merlin engine and exited my cowling. The Rolls-Royce engine was a damn fine motor, but once it sprang a leak, it was only a matter of time before it bled itself dry.

I climbed as fast as I could and turned for home. I was able to make it to 8,500 feet before the engine sputtered and conked out. I declared an emergency and called for help. The controllers told me I was forty miles from our lines and asked if I could make it. Regrettably, the Mustang glided like a grand piano so I barely made it forty yards before I threw the hood off and jumped. As I floated down, all I could think about was that a damn rifle bullet had shot me down! I wondered what it would be like to be a German POW, and who would be waiting for me on the ground. I was jolted back to reality when I saw my beautiful P-51C crash below. I could also see fighting going on below and hoped the Germans wouldn't notice me.

When I finally landed, I found myself near a road with only some small shrubbery to conceal me. I was on the ground for a couple of minutes when I saw a German halftrack heading my way through an open field fifty yards away. I got down as low as I could. The halftrack stopped and two soldiers armed with rifles began searching for me. I knew my time had come and hoped that my family would hold out hope that I was still alive when my group reported me missing in action. I stood up with arms raised over my head and began walking toward them. When I got closer, I spotted a crude white star painted over the halftrack's Iron Cross and saw that the two soldiers were wearing American uniforms!

It took a little convincing for the GIs—who were from New York—to believe me, but after I rattled off a bunch of baseball trivia, they loaded me up and took me back to their unit. The very next day I was stuffed into a military version of the Piper Cub, an L-4, and flown back to my squadron. Once there, I encountered a very big change.

FIGHTER SWITCHEROO

I had owned and ridden horses before the war, and lived by an old saying: "When you get bucked off, get right back on before you lose your nerve." The day after my return I took a P-51 up and found my nerve was in fine shape. Little did I know that that would be my last time in a Mustang for a while. Command had decided that the Eighth Air Force needed Mustangs more than we did, so the Pioneer Mustang Group was reassigned to P-47 Thunderbolts. We flew these into early 1945 and did mostly dive bombing and strafing, especially in the Battle of the Bulge during December '44 to January '45. I didn't really care for the P-47 much, but I have to admit it could take a lot of ground fire and keep on going.

During a P-47 dive-bombing attack against some Tiger tanks near Bastogne, I took a 20mm cannon round right smack in the engine, and it completely blew out two cylinders from the motor. Heck, I didn't even know I had been hit until I taxied in after the mission and all the ground crew guys were pointing and shaking their heads at me. Had I been in a Mustang, well, let's just say I wouldn't be here telling this story! The P-47 was an awesome dive bomber and a monster of an aircraft. If you talk to a full-time Thunderbolt pilot, they swear by it. But if you ask someone who flew both the P-47 and P-51 in combat, they will say that the Mustang was king. We were pleased when we got a reprieve in early 1945 and got our Mustangs back. In fact, we got the latest and greatest model, the P-51D.

The D models were improved versions of the B/C models. The D had a teardrop canopy, tail-warning radar, and six .50-caliber machine guns instead of four. To me, it was the ultimate in Mustangs and I ended the war with them, but not until I scored a victory over one of Hitler's wonder weapons.

On April 14, 1945, I was leading the 355th FS on a search and destroy mission over Germany near Mühlhausen, at around twelve thousand feet. I split our formation up to take four Mustangs one way and sent the others hunting in another area. It didn't take long for me to spot movement below. I could tell it was a twin-engine aircraft moving quickly below us at two thousand feet. The only thing that moved that fast had to be a jet—a Messerschmitt Me 262! I had encountered them a couple of times before and was amazed at their blazing speed. A ten-thousand-foot advantage was the only way a prop plane could score a jet. I told the rest of the group to follow me as I rolled my Mustang over and dived at the 262. As I picked up momentum, I glanced at the airspeed indicator as it climbed past 450 miles per hour. At about the same time, my control stick began to "feel funny" and I realized I was experiencing high-speed compressibility—great velocity that puts dangerous stress on a wing. I forgot about the jet and wondered if I would survive my dive!

I said a couple of prayers and moved the throttle forward and backwards. As I neared the ground, I felt the stick budge a little as I tried to pull out of my screaming dive. I thought for sure I was going to tear the wings off and drive the Mustang deep into German soil! As I pulled out, I found myself right on the 262's tail. In a split second I lined him up. At a hundred feet away, he was hard to miss. I gave him a little squirt that tore up his left jet engine and shredded his left wingtip. With a moment of greater forward speed than the jet, I overshot him and pulled off to the right. The 262 pulled straight up and I knew the Mustang couldn't catch him no matter how fast I was going. I thought I lost him as he pulled over a thousand feet away, but I was watching as he stopped in midair and began to tail slide back down. His canopy came off and out popped the pilot. I finally got a jet! My elation was short-lived, however, because we were now over a German airfield. Every flak gun down there began to hammer on us. Our Mustang flight pushed the throttles forward and climbed for the safety of higher altitude and headed for home.

I ended the war with six victories during my two tours. I owe my survival to the P-51 Mustang. The Pioneer Mustang Group was officially credited with 701 aerial victories and we were crowned the top-scoring fighter group of the European Theater of Operations (ETO).

THUNDERBIRD
Capt. Ted E. Lines Sr., USAAC
4th Fighter Group, 335th Fighter Squadron

When I arrived in England in the spring of 1944, I had a whopping twelve hours of experience flying the P-51, and all of that time was in the P-51A back in the States. To me, the Mustang was like a young woman: beautiful but vulnerable. With its thin skin of aluminum wrapped around the engine, there wasn't an ounce of protection. One little nick from flak or small-arms fire and we were out of the ball game. But I have to say that flying the Mustang, especially in combat, was one of the two greatest thrills in my life. The other was when I flew as wingman for my good friend Pierce W. "Mac" McKennon.

For whatever reason, Mac took a liking to me the day I arrived in England. He chose me to fly on his wing when we went out on our missions. Mac was a real character. After we got into big dogfights with the Luftwaffe and made our way back to England, the whole squadron would be scattered about. Mac had a real knack for finding me anywhere over Europe. He would come up alongside and for fun he'd try to flip me over by placing his Mustang's wingtip under mine and then bang it up and down. When I'd land at our base in Debden, the flight engineer, a lieutenant colonel, would ask, "Why is it that every time you and McKennon fly together you both come back with your wingtips beat up?"

Mac would be off in the distance, laughing, as I explained, "Must be turbulent winds, sir." I don't think that lieutenant colonel ever believed us!

Our wingtips weren't the only things we beat up when we went head to head with the Luftwaffe. I remember one of my first missions as we escorted B-17s into Germany because I was scared to death! Someone in the group called out that more than 150 German fighters were ahead of us. Although there were only twenty-four of us P-51B Mustangs, some joker came across the R/T and said, "Just about even!" Because we flew the Mustang, that was the attitude of the pilots in our group. We tore into the German fighters and had us an old-fashioned free-for-all.

ENCOUNTER REPORT: APRIL 8, 1944
335th Fighter Squadron, 4th Group
1430 HOURS
NORTHWEST OF BRUNSWICK [BRAUNSCHWEIG]

I was flying Greenbelt White 3 when we saw a large formation of about 85 plus A/C [aircraft] flying SW about 2,000 feet below us. They passed under us, headed for the bombers, getting a few before we got tangled with them. I cannot give a very coherent description because it's the first time like it I have ever been in. Fw 190s were all over the place and every time I turned around I started shooting. I made attacks on about 5 different 190s; one of these I got strikes on. Looking over at one side of the fight there was a 190 and a P-51 going round and round, neither getting deflection on the other. I dived towards the 190 and clobbered him pretty good (about a 40° shot). He straightened out and I got in some more strikes on wing root and fuselage around the cockpit. He went into a sharp dive and then I overshot him. I turned sharply and, looking down, saw him hit and litter a field with pieces of his A/C. The fight started about 23,000 feet and finally ended up on the deck.

A/C used: P-51B 7NA 43-6896
Pierce W. McKennon
1st Lt. Air Corps

ENCOUNTER REPORT: RED-NOSE SWEEP
HQ 4th Fighter Group

April 24, 1944, found me leading the group on a freelance sweep to the Frankfurt area, in conjunction with a bombing attack in the Munich area. We arrived in the vicinity of Frankfurt at 25,000 feet at 1233 hours, turned south, and started to lose altitude to 10,000 feet. A gaggle of about thirty-five Fw 190s were reported as being at 10,000 feet going south toward the bomber track. There were two Fw fighters above and to the rear of the main formation. We turned starboard into the sun and climbed above and behind them. As we did this the two Fw aircraft dropped their [auxiliary fuel] tanks and weaved violently above the enemy formation. However, the main gaggle continued to proceed on their southerly course and did not take evasive action.

335 and 334 Squadrons attacked in more or less line abreast formation with 336 Squadron giving top cover. I picked out an Fw 190 third or fourth from the port side of the gaggle and opened fire, obtaining strikes. The enemy aircraft broke hard left and up, and then evaded to the deck. I started to give chase but had several others on my tail so I broke off and engaged another Fw 190. We went around in tight circles and I got in a few bursts. When he headed to the southeast I got on his tail, opening at 300 yards with a second burst, finally closing to 150 yards. I was getting strikes on him when I saw him jettison his hood and helmet. I overshot him, and as I did so I saw him unfastening his straps and watched him jump out at 600 feet. His chute opened just above the ground.

I climbed to rejoin the battle and at 6,000 feet I saw an Fw 190 diving away to the south. I dove after him and at 2,000 feet he started a left turn. I opened fire at 300 yards, closing to 200, and saw strikes along the cockpit. The enemy aircraft then straightened out and glided for an open field as if to crash land. I got on his tail and was ready to open fire again when Captain Schlegal of 335 Squadron came in and got strikes in the cockpit. The enemy aircraft went straight into the ground and exploded.

I then joined up with other P-51s, reformed the group, and headed back for base.

Col. Don J. M. Blakeslee

STARCK MAD!
Col. Walter "Wally" Starck, USAF (Ret.)
352nd Fighter Group, 487th Fighter Squadron

As an original member of the 352nd Fighter Group, our squadron had cut our teeth in combat during 1943, flying the P-47 Thunderbolt. The Jug was big and roomy, and had eight .50-caliber machine guns. It could take a lot of punishment from the Germans and give back even more. I scored some of my early victories flying the P-47 and was quite satisfied with the big brute of an airplane. In the spring of 1944 we were ordered to trade our Jugs in for a new fighter called the P-51 Mustang. To say I was a little apprehensive about swapping fighters is an understatement. I felt very cramped sitting in the P-51B, compared to the wide, comfortable confines of the P-47. When I started the Mustang's Merlin engine for the very first time, the noise coming from the exhaust stacks that stuck from both sides of the cowl reminded me of a bunch of rattling tin cans; all I heard was a constant, annoying popping sound. But once I poured the coal to the Mustang and took off, it was an entirely different animal. In the sky, the Mustang had real positive control and was a joy to fly. It was very maneuverable and forgiving, too. I especially liked the Malcolm Hood version of the P-51B because the clear teardrop canopy gave improved visibility. The Mustang also topped the Thunderbolt in range. Now we could stay with the bombers all the way in to the target and fight the Luftwaffe on our terms.

ENCOUNTER REPORT: MAY 27, 1944
487th Fighter Squadron
1230 HOURS
VICINITY, STRASBOURG, 25,000 TO 6,000 FEET

I was leading Yellow Flight in the lead Squadron escorting the lead box of bombers at 25,000 feet. Suddenly the sky up ahead was filled with a huge glob of planes. They were Fw 190s and Me 109s, 100 plus. In a moment we were in the middle of them and the fight started. We swung over to the right and soon I and my wingman were alone in the middle of a Lufbery [defensive circle] of 12 Me [fighters], flying in three flights of four each. I reefed in [reduced diameter of approach] hard all the while and was actually making a smaller circle within the 109s. Whenever I started to get sights on one ship I noticed a flight of 109s ready to come in on my wingman or myself and so I had to break off. Finally I saw a 109 break away and head due east. I tore out after him and stayed a little below so he would not see me and thus give me a chance to close in on his tail and let him have it. We flew for about five minutes, wide open throttle, when the 109 pilot saw me and turned sharply to the left. I tried to cut him off but he turned the opposite way and we were right back where we started. Then the E/A [enemy aircraft] broke down and made a sharp turn to the left and then to the right. I swung my ship around as he turned to the right. I managed to get in to about 150 yards from him, measured off about twenty degrees deflection, and opened fire. Strikes showed up all over the cockpit in one brilliant mass and the E/A caught fire and did a half roll and spun slowly towards the earth where it crashed, in a burst of flames. The pilot did not get out—ever. I went down to take a picture of the wreckage and then headed back upstairs and went home, all alone.

Walter E. Starck
Captain, Air Corps

3

Prelude to Overlord

Spring 1944. Allied heavy bombers and their airborne "little friends" had been hammering away at Fortress Europe since early in the year. Around-the-clock strategic bombardment missions, in concert with low-level "Chattanooga Choo Choo" strafing missions by Allied fighters, helped soften up intended targets. As fliers, our objectives were railways, airfields, and German emplacements, and to knock the Luftwaffe out of the sky.

The battle-tested P-38 Lightnings and P-47 Thunderbolts of the United States Army Air Corps had recently been joined by a newcomer, the North American P-51B Mustang. With its "long legs," the Mustang could stay with the bombers all the way to the target. Once the bombers released their loads, the Mustangs were set free to roam, and search out and destroy targets of opportunity.

As the fighting intensified on two fronts, Hitler's Germany was in a stranglehold. This was the eve of D-Day, the greatest and mightiest invasion the world had ever known. The final knot in the hangman's noose was about to be tightened.

ENCOUNTER REPORT: BLUE-NOSE CIRCUS
352nd Fighter Group, 437th Fighter Squadron

As the bombers approached the vicinity of Magdeburg, Germany, on May 30, 1944, I led a section of seven ships giving close support to the rear box, which was quite a way behind the main formation. I noticed twenty to thirty single-engine fighters attacking the front boxes so I dropped [auxiliary fuel] tanks and headed toward them. We came up behind three Me 109s in rather tight formation. I opened fire on one from 300 yards and closed to 150. The enemy aircraft burst into flames and went down. I then slipped behind the second 109 and fired from 200 to 100 yards. This enemy aircraft started burning and falling apart. He went down spinning. The third enemy aircraft saw us and broke down. I followed him in a steep turn, diving and zooming. I got in many deflection shots, getting hits on the wings and tail section. I ran out of ammunition so my element leader, Lieutenant Whisner, continued the attack getting in several good hits. At about seven thousand feet, the pilot bailed out.

I claimed two Me 109s destroyed and one Me 109 destroyed/shared with Lieutenant Whisner.

Maj. George Preddy

LONGEST MISSION, LONGEST DAY
Capt. C. E. "Bud" Anderson, USAAC
357th Fighter Group, 363rd Fighter Squadron

"Staying alive was no simple thing in the skies over Europe in the spring of 1944. A lot of men couldn't. It was a bad thing to dwell on if you were a fighter pilot and so we told ourselves we were dead men and lived for the moment with no thought of the future at all. It wasn't too difficult. Lots of us had no future and everyone knew it."

—C. E. Bud Anderson

During the spring of 1944, I could see the military buildup in England and figured the [channel] invasion would take place soon. I was returning from a mission on June 5, 1944, and as I neared Pas-de-Calais, France, I noticed more boats than I had ever seen before. I shouted over the R/T [receiver/transmitter], "Oh wow!" The group leader ordered radio silence; he didn't want me tipping off the listening enemy!

After we landed, our P-51Bs were swarmed over by ground crews carrying paint buckets and brushes. They hand-painted black-and-white bands around our wings and fuselage, turning our olive-drab Mustangs into hybrid zebras. We figured something was up for them to go to all that trouble. We learned hours later that the boys on the ground would land on Normandy early the next day. The invasion was on!

Our group, the 357th, was assigned to launch thirty-two P-51Bs at 2:15 a.m. We were to patrol an assigned area south of Normandy and wait for some action. It never came, because the Luftwaffe missed the invitation to the party and never showed up. I was taken up with the excitement, and since it was really dark outside I did a very poor preflight of my P-51B, *Old Crow*.

I didn't notice that the coolant radiator doors were in the automatic position. Normally, my ground crew ran up *Old Crow* and left the radiator doors in the manual position. A Mustang could overheat if it remained on the ground for extended periods of time with the prop turning. But I didn't think I was on the ground all that long.

I was the fifth Mustang to take off. I advanced the throttle forward and my P-51B raced down the runway, gaining flying speed. I was fully loaded with gas and ammo as I lifted off into the black, moonless night. That's when the radiator cap blew. The vapor spread across my windscreen, blinding any forward vision I had. I quickly opened the coolant doors and the temps came back into the green. My mind raced back and forth: *Why didn't I do a better preflight? What the heck should I do now?*

There was no place to land, as all the runways were clogged with other Mustangs waiting to take off. The coolant temperatures were holding steady and I decided to take the risk and keep on flying. Besides,

Old Crow and I had never had an abort, and I didn't want to break our record on the greatest day in history.

My windscreen began to clear as I gathered my flight together and tucked them in a close trail behind the group leader. There were red and green navigation lights all over the sky; they looked like a bunch of crazed fireflies buzzing around. After the group was assembled, with every flight in its proper place, the group leader announced, "Turn out your navigation lights and start patrolling!" That's when it all fell apart.

I kept close watch over the blue exhaust flame on the lead Mustang ahead of me. I looked around for my fellow wingmen and found they had disappeared. I wondered who else was lost as we droned around over parts unknown. Then the Germans opened up with their antiaircraft guns; I knew we weren't over England anymore! Every once in awhile I asked the group leader to flash his navigation lights so I could get back into position.

The early morning light began to push the darkness away. There were over thirty Mustangs that launched from our base at Leiston and now, to my surprise, counting myself, there were only four of us: the group leader and his wingman, and another flight leader, "O'bee" O'Brien, sitting under my tail. Either we were really lost or we were a bunch of crack navigators! At that moment, through the breaks in the clouds, we saw the entire Normandy beach area.

It was an awesome sight. The landing barges were still approaching the beaches and I could see the white wake that followed each vessel. We were a long way away, but I could see the fighting and activity on the ground below. I could only wonder how the guys on the ground were doing, and prayed for their success.

After six hours and fifty-five minutes of flying, I touched down at Leiston. It was the longest mission I had ever flown during the war. D-Day had been "dull day" as far as enemy action was concerned, but we had been part of history, and that was satisfying to me. I had had some exciting moments and saw places and things that I would never forget.

To learn more about Bud Anderson's combat experiences, see his book, To
Fly and Fight.

BY DAWN'S EARLY LIGHT
2nd Lt. Carlton "Bud" Fuhrman
352nd Fighter Group, 486th Fighter Squadron

Something big was about to happen, but we were all kept in the dark.
The telltale sign was when we saw the Bodney ground crew painting
ugly black-and-white stripes on our Mustangs. Our "thoroughbreds"
had the look of deformed zebras!

On June 5, 1944, a bunch of us were down in the officer's club telling "tall tales" of combat. Around 7:00 p.m., our CO, Colonel Mason,
came in and said, "Boys, you better get to bed 'cuz you're gonna need
the sleep." By the time we got settled in our bunks, an orderly came in
and said breakfast was ready. It was only eleven o'clock at night. Who
the hell wanted breakfast that early? We were also told our briefing was
scheduled for midnight.

Our heads became a lot clearer when we saw the big map at briefing. The invasion was finally on! After we had been given our areas of
responsibility along with "angels [altitudes] and headings," we walked
to our planes, where I adjusted my instrument lights and set my gauges.
Then we stood around in the darkness so our eyes would adjust. A light
rain began to fall.

By the time we cranked up our engines, it was now spitting rain. It
was also the first time we took off at night. The standard daytime procedure of launching four Mustangs abreast would also be used on this
night mission. Red and green identification lights moved all around in
the darkness. The real "fun" was trying to pick out the ones on the guy
you were supposed to join up with.

At 2:30 a.m. our squadron would be the first to launch. I was the
number-four man in the second flight of four waiting to depart. Next
to me in the number-three position was Lt. Bob Frascotti, flying his

P-51B named (Durante-style) *Umbriago*. This was Lieutenant Frascotti's eighty-ninth and final mission before he was to rotate home. Sadly, he never made it.

A brand-new control tower had just been built and completed the day before. It would be a couple of days before the interior work was done and the tower operational. In the meantime, a small string of lights was erected on the field to aid our takeoff. The first flight of Mustangs clipped the lights and took them along as the planes departed the field. Bodney air base was now pitch black.

Holding my brakes, I began to advance my throttle forward. I could feel the rest of my flight begin to throttle up, too. We would need all the horsepower we could get because of the extra weight we carried in the form of drop tanks and internal fuel. My eyes were glued to Lieutenant Frascotti's lights as we trampled across the airfield. No one in our flight knew we were lined up off center.

My Mustang "bounced" into the air and for a split second I almost pushed it back down to gain more speed. Something in my head told me to "keep it up." I was looking left, watching my wingman, Lieutenant Frascotti, waiting for him to climb. Suddenly, I was engulfed in a huge fireball of brilliant light and flame. I instinctively pulled back hard on the stick and felt the Mustang shudder. I was pulling too damn hard and was almost stalled out!

My vision was completely "whited out" by the flash of light. And for a few seconds, which felt like an eternity, I flew blind. By the time my vision came back, the rest of the flight was disappearing into some clouds above me. I swung off to the right, climbed up through, and waited for everybody. No one showed up.

I was all by myself for quite a while. I saw a set of lights on up ahead and we went around and around each other like a couple of fireflies trying to ID one another. It was a fellow "blue noser!" I latched onto him for the rest of the mission. As day began to break, I looked out across the channel and saw a massive formation of ships on the water heading for France. I wondered if there was enough water to keep them afloat!

With fuel running low, we returned to Bodney. The control tower was still smoldering when I landed. The only thing left of Lieutenant Frascotti's airplane was the Rolls-Royce engine lying on the floor in the control tower. With full fuel, he had plowed right into the darkened tower. My Mustang had been scorched as it flew through his fireball. Frascotti's flame burned bright, enabling the rest of the 352nd to launch safely. Although we never encountered a German airplane on that first mission, Lieutenant Frascotti became one of D-Day's early casualties.

ZERO HOUR!
1st Lt. Raymond T. Conlin
357th Fighter Group, 362nd Fighter Squadron

At 10:00 p.m. on June 5, 1944, everyone was assembled to hear an address from General Eisenhower. H-hour was only hours away, and the general told us that this would be the most important mission that anyone would ever take part in. Our job was to protect those brave GIs who were to execute the actual landings. Our primary goal and reason for being there was to disallow any German aircraft from spoiling Ike's plan.

We were then briefed and told that our assigned area was twenty-seven thousand feet over the Jersey and Guernsey Islands. I was assigned to fly wing on our squadron leader, Capt. Joe Broadhead. Takeoff was scheduled for 5:00 a.m. on June 6. No one could sleep. All thoughts were focused on the mission at hand. I sat and wondered how many German aircraft we would encounter. I mentally prepared myself for this historic mission, playing scenarios over and over in my head so I wouldn't make any mistakes.

We reported to flight-line operations for breakfast, then to flight prep prior to takeoff. As I walked out to my plane, I had a nagging feeling I was forgetting something. I climbed into the cockpit of my P-51B and noticed the hastily applied black-and-white stripes. That nagging feeling was now in the pit of my stomach. As I sat strapped in the cockpit, ready to crank up, I realized I had forgotten to use the bathroom.

I tried to focus on other things. I resolved to myself that once I got to our assigned altitude, I'd avail myself of the relief tube that North American Aviation had so thoughtfully provided for such an emergency. At precisely 5:00 a.m. my Mustang roared down the runway at Leiston, launching into the unpredictable English weather.

Clinging to Captain Broadhead's wing, we ran smack into a low, heavy overcast. We had to fly on gauges, but at least my mind was focused on something other than my physical discomfort. For more than forty minutes we climbed through the soup and finally broke into the clear. We were on time and on station as H-hour was about to unfold below.

As our flight settled into patrol formation, I received a call over the R/T from Captain Broadhead. The dear captain informed me that we were going down to take a look at the invasion. I'd been seconds away from using the relief tube and had to put everything back in its place. It also meant we had to fly five miles back down on the gauges and then five miles back up. Orders is orders, so down I went.

We broke out of the overcast at two thousand feet, near the west end of Omaha Beach. On our way down, we heard over the R/T that two enemy Bf 109s had made one pass down the beach, strafing from west to east. We had missed them by just a few seconds!

As the captain and I drifted and stooged around over the beach area, I could see a lot of fierce fighting down below. Tracer fire was going in every direction and there was smoke and explosions all over the beach head. The channel was thick with an armada of countless ships and invasion vessels. Each had departed from England so loaded with equipment and men that I was amazed that the whole of Britain hadn't sunk beneath the weight!

I doubt if anybody on the ground even looked up at us. Our GIs were busy handling their own set of problems and had no time to worry about gawkers like us. After a few minutes of sightseeing, we went back upstairs to join the rest of the boys. With all the action and excitement down below, I forgot about my bladder problem, which was finally resolved when I returned to base three hours later. I flew another mission later that day, but this time I was fully prepared and my bladder completely empty!

REQUIEM FOR A PRINCESS
1st Lt. Robert K. Butler, USAAC (Ret.)
352nd Fighter Group, 487th Fighter Squadron

I arrived in England in early January 1944 as a replacement pilot. After I did my familiarization flights out of Atcham in P-47 Thunderbolts, I was assigned to the 352nd Fighter Group, 487th Fighter Squadron. I was one of five men sent to Bodney air base as replacement pilots in the group. We received a rather cold welcome from the other pilots. It was nothing personal; it was just hard for the old timers (those with twenty missions under their belts) to admit they were losing people. We were a reminder of that fact.

I flew a handful of missions in the P-47 "Jug," most of which were in the bomber-escort role. We carried drop tanks to extend our range as we fought desperately, early on, to put enough fighters in the air to keep the Luftwaffe off the bombers' backs. Before the drop tanks were added, it was always a hard-fought battle for the bomber crews when we had to break off and return to base because of our dwindling fuel supply. The bomber losses were terrible, but, fortunately, that was about to change.

In early spring of 1944, three brand-new, highly advanced fighter planes arrived at our base in Bodney. The manufacturer called it the North American P-51B; we called them Mustangs. We were soon informed that each one of us would get one hour of stick time to familiarize ourselves with our new mount. Before we could take it up, though, we had to meet and agree to certain conditions.

The first condition was that under no circumstance would we bend, break, or damage anything on the Mustang. The second condition was even more stringent: we had to return it! Compared to the Rolls-Royce feel of the P-47, the Mustang was like driving a race car. The P-51 had better visibility over the nose and was more agile. When you were strapped into it, you felt like an extension of the airplane. Everyone behaved themselves and we were given our endorsements after our none-too-lengthy checkout. It didn't take us long to show the Luftwaffe what this new fighter could do.

May 12, 1944. Our group was just finishing a bomber-escort mission southwest of Koblenz, Germany. Lieutenant Fred Allison was leading red flight and I was his wingman. As we turned for home, Lieutenant Allison spotted a Luftwaffe airfield with German fighters landing and taking off. We racked our Mustangs over and came screaming in behind the Bf 109s that were about to touch down on their home field. They never knew what hit them.

Lieutenant Allison picked out one 109 that was spitting and sputtering as it tried to get out of the air. Allison hit him several times with his four .50 calibers. I was off to one side as Allison made his gun run in. We were really hauling, with a lot of forward speed and energy, and I realized he was going to overrun the 109. Lieutenant Allison soon overtook the 109 and pulled up over him. I instinctively hauled my throttle back so that my four propeller paddle blades could act like a speed brake to slow me down.

I lined up behind this guy and hosed him all over with my guns. There wasn't much left of the smoking 109 as he bellied into a field. Looking backwards, I saw the pilot get out of his fighter; at least he had a short walk back to his base. Our own mission destinations soon became shorter, too, as we shot up German trains, troops, and convoys in central France as the preparation for the invasion intensified.

June 5, 1944. We landed back at Bodney after another day of strafing anything that carried a German soldier. We took our showers and cleaned up to get ready for evening chow. When we walked outside, we looked at our Mustangs and said, "What the hell is going on out there!?" The field of airplanes looked like a bunch of deformed zebras with black-and-white stripes painted on their wings and fuselage. The invasion was on!

At 11:00 p.m. we received our formal briefing for the next day's mission. We were to take off in the early morning hours and escort B-24 Liberators behind the beachhead as they carpet-bombed the German defenses. Our job was to orbit at twenty thousand feet and keep the Luftwaffe off of the bombers. The Luftwaffe would be no problem that day, but getting safely airborne would be.

By the time we cranked up our engines early on June 6, it had begun to spit rain. It was also the first time we took off in darkness. Our standard daytime procedure of launching four Mustangs abreast would be carried over and used on our "virgin" night mission. Red and green identification lights mounted on our Mustangs moved all around in the darkness. The real "fun" was trying to pick out the ones on the guy you were supposed to join up with!

After I got airborne, I cruised around Bodney, trying to find somebody to join up with—anybody! After ten minutes of chasing red and green lights around in the sky, a few of us were able to join up. We rendezvoused with the bombers and did our escort mission. There was no sign of the Luftwaffe anywhere as we stooged around high above the epic battle below. Our final order of the day was simple and to the point: stay off the deck! All the men and machines on the beach and the countless ships in the channel were unforgettable sights.

With one D-Day mission under my belt, I prepared for my second flight of the day. At least this one would be in the daylight hours (6:00 p.m.). Because so many P-51s were flying this day, with most handling two missions and some flying three, I was given what was available. I drew Lt. Bill Whisner's *Princess Elizabeth* (P-51B-10 Serial #42-106449). She was named in honor of the future Queen of England. Already a proven fighter, she carried a handful of German crosses on her side, and I hoped to add a few of my own as we prepared to go hunting.

Our mission was originally planned to have sixteen P-51s from our 487th squadron escort nine P-38 Lightnings on a dive-bombing mission south of Paris. I was slotted to fly element [section] leader in the last flight of four Mustangs. For whatever reason, our flight leader had to abort due to mechanical problems, so I took over the Tail-end Charlie flight of Mustangs with a P-51 on either side of me. As we flew on toward France, we joined up with the bomb-laden Lightnings.

The P-38s were concerned that the Luftwaffe would try to jump them on their way into the target, forcing them to prematurely dump their bombs. Just like the first mission of the day, there were no German fighters around, as the P-38s dropped their bombs on target. We were now cleared to leave the Lightnings and drop down to the deck for a little "housecleaning" of our own. German vehicles seemed to be every-where; it looked like controlled chaos as the Germans were racing men and machines to the beach. It was our job to make sure they would never arrive. We strafed and chewed up trucks, tanks, and convoys, cutting a swath across the French countryside. Anything that moved prior to a preset line from the beachhead was fair game. The Germans tried to stand and fight by throwing a lot of flack and small-arms fire at us as we screamed overhead.

As our flight of fifteen Mustangs joined up for the trip back home, we climbed to a safer altitude and prepared to cross the beach. I was in the back of the formation leading my flight when I noticed a train out of the corner of my eye. The locomotive and several boxcars were sitting idle on a turnaround in a small valley. It looked like easy pickings for some hungry Mustangs! I called the boss man leading the squadron and he gave me the go-ahead for the three of us to go down and shoot it up.

I didn't want to alert the Germans, so I took my flight and flew a mile ahead of the train. I hoped they thought we weren't interested in them. I thought we'd have the element of surprise on the way back, coming in low and fast. I thought this would be an easy target. I thought wrong.

I cranked *Princess Elizabeth* over and dropped her down to the deck. The three of us were "cuttin' grass" through the valley floor as we leveled off. The train was dead ahead, sitting quietly at the end of a peaceful val-ley surrounded by hills. The hills on one side were lined with trees. On the other side was a quaint-looking church that overlooked a cemetery. It was almost picture perfect, until the flak opened up on us.

As our flight neared the church low on the deck, all hell broke loose. We took fire from 20mm and 40mm guns, and from small arms. The fire erupted from the trees, the church, and the headstones. We had flown into a trap and I was the rat caught in the valley of death! I could see the streams of tracers racing toward me, going over my airplane, and all I could think was, *This isn't going to work*! I still had a little luck left with the *Princess*. I was so low the gunners misjudged my height. White-hot balls of lead streaked over my canopy. Then my luck ran out.

Those harmless-looking boxcars turned into "flak flat cars" when their canvas sides dropped and their guns swung in our direction. We were still too low for the train's guns, but more rounds were pumped over our heads. There wasn't much room for the three of us to maneuver as the trees began to rise. My two wingmen pulled up and got out of there while the getting was good. I was now alone and running out of options.

Actually, I had two options available to me. I could either fly over the top of the train and get chewed up by all the incoming flak or I could fly through the train and die! I may have been young and foolish, but I wasn't stupid. I prayed I would become much older! It was now or never, so I jinked the stick back. Bang! I took a big hit in the belly and the *Princess* lurched upward. Hot oil that streamed into the cockpit through the ventilators caused the Plexiglas canopy to fog up.

I was now literally blind as I pulled back on the stick to gain as much altitude as possible. The scalding hot oil showered over my shoulders and I knew I wasn't going to last long with my engine's lifeblood pouring out the bottom of *Princess Elizabeth*. I slowly pulled my power back as the needle on my oil pressure gauge raced for the zero mark. The Mustang was going fast and it wouldn't be long until the engine seized up.

One of my observant wingmen joined back up with me and told me I had oil leaking all over the place. *No kidding*! If he'd been any closer, I would have reached out and wrung his neck! I told him I didn't think I was going to get this crate back to England, and added, in no uncertain terms, that he was *not* to follow me down. One Mustang loss was enough for the day. I didn't need him to get his ass shot off, too!

I was trying to make the beach about nine miles up ahead. I was at 1,500 feet with the engine shaking, popping, and rattling around. I could see all the "hell-raising" going on up at the beachhead and I wondered how much farther I could get the *Princess* to fly. That's when the prop stopped dead, locked up tight. Boy, did it become silent! The P-51 was never designed to be a glider so I opened the canopy.

I kicked the Mustang around a little and got sucked right out. After a few seconds, I pulled my ripcord and floated under a billowing canopy. As I hung in my parachute, I could see *Princess Elizabeth* overhead, arching downward, trailing thick, black smoke. My P-51 slammed into the ground, right onto some railroad tracks. It was an unbelievable sight, and ironic, too. A damn train shoots me down and in its last dying act, *Princess Elizabeth* grinds up some train tracks. You take what you can get!

I came down near some trees and stepped out of my harness. I buried my chute the best I could and then ran as fast as possible for a quarter mile. When I found a large tree with good foliage, I scurried up to the top, hidden from the ground. I sat there and belted myself to the trunk. It didn't take long for the Germans to arrive. Thankfully, they never looked up. I was twenty-one years old, tired, and beat up and burned. What else could go wrong? Then it started to rain.

When I awoke the next morning, cold and wet, I saw an old Frenchman below me, acting very nervously and looking from side to side as he walked through the woods. I watched him for over an hour. The Frenchman began to cook something, so I quietly climbed down to see what he was up to. I walked toward him looking like hell, with fresh oil burns over my body. The Frenchman was busy cooking a still, making booze. I used my escape and evasion book to tell him I was an American and not a German. The wide-eyed Frenchman mumbled something and left. I figured he didn't believe me.

I thought he went to get the Germans, but he showed back up with guys from the French Underground. The smiling old man gave me a teacup filled with his finest home brew. I was taken to a farmhouse, where the Frenchmen began to celebrate and toast America over and over again. Each time a glass was raised, another would be poured down my throat. Right before I passed out, I could feel my clothes being taken off. Then everything went black.

When I came to later the next day, I was told that the Underground had gotten me gassed because they had to move me. They'd put me in French peasant clothes and thrown me on a hay wagon. I went through three German checkpoints. I was so drunk, all I could do was moan and mumble every time a German soldier tried to talk with me.

For the next seventy-nine days, I stayed on as a guest of the French and worked with the Resistance on clandestine missions against the Germans. I was liberated by advancing Canadian troops and returned to the 352nd Fighter Group and Bodney. I continued to fly combat missions right up until V-E Day. I named my new Mustang *Channel Belle*, in honor of my delayed crossing back to England.

CONTROL OF THE SKIES
Capt. William B. Overstreet Jr., USSAC
357th Fighter Group, 363rd Fighter Squadron

Although our group had trained in P-39s back in the States, we were in for quite a surprise when we arrived in England in late 1943. Our group was supposed to be assigned to the Ninth Air Force, but by then the P-51B Mustang was arriving in England. There was some horse trading going on and we got traded to the Eighth Air Force for a P-47 outfit. I flew the Mustang for the very first time on January 30, 1944. I had heard very little about the P-51, but was immediately impressed with its looks. Like any other fighter plane, it had a single seat, so to get acclimated to its characteristics you hopped in, fired it, up and took off. When I flew the Mustang, I felt as though I'd put on a favorite coat; it just became a part of you.

My original flight leader had been killed while strafing a German airfield. Our flight was split up and I became the number four—Tail-end Charlie—in Bud Anderson's flight. I have yet to meet a finer pilot, leader, or man, and I tried to fly with Bud as much as possible. By March, we were flying over Berlin on bomber escorts, and I eventually received one of Bud's original P-51B Mustangs, *Old Crow*. I changed the name to *Berlin Express* because that's where we always seemed to end up. Both Bud and I painted white sidewalls on our tires and sported red rims in honor of the convertibles we had back home.

I thought that the P-51 Mustang was the finest fighter in the war; it certainly changed the air war in Europe. The Mustang could fly anywhere and beat the Luftwaffe wherever they were. On one of our early Berlin raids, we missed connections with the bombers. They weren't where they were supposed to be. We flew past Berlin for a while and turned around just in time to find the wayward bomber group getting bounced by upwards of 150 German twin-engine and single-engine fighters. We came in from behind and they never knew what hit them. That really seemed to shake the Luftwaffe up because we shot down twenty of their fighters and never lost a Mustang.

I attribute our success to a couple of things. Number one was the fact that our group always performed liked a team. If you were ever in trouble, somebody would be there to help you out. When you're in the middle of a dogfight and bullets and airplanes are flying every which way, it becomes a little hectic, to say the least. Most of us thought of ourselves as hot pilots. You had to have that attitude to survive; otherwise you had no business being in the middle of it. But help was always appreciated.

Another reason for our success was the P-51B Mustang. My favorite model was the B or C with the Spitfire/Malcolm Hood canopy. It provided much greater visibility than the original birdcage canopy. I also thought the B/C Mustangs were much better fighters than even the D model. I didn't like the P-51D as much was because the gas tank was installed behind the pilot's head. You were kidding yourself if you thought that you could dogfight with a load of fuel back there. The center of gravity was so heavy and in the wrong place that you couldn't turn and you couldn't do anything right. But in the P-51B/C, I thought, I could do everything right. It was the perfect fighter.

COMBAT REPORT: JULY 29, 1944
35th Fighter Group , 363rd Fighter Squadron
1030 Hours
West of Merseburg

I was flying Cement Red #3 and my wingman and I were making a pass on a large field. As we did, an Me 109 dove on us slightly to our right. I turned into him as soon as I was across the field and he was fairly close. He turned right also leaving me right behind him. Using the gyro gun sight I fired about thirty-degree deflection and got hits. I think the range was about 350 yards. I closed in still firing and hit his coolant. He dropped down right on the ground and as my wing was in the grass I had to pull up. Pieces of the 109 made holes in my canopy. The gyro gun sight (K-14) worked extremely well and I think was responsible for getting the hits at first. I claim one Me 109 destroyed in the air.

William B. Overstreet Jr.
1st Lt., Air Corps

WINNER TAKE ALL . . . AND AN ACE UP MY SLEEVE!
Lt. Col. Donald S. Bryan, USAF
352nd Fighter Group, 328th Fighter Squadron

By the time I flew my first combat mission out of England in September 1943, I probably had more time just "practice dogfighting" than most of my fellow pilots had in total air time. One of my first assignments was to instruct new fighter pilots in Curtiss P-40 Warhawks and Bell P-39

Airacobras over the sunny skies of Florida. I thought the P-40 was a bastard when it came to flying , because it was one of the hardest planes to land. I thought even less of the P-39. But I have to say that, without a doubt, I learned at least one valuable lesson while flying the P-40, a lesson that would save my butt a year later.

I was up on a training flight with one of my students over Pinellas County, Florida, as we chased tails with one another in our P-40s. I was able to get behind him and was just about to "fire at him" when he suddenly disappeared. I knew I didn't shoot him down because our guns were unloaded. I found him a short time later and reengaged him again. Same thing: I got on his tail, brought my guns onto him, and bingo! He was gone! At the time I thought I was a pretty good pilot, but, man, this guy was waxing my butt! We flew back to the base and I was dying to know what the heck he did up there with that P-40. My student, or should I say my "instructor for the moment," called it an inverted vertical reverse.

After he explained it to me on the ground, we went up again for some classroom work. It turned out to be a fairly simple maneuver and it worked like this. When you had an enemy plane behind you and they got their guns on you (not *through* you, so they could fire at you, but *on* you), you started the maneuver. I was in a left-hand turn and brought the P-40 up into a stall and then snapped the stick back hard, into my gut, as I hit full left rudder. I immediately slammed the stick full forward and the P-40 turned wrong side out. My head hit the top of the canopy as the P-40 turned 180 degrees in less than a second. The airplane flipped and twisted around the propeller's torque, and in an instant, I vanished. It was a trick I would never forget.

JOINING THE BLUENOSERS

When I joined the 352nd Fighter Group, 328th Fighter Squadron, in early 1943, we had been sent to Bodney, England, to fly combat in the Republic P-47 Thunderbolt. I liked flying the "Jug." Although you could really feel the seven tons strapped to your shoulders, it was a very docile, easy-to-fly airplane with more than enough firepower. My crew chief,

Sgt. Kirk Noyes, liked to tinker with the Thunderbolt and in doing so created a "hot rod" of a fighter. Whatever magic he put into the Jug, it made it the fastest airplane on the field and in the sky against the Luftwaffe. More than once, I did things at low level in the Jug against Fw 190s and Bf 109s that were thought to be next to impossible. I owe all the credit to my crew chief, who stayed with me when the group switched over to the P-51 Mustang in April 1944.

I had already shot down four German aircraft by the time we traded our P-47s for Mustangs. The first Mustangs we got were P-51Bs, which I despised. The damn things only had four guns compared to the eight we carried on the Thunderbolts. The guns on the Mustang would constantly jam whenever you pulled negative G, because in combat, you were always pulling either positive or negative Gs. If you were foolish enough to fly straight and level against the enemy, your chance of finishing your tour was slim to none. Simply put, you were dead.

The P-51Bs had a horrible heating system, and at high altitude the cockpit was colder than a well-digger's ass! The other thing I hated about the B model was the seat; the thing was straight up and down, and after three to four hours of sitting like that, with a parachute strapped to your shoulders, your back was killing you. The best thing I can say about the P-51B was that I didn't have to fly it much because in May 1944 I was sent home on R&R.

BACK IN COMBAT

When I returned to the group in September of '44, I was given a brand-new P-51D Mustang that I named *Little One III*, after my petite wife, Francis. The D model was everything the B wasn't. For starters, the visibility through that big bubbletop canopy was outstanding compared to the "French widows" on the B. The D carried six guns—still not as many as the Jug, but at least these were mounted at an angle and most jamming issues ceased to exist. The cockpit layout was designed for a fighter pilot with everything, including throttle, mixture, flap handle, gear handle, gun switches, gun sight, and relief tube just exactly where

I wanted them. It was the perfect cockpit, with ample heat and a seat that angled back. When I flew the D, I felt as if I put the Mustang on and wore it like a favorite overcoat. The P-51D was by far the most comfortable fighter aircraft I ever flew. Period.

I got my first victories in the P-51D on September 27, 1944, when I shot down a couple of Bf 109s near Frankfurt. I don't know what kind of magic my crew chief put into the Mustang, but when I firewalled the Merlin engine, the Mustang walked away from everyone else in my flight.

ENCOUNTER REPORT: SEPTEMBER 27TH, 1944
1003 HOURS
VICINITY, FRANKFURT

I was leading Yellow Flight which was composed of three ships: F/O Montgomery as number 2, and Lt. Brookings as the number 3 man. The Squadron Leader had to abort and I took over the Squadron in the Frankfurt area.

At 1000 hours the 487th Fighter Squadron, 352nd Fighter Group called in many Me 109s and Fw 190s. I was not with this Squadron but I figure that they were somewhere in the immediate area. I was then at 20,000 feet. Seeing some contrails to the south and high I turned into them and started to climb. At 24,000 feet, between 100 and 150 Fw 190s and Me 109s passed over my head about 2,000 feet above. I swung in behind them and was able to get above them at 27,000 feet. I was then about 3 miles behind them.

When I made the 180 degree turn I lost or out-climbed the rest of the Squadron and my number 3 man. My number 2 man and I overtook the last box of enemy fighters—about 50—just as the first part hit the bombers. I picked out an Me 109 and attacked it. I opened fire at about 200–250 yards and stopped at about 50 yards. I observed many strikes on the fuselage and wing roots almost the entire length of the burst. Smoke poured out and the enemy aircraft burst into flames just as I broke off the attack. I then picked out another Me 109 and opened up at about 200 yards. I didn't hit it very good at first but as I closed I began to get hits. From 100 yards to where I broke off—at about 30 to 40 feet—I got many very good hits. This enemy aircraft snapped into a spin and went down spinning and in flames, through of the overcast at 8–9,000 feet.

The entire box of enemy fighters broke up then and dived for the overcast. Only a very few made a half-hearted attempt to fight. I lost my number 2 man at this time. All this combat took place at about 26,000 feet. A lone Me 109 then tried to get on my tail but I was easily able to out-turn him. He tried to tighten up his turn and at 24,000 feet snapped into a very violent spin. As he was spinning down I made two attempts to shoot him down; one from the side and then after he flattened out into a very flat spin I made a pass straight down on him. I observed one strike on the tail of the fuselage. He spun right on down into the clouds. I didn't attempt to follow him through but later I found that the tops were at 9,000 feet and the bottoms from 6–8,000 feet. I claim this enemy aircraft probably destroyed.

I believe the enemy pilot was trying to get it out of the spin, for I could see that he had the throttle out back. If he was, I doubt if he could get it out in the 6–8,000 feet remaining before he would reach the ground; especially after trying unsuccessfully for some 15,000 feet. However, if he was using the spin for evasive action, it was very good, for I couldn't hit him in it.

I chased several other ships through the clouds and fired at one, an Fw 190 without observing results. He climbed back into the clouds. I then joined up with 487th FS and came home. At no time did I have any trouble either overtaking or out-turning the Fw 190s and Me 109s. I claim 2 Me 109s destroyed and 1 Me 109 probably destroyed.

Don Bryan

Lessons Learned

I never worried about being out in front, mixing it up with the Luftwaffe. I knew the rest of my flight would catch up, so I didn't concern myself about who was on my ass! I flew a lot more missions in the P-51D during the fall of 1944, but it seemed the Germans were in hiding or licking their wounds; the Luftwaffe was very scarce. It wasn't until early November that I encountered the Luftwaffe in large numbers again, and nearly doubled my score in the process—on one mission. It was also a mission that I used everything I had learned in training and in previous combat, along with a little luck.

Our squadron, the 328th, was led by our new CO, Maj. George Preddy. On November 2, 1944, we were assigned with the rest of the 352nd Fighter Group to provide escort for over one thousand bombers as they made their way into Germany, many of them bombing German oil targets. There were a bunch of other fighter groups from England that flew along with us that day; our numbers almost equaled that of the bomber stream. It was a huge air armada, with almost two thousand aircraft of various sizes, heading for multiple targets inside Germany. Needless to say, our arrival did not go unnoticed. The Luftwaffe came at us with numbers not seen since September, with some of the squadrons reporting jets in the area. I didn't see any of them in my section, but I did see plenty of other Luftwaffe fighters to engage.

Let's face it: I was never a good pilot. My wingmen were hotter pilots than I was and they could always wax my butt. I did have a couple of advantages over them, though. I had better eyesight and I was a flight leader. Both of these attributes came into play when I saw the contrails up ahead and called them out as Me 109s. I was leading Yellow Flight with lieutenants Hill, Montgomery, and Briggs as my number-two, three, and four men, respectively. We were flying at about twenty-eight thousand feet in the vicinity of Merseburg, Germany, when I saw the 109s. I turned on my switches and prepared for combat. Significantly, this was the first mission I had flown with the new K-14 computing gun sight, mounted right in front of me.

There seemed to be about fifty 109s ahead, with forty of them in a box and several more above them as top cover. By the time I could get into position for a bounce, ten to fifteen of them pushed their noses over and started down on the bombers. The other 109s were preparing to follow the first wave. I figured that if I hit the middle of the pack, I could break up their attack. I led my flight in a diving attack into the midst of the 109s and closed to about one hundred yards on one of them. As I peered through the K-14 gun sight, I observed a few strikes on one of the 109s as I gave him a quick squirt. I overran the 109 and dived under him. I was only twenty feet away from him, heading downhill, when I glanced up and saw that his coolant system was shot out. I couldn't stick around to watch what happened to him because at the same time my number three called to say there was a 109 on my tail.

I snapped-rolled the Mustang and quickly lost the pursuing 109. But I lost the rest of my flight in the process, and for the next ten minutes I was probably in at least fifteen separate combats. I made a stern attack on eight 109s that were flying in a string, playing follow the leader. I attacked the last 109 and observed many strikes on him before he went down in flames. I found another 109 and proceeded to attack it, and observed many good hits on the fuselage and wings. Many large pieces began to fly off the 109 as thick black smoke poured from his engine. I watched him fall off into a steep dive from ten thousand feet, going through the under-cast with a great deal of smoke still pouring from him. During the melee I attacked another 109 and observed strikes on him as well. While I was making these attacks, I was engaged by other 109s the whole time. And one of these guys must have been an old timer because he flew circles around me.

He came at me from behind and I thought, *Hell, this 109 is easy meat.* I knew my P-51D was superior, especially against a little ol' 109. But buster, this guy was better than I have ever been and ever would be! He outperformed me as I twisted and turned that Mustang wrong side up and wrong side down. He was only a hundred yards away from me when I saw him pull his guns onto me. I did everything I could think of to lose this guy, except one. I knew I was had, so I used the old P-40 trick and initiated an inverted vertical reverse. In an instant I was gone, and left him wondering where the hell I went. I never met up with him again, and I sure wasn't going to go looking for him either. That son of a gun was good. He had a good airplane and he knew what the hell he was doing. He was certainly an exception because my next one didn't have a clue.

I observed a single 109 and a P-51, flown by Lieutenant Cramer of my squadron, in an engagement, bobbing in and out of clouds. When I made an attack on the 109, it dived into the clouds at four thousand feet. The 109 came out of the clouds shortly after my attack, and I made several more on him as he flew in and out of cloud. After several more tries on him, I thought I was going to make a head-on pass, but as it turned out, I was ninety degrees to the 109. I opened fire at about 500 yards and closed to about 150 yards, observing strikes in the cockpit and wing area. The 109 nosed over sharply and went down through the under-cast with gas pouring from his wing root. As I followed him down, he went into a very steep dive toward the ground from one thousand feet, indicating 350 to 400 miles per hour. I later learned from Cramer, who had joined me on my wing, that the 109 had crashed and exploded.

I started back up toward the bombers with Cramer, and as we passed through ten thousand feet, I saw two 109s, either F or G models, flying just above the under-cast at five thousand feet. I moved into position and split-essed onto the last one (a rolled, descending half-loop). I only had two of my guns firing as I made my attack. I opened fire at five hundred yards and hit the 109 very hard around the fuselage and wings. As I closed to three hundred yards, I hit him on the wing and the wingtip, causing the top of his wing to fly off. The 109 snapped into a violent spin to the left and went through the under-cast in flames, spinning the whole way down. I turned my attention to the other 109 and began to get strikes on him when one of my two guns stopped firing.

This threw me off a little bit and I found it difficult to get many strikes as I closed on him from 350 to 150 yards. When I closed the distance to 80 yards, I began to get strikes through the fuselage and wing roots. I broke off the attack as the 109 went through the under-cast at four thousand feet in a very steep dive, indicating 350 miles per hour, with large amounts of black smoke pouring from the engine. I was wringing wet with sweat, was almost out of ammo, and had only one gun that worked. Needless to say, I didn't go looking for trouble as we made our way back to our base at Bodney.

I claimed five 109s destroyed and two more damaged.

The 328th Squadron as a whole got twenty-five that day, a new Eighth Air Force record for a squadron on a single mission. The other two squadrons in the group, the 486th and 487th, racked up thirteen more between them. All told, the Germans lost 134 fighters that day. I'm pretty sure that by then the Luftwaffe was made up of just a few real hot pilots; the rest were just "new boys." If they had been in our outfit, they wouldn't have been allowed to go to the john without an escort! On most of my encounters, I could count on one hand the number of German pilots who did anything to evade being shot down. I often wondered if the hot pilots, like the one who almost got me, weren't dragging the new guys along to use as bait. Maybe these unseasoned guys were good enough to shoot down bombers, but they weren't much to depend on in a dogfight.

Right time, right place? Who knows, but I can tell you this, it had been the longest ten minutes of my life.

THE MEANING BEHIND THE NAME *WORRY BIRD*
1st Lt. Robert Frisch
339th Fighter Group, 503rd Fighter Squadron

Our biggest enemy was weather. We started out as a group and went into combat in April 1944. By the end of that year we had lost eighty-four aircraft. Everybody seems to think that your big losses are in aerial combat. They are not. Big losses were due to ground fire, weather, and mechanical failure. I mean, you got one engine. Once that goes, you're done!

I needed all the luck I could get to make it through the war in one piece. My lucky charm was a "worry bird" my girlfriend had sent me from back home. My worry bird was a small figure that you could mount on top of a glass and let it tilt forward, as if it was sipping your drink. I carried it with me on my missions. When my crew chief saw it on my instrument panel, he was afraid I'd lose the bird during a high-G turn, so he manufactured a bracket for it and screwed it into my panel. I guess it was easy to come up with a name for my P-51 Mustang—and *Worry Bird* looked good on the nose, too!

Lieutenant Frisch ended the war with six victories.

PLANES, TRAINS, AND TRUCKS
Capt. James R. Starnes
339th Fighter Group, 505th Fighter Squadron

339TH FIGHTER GROUP HISTORY

The 339th Fighter Group was actually supposed to be a bomber unit. When it was formed in August 1942, it was known as the 339th Bombardment Group (Dive). While it trained in Tampa, Florida, it flew A-24 Banshee and A-25 Shrike dive bombers. In July 1943, it began converting over to P-39 Airacobras. In August 1943, a new commanding officer, Lt. Col. John B. Henry Jr., took over as group commander. Colonel Henry was my CO throughout my time in the 339th. You would be hard pressed to find a better leader.

The group changed its name again, becoming the 339th Fighter Bomber Group. It was comprised of three fighter bomber squadrons: the 503rd, the 504th, and the 505th. In September 1943, the whole group moved to Rice Field, California, to supply air support for ground troops training in the Army Desert Maneuver Area. I joined them in California in January 1944, and flew the P-39s over the hot deserts. Most of us thought we would head for the Pacific Theater or be broken up completely and sent to combat units as replacement pilots. We all thought wrong.

By early March 1944, we were sent packing again, and this time our destination would be with the Eighth Air Force in England. Arriving in early April 1944, we were introduced to our new base and new fighters at Fowlmere. The P-51 Mustang was sleek and fast-looking even on the ground. As we hurriedly prepared for aerial combat with our new mounts, we found that the plane was even nicer in the air. Our early missions, beginning on April 30, 1944, were fighter sweeps over France and Belgium, designed to acquaint ourselves with our new surroundings and to experience some light flak—the heavier stuff would come soon enough.

FIRST BLOOD

Early on, almost right from the get go, our basic missions were bomber escorts. Most of the early ones picked up the B-17s and B-24s during target withdrawal, as they staggered back home from deep inside Germany. We couldn't go all the way in with them because our P-51Bs didn't have drop tanks yet. That all changed in mid-May 1944. After that, we were finally able to stay with the bombers all the way to Berlin! It also happened to be May 19, the day I got my first kill.

We were on bomber escort. I was the number-three in our flight. We began dodging flak early into the mission; lucky for us, we didn't have to fly a straight-line course like the bombers. They had to go right through the middle of it. The closer we got to Berlin, the heavier the flak was. As we skirted outside of that black ring of death, just outside the bomber box, someone in our flight noticed two enemy airplanes up high, four thousand feet above, heading west in the other direction. We began a slow climb to their altitude. It took us awhile, but we finally got on their tails without them noticing us.

They were Fw 190s. My flight leader told me to take the one on the right and he would deal with the guy on the left. When we opened up on them, I saw that my flight leader hit his 190 hard; it began to smoke immediately. I was a split-second late as I hosed the other 190 in front of me. He was smoking when he did a split-ess out of there, to the left. I rolled the Mustang over and followed him down, catching him rather quickly—in fact, I almost ended up ramming him.

Just as I was about to let him have it again, his hood came off and flew at me backwards. I jinked the stick to avoid hitting it. A second later the pilot popped out, his parachute streaming open right in front of me. Jeez, it was close. I almost took that guy's legs off! It was that quick, as most combat encounters are—and it was also a valuable lesson learned, one that I would carry with me until the end of the war.

CHATTANOOGA CHOO CHOO

After we had safely escorted the returning bombers out of harm's way, we were encouraged to drop down to the deck and strafe anything that moved. Road traffic, airbases, barges, and trains—especially trains. They carried a lot of German supplies across Occupied Europe and were very lucrative targets. You just had to be careful for the ones that carried flak guns. They could ruin your day in a hurry.

General Jimmy Doolittle, who had been reassigned and was now attached to the Eighth Air Force, came up with a special mission for all of the fighter squadrons to carry out on May 21. It was called Operation Chattanooga Choo Choo. The bombers were ordered to stand down while each fighter group was given a specific area of Occupied Europe to attack at low level. Our targets were German airfields, train yards, marshalling yards, communication lines, and any other military vehicles we could find.

Our area of responsibility was between Leipzig and Dresden. It was a target-rich area, with at least five German airfields scattered about. We roared in low over the airfields and caught the Germans napping. I latched on to a slow-flying trainer and hit him with a few rounds. But I was way too fast and he was way too slow. I quickly overtook him and passed on by. My wingman took care of him, though, so we each ended up sharing a half credit.

The flak below was intense, and our group lost four airplanes that day. We ended up shooting down fourteen of theirs and destroyed ten on the ground. Some of the guys flew so low that day that they came back trailing high-tension wires that were tangled on their wings. But it was all worth it because we softened up the area in preparation for the upcoming D-Day invasion.

BOMBS AWAY!

I had flown three missions on D-Day (June 6, 1944) as a second lieutenant. Two days later, I was promoted and became a brand-new first lieutenant. That and two bits would have bought me a cup of coffee. We were flying almost nonstop in support of the guys on the beach, as they tried to push their way through the stiff German resistance. Our targets were transportation, trains, and convoys as the Germans rushed troops to the beachhead in an all-out thrust to halt our advance. It was no surprise to discover that France was a target-rich environment.

Our first mission of June 8 took us to a sector well inland from the beachhead. Taking off in the predawn darkness, my red-and-white-checkered P-51B (named *Tarheel* in honor of my home state of North Carolina) had a 250-pound bomb hung below each wing. In the clouds and darkness I became separated from the rest of the squadron. I proceeded to our "block of France," knowing full well there would be plenty of targets to choose from. It was barely light when I spotted a train parked at a rail station down below. I rolled the Mustang on over and began my dive toward the target. I released both bombs and had good hits on the train. With my target now burning, I came screaming back around for one strafing pass. As I roared overhead, my .50 calibers sent slugs dancing across the station.

I began my climb back up to altitude. When I reached five thousand feet, I noticed a thick patch of ground fog on my left. Suddenly, the fog began to vibrate and out popped a Bf 109. With its distinctive slender outline, the 109 was very easy to identify. This German pilot was definitely not a morning person; he was oblivious to me overhead and just continued in a straight line, zipping along half asleep.

With my altitude advantage I simply pushed the Mustang's nose over and initiated a bounce. I fell in behind him and closed rapidly on his tail. I gave him a few short bursts, and he began to smoke and roll over. I'd ruined a fine German aircraft.

Later that afternoon, I caught the third mission of the day. It was another bombing run behind the beachhead, in the vicinity of Rennes. This time, each of us in the 505th Squadron carried a one hundred–pound bomb under each wing as we went looking for rolling stock—trains and truck convoys. This time I stayed with the squadron. We quickly spotted a convoy of armored vehicles and trucks on a highway below. Our P-51Bs fell into a trail as we prepared to bomb them.

The CO, Maj. Don Larson, began to "fishtail" his Mustang, giving us the signal to dive, and follow him down on the bomb run. Just as we were ready to release our bombs, a bunch of Fw 190s showed up and jumped us. The CO was having radio problems so I called for the rest of the flight to "break and release bombs." I fell into an Fw 190 that was trying to get Larson's plane. As I went round and round with him, another 190 fell in behind me. Our number-three man fell in behind that 190, and then he had *another* 190 on *his* tail. When our number-four tacked onto number-three, our defensive Lufbery circle really began to grow.

Only every other airplane in the group was a P-51B. We "rat raced" over the French countryside, in a round and round, swirling dogfight. We'd only been at five thousand or six thousand feet when we got bounced by the Fw 190s. But in less than five minutes, when it was all said and done, we lost one man and the Germans lost seven. I got credit for 1½ kills.

As we rejoined Major Larson, I glanced over at his Mustang—he still had his damn bombs hanging under his wings! He didn't want to return to England with them, so we followed him down as he bombed the convoy below. The rest of us strafed it with what little ammunition we had left. We flew on back to England and prepared to do it all over again the next day. June was turning into a very busy month for us.

Cloud Dancer

I was leading Upper Yellow flight on a ramrod (bomber-escort run) to Merseburg on July 29, 1944. As we neared the target at twenty-five thousand feet, a Bf 109 passed below and off to the right of our formation. The 109 made an attack on a lone B-17 that was at fifteen thousand feet heading west from the target area. I pushed the Mustang over and broke down after this guy. I couldn't overtake him until he had already completed his attack on the B-17 straggler. The 109 made a diving turn to the right and tried to make a break for it and escape into the undercast at nine thousand feet. I didn't want him to get away so I fired several long bursts at him before he got safely into the cloud layer.

The 109 must have chopped his throttle in the clouds because I chopped mine immediately when I entered the cloud layer, and was only a hundred yards behind him when we came out of cloud. I pushed my throttle forward and closed to fifty yards before I began to fire—I didn't want to miss a second time! My rounds danced all over his fighter, and I noticed strikes on his fuselage from my left wing guns. I broke off my attack while my second-element leader had a go on him; I witnessed hits from his firing pass. The element leader broke off his attack and I went in again, trying to knock this guy down. Just as I was about to fire, the 109's canopy came off and the pilot popped into view. I was amazed that despite all the hits we made on the 109, we couldn't get the plane to burn. I watched it arc earthward, several pieces coming off before it finally hit the ground.

SEEK, AND YE SHALL FIND

Little did I know at the time that on August 4, 1944, getting lost would create so many milestones for me. I was part of a bomber escort mission flying Upper White 3 on a ramrod to Hamburg. For some reason or other, I became separated from the squadron and climbed up to eighteen thousand feet to see if I could find them. As I scanned the sky around me, I looked down and saw a Bf 109. Like me, he was all by himself. The 109's outline was unmistakable, and from my lofty perch I clearly saw the black crosses on his wings.

The 109 was zigzagging back and forth, trying to clear his tail, but for whatever reason, he failed to look up. I rolled the Mustang over and initiated a bounce on him. I came down rather quickly and zoomed below him before I pulled back up. As I glanced up at his belly, I could see that his right wheel wasn't inside the wheelwell; it looked as if the fairing door had closed ahead of his wheel. His left landing gear, however, was in the normal retracted position.

I was pretty close to him so I chopped my throttle and let him pull away from me. At a hundred yards I let loose with my machine guns and gave him a quick squirt. My rounds tore into his left wing root as I hit him hard and fast. A stream of coolant began to spray from his exploded radiator. I pulled off to the side because for a moment his vapor trail obscured my vision. I also wanted to see what this guy was going to do. When he made a wing-over to the left, I noted more hits to his left side.

He began to spiral as he entered a small cumulus cloud. I broke off my attack and met him below the cloud.

He was over his own country and I'm sure that made his decision to bail out much easier. He rolled the 109 over and fell earthward. In a way, I felt sorry for the inexperienced, minimally trained German pilots. Most of the old pros had been in combat for over four years and there weren't many of those guys left by the end of 1944. Most of our engagements were with the guys who had no experience. In some cases, they would throw off their wing tanks and bail out if they knew we were behind them; some of the time we never had to fire a shot!

The Luftwaffe had more airplanes than pilots, anyway, and it was a much more desperate situation for them than for us. After my August 4 mission, I became an ace with five confirmed victories. I also became the first pilot in the squadron to reach three hundred hours of combat time. Instead of accepting the offer to go back home, I promptly signed up for fifty hours more. I was a young, experienced fighter pilot and I wanted to see this thing through to the end!

JET JOBS

Our group was on a bomber escort on March 30, 1945, cruising along at twenty-nine thousand feet, when our CO, Col. John B. Henry, spotted a German jet below us, climbing fast toward our group. Colonel Henry dived into him and gave him a squirt at twenty-two thousand feet from over 1,000 yards out. Black smoke soon appeared on the Me 262, which reversed course and dived into the safety of some clouds at twenty thousand feet. The 262s were definitely a menace and showed weakness only when they took off or landed. Other than that, they were as fast as greased lightning, able to top out at 541 miles per hour!

I was leading the 505th's Upper Yellow Flight when I spotted more 262s and dived to attack them with the rest of my flight. The P-51 Mustang was fast, but the Me 262 was even faster; they walked away from us as if we were standing still. Unfortunately, we were so fixated on the jets in front of us that we didn't notice the one behind us. My number-four man tried to warn us, but it was too late. I saw yellow streaks of 262 tracers zip by my wing and slam into my number-two man, Lt. Evergard L. Wagner. His Mustang was hit hard and began to burn. Evergard bailed out okay, but his chute didn't stream and failed to open properly. Although we lost a fine pilot that day, the rest of the group made up for it when we were able to claim a handful of 262s as destroyed, damaged, or probable.

Thankfully, the Germans were almost out of gas, and the war was nearing an end for the Luftwaffe. As the jet menace flickered out, we turned our attention to attacking them on the ground. The war finally ended for our group on April 21, 1945.

Captain James Starnes ended the war with six victories.

The 339th Fighter Group recorded 657 aerial and ground victories during the 264 missions they flew from April 1944 until April 21, 1945. The average number of enemy aircraft destroyed per mission was 2.488, the best in the Eighth Air Force Fighter Command.

4

Aloft over the Mediterranean

Although the air war over Italy and the surrounding Axis-controlled countries was overshadowed by the colorful exploits of the fighter groups based in England, the war in the air—machine against machine—was equally deadly, no matter what country or ocean it was fought over. Some will argue that the "boys in England" lived like royalty compared to the somewhat harsher living conditions endured by the Mediterranean squadrons. But one thing was for sure: the fighter pilots operating in the Mediterranean Theater were equally as skilled as their Eighth Air Force counterparts. They flew the exact same model of airplane and were just as bored droning along on an almost eight-hour bomber-escort mission with no German fighters in sight. The simple truth of the matter was, all of these men, no matter what ground they stood on or the sky they flew in, were all trained to perform the same task: seek out the enemy and destroy them. Strap on your parachute and buckle up as you fly along in a yellow-and-black checker-tailed P-51 Mustang while you protect the bombers and slug it out with the Luftwaffe over the oil fields of Ploesti and beyond.

MEMORIES OF A CHECKERTAIL ACE
Col. Arthur J. Fiedler, USAF (Ret.)
325th Fighter Group, 317th Fighter Squadron

By the time I got to the Mediterranean in April 1944, I had more than 370 hours of fighter time as a P-47 Thunderbolt instructor back in the States. I consider that fact, along with my 20/10 eyesight and the P-51 Mustang, the three contributing factors to my success against the Luftwaffe. Being in the right place at the right time sure didn't hurt anything either!

ENGINE TROUBLE

On June 24, 1944, I was returning early to our base at Lesina, Italy, because of a rough engine. As I flew in the opposite direction of the bomber stream at twenty-four thousand feet, I looked down to my left and saw eight B-24s three thousand feet below me, heading for the oil fields at Ploesti. What caught my attention were six Bf 109s queuing up to make an attack on the bombers. I decided to make a head-on pass through the 109s in an attempt to scatter them. By the time I got in range, I was only able to tack onto the last guy in the flight. I pulled 4 Gs as I whipped my Mustang in behind him—and that's when my gun sight burned out.

I had been so used to putting the nose of the P-47 on the target, pulling the trigger, and shooting that the loss of the sight threw me off. I didn't compensate for the downward slope of the P-51's nose and was having a helluva time getting hits on this guy as I pumped the stick up and down, trying to figure out where to aim. As we crossed over the bombers, I saw what looked like a thousand bees floating just outside of my cockpit. I quickly realized that the gunners on the B-24s were firing at both of us. I now had a total understanding of what a German pilot must have gone through as he attacked a bomber stream! I finally settled down and got some good hits on the 109, and watched him as he caught fire. I saw him go into a vertical dive, but our instructions and orders were not to follow them below fifteen thousand feet.

I claimed one probable.

STARE-DOWN

June 28, 1944. While up on a fighter sweep, we received reports of many 109s above thirty thousand feet. I started climbing with the squadron through the overcast, but lagged behind because I had a left wing tank that had hung up and refused to drop. As I passed over a clear area in the overcast, I spotted two birds off to the left. I dived down to get a look at them, and when I saw the water coolers under each wing, I knew they were 109s. I attacked and got good hits on the first guy, who spiraled down and crashed. I ignored the order and followed him down to take pictures that would confirm my victory. I started back up and I saw what I presumed to be the other 109 pass right in front of me.

I cranked the Mustang into a vertical bank as I got six to eight hits on him. I began to pull a lot of Gs as I tried to keep him in my sights. Then my guns jammed. Because I was climbing, I was at a lower air-speed than normal. In a moment I found myself sliding into formation with this guy, just forty to fifty feet away. We stared at each other, both of us in shock and with no idea of what to do next. To this day I couldn't tell you how that 109 was painted or what his markings looked like, but I can sure as heck can tell you what his oxygen mask and helmet looked like! It felt like we stared at each other for five hours, but it was probably less than thirty seconds. Then I came up with a brilliant idea: I'd shoot him through my canopy with my .45-caliber pistol!

My intent was to scare him so he'd veer away from me, so I could then veer off in the other direction and get out of there. The .45 was tucked into my shoulder holster. I grasped the butt and began to pull it out. I must have really scared the hell out of the guy because I was astonished to see his canopy come off as he bailed out.

I claimed two Bf 109s.

OUT OF GAS

July 9, 1944. I was flying on Col. Hershel "Herky" Green's wing on a mission over Ploesti when we saw eight 109s yo-yo-ing off of a group of

B-24s that were at twenty-four thousand feet. The 109s were at twenty-eight thousand feet, diving on the bombers and then pulling back up to do it all over again. The 109s saw us coming in as they hightailed it north. About thirty to fifty miles on the other side of Ploesti, we finally caught them. I had a slight problem though: I couldn't get my left wing tank to feed. This was annoying because I'd already aborted two other missions with the same problem. Although I decided to stay and fight, I knew that I was now 108 gallons short on fuel.

All of the 109s started to climb except one guy who thought he was going to turn right and fly over the top of us; he thought wrong. I made a firing pass at him that I started at ninety degrees and hit him when I was at seventy degrees. I got so many hits on this guy that I thought someone else was firing at him. He started to stream thick gray smoke as his right gear came down and flopped in the breeze. I passed over the top of him and saw that his canopy was gone. Clouds of smoke poured from his airplane. I don't know if he got out or not, and I didn't stay around to find out because I had my own problems. We had been instructed to turn for home over Ploesti when we had ninety gallons of fuel left; I only had sixty. I called Colonel Green and told him I wasn't going to make it back to Lesina. Herky told me to divert to the closest bomber base I could find.

I remembered the reports on fuel conservation made by Charles Lindbergh while he was with the fighter units in the Pacific. I set up the Mustang using maximum manifold pressure as I pulled the rpm back as low it would go. I was all set up at thirty thousand feet, with 160-mile-per-hour airspeed in a two-hundred-feet-a-minute rate of descent. With my fingers crossed, I must have looked at my fuel gauges five hundred times. As I cleared the mountains, I saw the bomber base ahead but was denied permission to land because they were recovering bombers. I ignored the control tower and told them I would take the right side of the runway. I set the Mustang down, and as I taxied off the runway, my engine quit from lack of fuel. Funny thing was, I never did see a bomber land as I waited to get towed back to the ramp!

I claimed one Bf 109.

CANYON CHASE

July 26, 1944. There were twelve of us in three flights of four on an escort mission for the B-24s of the 55th Bomb Wing. Although we hadn't reached the rendezvous point as we neared Klagenfurt, Austria, we stumbled upon a group of B-17s from the 55th Wing that were still climbing to an altitude of twenty-eight thousand feet. As we passed over the Forts, I looked down through an opening in the clouds and I saw sixty-four airplanes in rows of eight, flying line abreast. Some of the other guys in our flight called them out as P-51s when two of them broke away from the formation, but the wingtips didn't look right to me. I was still fairly new to the squadron so I kept my mouth shut, but I kept one eye on the formation below. I lost them in the clouds, and as we flew on for a little while, I looked back toward the last group of B-17s and saw a bunch of explosions. There were wings falling off and tails breaking apart as B-17s began to spin out of control. I called out on the R/T, "They're bogeys and I'm gone!"

I rolled over into a vertical dive and found a bunch of Fw 190s right in front of me. Habits from my duck-hunting days took over as I began to "flock shoot" the 190s. I came right through the center of their formation and saw a 190 about two hundred yards in front of me. I was half-assed upside down at the time, and when I rolled upright, the 190 went into a vertical bank to the right. I knew he couldn't get a shot at me so I dropped my right wing and waited for him to reappear, so I could drop down on him. The problem was, he never showed up. I rolled inverted and found a 190 coming straight up at me with all of his guns blazing away. He passed by me, and how he missed me I will never know.

I kept turning the Mustang until I was on his tail. I followed this guy down as he whirled, veered, and twisted. He kept his stick in one corner and the rudder in the other, both of us rolling downward. I quickly realized that I wasn't dealing with just one Fw 190 either, because I was getting shot at from the rear. As we flew right down to the deck, I was able to get about five hundred yards behind the second

190. I was just about to open fire when I suddenly remembered what an old World War I pilot back home had told me before I left for combat:

"The easiest time to shoot down an enemy airplane is to do it when the enemy is trying to shoot down one of yours. That guy can't afford to look behind him because he's trying to concentrate on the airplane ahead of him. Young man, if you ever get ready to shoot down an enemy airplane, take a quick glance at your six o'clock to make damn sure no one is coming down on you."

I looked back and there was the other 190 at my seven o'clock, barreling in from a hundred yards away. I jerked the stick back and went into a vertical climb, rolled 180 degrees, pulled again, and rolled another 180 degrees right side up. The 190 was right in front of me. He dived for the deck and I was right on his butt as we entered a canyon fifty feet off the floor. As the 190 pulled into a vertical bank to the right, I put my gun sight's pipper out ahead of him and let it drift back. I scored hits up and down his fuselage as he rolled to the right, upside down, and smashed into a barn that was a hundred feet off the canyon floor.

I began to look for the first guy again and saw another airplane coming right for me. I wondered how that 190 got turned around so fast. Someone suddenly called out over the radio, "If this is a P-51 coming head-on, wiggle your wings." I did, and saw that the intruder was my flight leader, Capt. Wayne Lowry. We joined up and climbed to eleven thousand feet, but didn't stay there very long. Lowry whipped his Mustang over and dived back down. I followed and saw a very long trail of thick, black smoke way ahead of us that poured from a Bf 109. Lowry tucked in behind this guy's tail and began to fire—and then his guns suddenly fell silent; he had shot his last fifty rounds! Lowry called me and said, "OK, you lucky SOB, he's all yours!"

I came up from 250 yards away and immediately saw an explosion as my rounds tore into the German fighter. My Mustang was covered in oil and my windscreen had a bunch of nicks in it. The 109 pilot suddenly popped his canopy and tried to bail out from ten feet off the deck. I saw his chute string out as he hit the ground and then bounced, traveling at over 380 miles per hour. He bounced twice more before he disappeared into the burning wreckage of his airplane. That was the first time I had faced the realities of combat. No longer was it airplane against airplane. Until now, I'd never considered the person-to-person aspect of aerial combat.

I claimed one Fw 190 and one Bf 109.

FRIEND OR FOE?

It was October 12, 1944. I had shot down a Ju 52 trimotor transport on September 15, but things were getting pretty scarce because we didn't get many good missions after the Russians took Ploesti. On today's flight we were sent out on a strafing mission between Budapest and Vienna. There was a thick cloud layer at nine hundred feet with a half-mile visibility in mist. We were flying over a rail line when I looked left and saw a very big airplane two hundred feet off the ground. At first I thought it was a B-17. I came up behind him, forty to fifty feet away, and saw that it was an He 111 medium bomber. I didn't fire because we had been told that the Russians had an airplane that looked very similar to the 111, and we knew that they were close to Budapest. The mystery plane was painted silver with black, wavy lines crossing the wing at forty-five-degree angles, about four inches apart, but other than that, the plane had no markings.

I decided to pull up closer to the tail section because I thought I could tell the difference between German and Russian writing. As I pulled closer, the tail gunner woke up and turned his machine guns toward me, firing wildly. As far as I was concerned, the game was over, and I didn't care what nationality the 111 was. My first blast tore into the rear-gunner area and then into the left engine. With the engine burning, I raked my guns across the whole aircraft and set the right engine on fire as well. The He 111 went down and exploded about twenty miles west of Budapest.

I claimed one He 111.

Playing the Odds

On January 20, 1945, I was leading a flight of P-51s on a B-17 bomber-escort mission to Regensburg. We were flying a racetrack pattern (straight and level flight in an elongated oval) over the bombers. I looked down at them and noticed they were flying a nice, tight formation. By the time I looked up, the sky had turned black, with over forty Fw 190s diving on the bombers from my two o'clock position. I ordered my flight to drop tanks. The movement seemed to catch the attention of the 190s, which turned toward us. I went back to my old bad habits and began to flock-shoot at them. As I fired my guns, I ducked down behind the windshield and kicked my rudders back and forth.

After my head-on pass, I climbed into a steep chandelle (climbing turn) and found myself behind two 190s. I opened fire on one of the guys and saw one hit on his tail section. He suddenly blew up into a ball of fire right in front of me. As I jerked the stick back to avoid hitting him, his leader went inverted and began to roll into a split-ess. I couldn't find the rest of my flight; I thought they'd been shot down. For the next five minutes, I had a jolly old time trying to get on the leader's tail. Every time I got into a firing position, I had two more 190s on my tail and had to break off my attack. The only thing that saved me was the fact that I was flying in a P-51 Mustang.

I could out-turn these guys with ease, but there was only one of me and a whole bunch of them. The final straw was when I got behind two 190s turning thirty degrees in opposite directions. I knew this game. It was called it the "mouse in the middle," and no matter which way I turned, I'd end up with a 190 on my tail. I decided I didn't like the odds so I broke off for home. That was the only time in my combat career that I pushed the throttle through the gate. At least a dozen of the 190s chased me for a while but gave up when I pulled away from them. When I got back to base, I found the rest of my flight safe and sound, though each of them had had their own mechanical or combat issues during the encounter.

I claimed one Fw 190, which was my final victory.

BLACK GOLD AT PLOESTI

There was no such thing as an easy target for the USAAC bomber crews stationed in the Mediterranean region during the early stages of World War II. A combination of long distances and the lack of long-range fighter escorts instilled a feeling of hopelessness and fear in the hearts and minds of the bomber crews as they crawled their way to target areas. Nowhere was this more evident than to the poor unfortunate souls who ventured out from remote bases in the bellies of B-24 Liberators to make a perilous journey to a place who resembled the gates of hell. A place called Ploesti.

The thick, black-liquid lifeblood of the German war machine was located in the Romanian oil fields and was one of the most highly defended targets in southern Europe. A defensive ring of flak guns and smoke screens supported the oil refineries on the ground, but an even greater threat came from the skies over Ploesti. The Luftwaffe, fielding Bf 109 fighters in concert with the Romanian-designed IAR-80, a radial-engined, ground-attack fighter of the Fortelor Aeriene Regal ale Romania (Royal Romanian Air Force), flew protective cover against any and all who dared to assemble over the target area. In the aerial game for freedom, the cost was high, with an endless stream of American bomber crewmen buried in the ground by the time escort planes became available. The savior came in the form of Fifteenth Air Force fighter groups flying North American P-51 Mustangs. The Mustangs' long legs were stretched to their operational limits as they shepherded B-24s and B-17s into harm's way and back out again, all while slugging it out with Axis fighters that rose to repel the Allied invaders.

After flying 337 hours of combat in sixty-six missions with eight con-firmed victories, Art Fiedler returned to the United States in March 1945.

ESCORT TO PLOESTI
ADVENTURES OF A MUSTANG ACE
Lt. Col. Robert J. Gobel, USAF (Ret.)
31st Fighter Group, 12th Air Force

"I could see the handwriting on the wall and I knew we were going to lose the war when I watched helplessly as over 1,200 American bombers and P-51 Mustang fighters flew over Hungary. What were we to do with only forty of us in our tired old Me 109s? It was the beginning of the end for the Pumas during that dreadful summer of 1944.

—Lt. Mihaly (Michael) Karatsonyi,
Royal Hungarian Air Force,
101/3 Fighter Group, the Pumas

HIGH ADVENTURE, FROM *B* TO *D*

By the time I arrived in the Mediterranean Theater of Operations (MTO), I had over 240 hours of fighter time in Curtis P-40 Warhawks and Bell P-39 Airacobras. I had dueled fellow squadron mates over the well-protected and Axis-free skies above Panama. I thought the P-40 was a great block of concrete with wings on it, but given a little time and opportunity, I thought I could do all right with it. The Airacobra was another story.

I was young and naïve, and christened with the title "fighter pilot." I thought the P-39 was a good plane, but at the time I just didn't know any better. It had some very tricky flight characteristics to it, and you had to honor those if you wanted to stay alive. In retrospect, I was glad I didn't have to go up against the highly maneuverable Bf 109 with it. Actually, the P-39 was a greater danger to American pilots than it was to the Germans. Years after the war, I mentioned to Luftwaffe ace Günther Rall about my flying the P-39 in training. Günther smiled at me and said, "We (the Luftwaffe) were very familiar with the P39—we loved them!"

When I was deemed combat ready, with no actual combat experience, I was shipped overseas. Shoehorned aboard a Liberty ship full of other combat-bound servicemen, we bobbed on the Atlantic for twenty-one days, dodging U-boats until finally arriving in Oran, Algeria, in early 1944. From there, I was sent to the Twelfth Air Force fighter training center at Telergma, Algeria, which was the former home of a French Foreign Legion outpost. Unfortunately, we were not living as comfortable a life as our brother pilots in the European Theater of Operations (ETO). About the only thing we did have in common was our great affection for flying the Spitfire.

I had just been assigned to the 31st Fighter Group, 308th Fighter Squadron of the Twelfth Air Force. Our group, along with the 52nd Fighter Group, was to receive training in the Spitfire Mark V in preparation for our role as a close-air-support unit flying Spitfire Mark VIIIs and IXs. The Spitfire was a recognized front-line fighter and a proven combat veteran. The Spit was a true joy to fly: light on the controls, very nimble, and highly maneuverable. I was elated while flying the Spitfire and looked forward to the day I would fly in combat. Unfortunately, that day never came.

After receiving twenty to twenty-five hours of familiarization time, our group of recently trained Spitfire pilots was moved to the 31st Fighter Group home at Castel Volturno, Italy. Our stay was very short. Without warning, we were removed from operational flying, told to turn in our Spitfires, and transferred to the 306th Fighter Wing of the Fifteenth Air Force. We were also told that our new combat assignment would be bomber escort, and that we'd be flying an airplane called the P-51 Mustang. The news of our new mounts brought with it both good news and bad.

The good news was that I recognized the P-51B as a different breed of cat than the P-40s and P-39s I'd flown earlier. And the Mustang was faster than the Spitfire—not quite as nimble, but all in all, a great fighter plane. There were two things I didn't like about the P-51B model, though. One was the fact that it only carried four .50-caliber machine guns, mounted on an angle in the wings. This slanted arrangement caused the guns to jam at high G loads. The other thing I didn't like about the Mustang was that it carried a seemingly endless supply of fuel—a fact that was great news for the bomber boys, who had been getting pounded day in and day out, but a mixed blessing for Mustang pilots, who had to deal with the fuel's considerable weight and potential for fiery explosion. But to the bombers, our extended range was the answer to their prayers.

An escort plane had to fly for more than six hours on each run, taking the big bombers to the target, fighting off the attacking Luftwaffe, and returning the bombers to the safety of home. For us, that was a long time to sit in a small, cramped cockpit. But when you're just twenty-one years old like I was, it didn't make a damn bit of difference as long as it was an *exciting* six hours!

MUSTANG BAPTISM OF FIRE

But of course, not every mission was a thrill. Typically, we would drone out for two-and-half-hours, escorting the bombers to Ploesti. Then we would fight the Luftwaffe for five minutes and then grind back home to base for another two-and-a-half hours, knowing full well that we had to do it all over again the next day. Some missions were a lot more hairy than others, while some seemed uneventful, including my first mission.

On April 16, 1944, I took part in the 31st Fighter Group's first operational mission with the P-51 Mustang. I was pleased with myself for staying with my leader and coming back home in one piece to our base at San Severo, Italy. I racked up more and more missions, and could feel my confidence growing by the flight hour. On May 29, 1944, I scored my first victory by downing a Bf 109 over Wiener Neustadt, Austria, using a thirty-degree deflection shot. My mother used to tell me there was no rest for the wicked; she must have been referring to the Luftwaffe, because they were relentless in attacking the bombers as we escorted them to the target.

By the middle of July 1944, I had destroyed five Bf 109s and had flown forty-four combat missions. At that time, the 31st Fighter Group transitioned into P-51D Mustangs. This new model was a vast improvement over the B. It carried six .50-caliber machine guns instead of four, and these were mounted in upright positions. This arrangement took care of the constant jamming problem due to high-G maneuvers in the B model. The D's other great feature was the bubbletop canopy that gave all-around greater visibility.

THE FLYING DUTCHMAN

Because of my seniority in the squadron, I had finally earned my own Mustang. All of our P-51s in the group were identically painted with red candy stripes on the tails and solid red spinners, with a thick red band behind it on the nose. I wanted my airplane to have its own identity, but had a very hard time deciding on a name for it. It seemed that most everyone had named theirs after a girlfriend or a wife back home; I wanted to avoid that.

I recalled a story about the Flying Dutchman, a phantom ship that sailed through the air on an eternal but unending quest to find a home port. I liked the story, and because a sizeable portion of the population in my hometown of Racine, Wisconsin, was of German extraction (the elders referred to themselves as "Dutchmen" [Deutsche Manner]), I christened my Mustang *Flying Dutchman* and went looking for German fighters to add to my scoreboard. It didn't take me very long to find just what I was looking for.

BLACK FLIGHT

August 18, 1944. The mission for that day, my fifty-fifth combat hop, was anything but typical. Normally, our squadron would put up four flights of four Mustangs, with two spares to fill in if needed. The squadron's planned mission was another escort of B-24s to and from Ploesti, but this time we had a trick up our sleeve. The squadron CO, Capt. Leland "Tommy" Molland, my close friend and mentor, received permission from the higher-ups to put up a rogue flight of four Mustangs called "Black Flight" (the Outlaw Squadron). Tommy would lead the flight with his wingman, and he asked me to fly the number-three position, with my wingman tucked in close. Our sole responsibility was to stir up and seek out and destroy any Luftwaffe fighters that came looking for a fight. Fortunately, the Luftwaffe didn't let us down.

We stayed with the squadron for most of the way into Ploesti, and finally turned off course as we entered the target area. Immediately, I spotted some tiny, fast-moving dots out to the Russian side of Ploesti. After calling them out, our Black Flight raced toward them but lost contact in the overcast. Our flight initiated a turn back toward Ploesti as we continued to scan the area. My body froze momentarily when I looked back and up and saw more than fourteen Bf 109s above us. When *they* finally saw *us*, the action really began.

I told Tommy to "Break left!" as I broke right. Half of the 109s tacked onto Tommy and his wingman, but had trouble keeping up with the Mustangs. I cranked my Mustang around and turned back into the 109s, looking for a target. I picked one out and closed the distance, pouring .50-caliber bullets into his airplane. I watched as the canopy on the 109 came off and the pilot bailed out. It was time to find another target.

I spotted another 109 as he pushed his nose over, diving for the deck. I pushed my throttle to the stops and racked my Mustang over in a headlong dive after him. I caught up to him at eight thousand feet and hit him pretty good on the first burst. Like his comrade before him, his canopy came off. I sent another burst into him but was a little slow getting off the trigger as he stepped out onto the wing. I cocked the Mustang up on a wing and watched the pilot fall, looking for his chute to blossom. The parachute never opened, and he fell to his death in a plowed field.

That scene kind of shocked me; I stared in disbelief. True, I had meant to destroy his airplane, but that was the first time I had seen one of my foes killed. I snapped my head back on a swivel where it belonged and started looking for more enemy aircraft. I cleaned up the Mustang and called Tommy over the R/T to find out where everyone, including my wingman, had gone to. I received no response from anyone in Black Flight, and noticed I was getting a little low on fuel. I started to climb to get some altitude under my wings, and began to turn the Mustang every thirty seconds to clear my six o'clock. Suddenly, my P-51 shook violently.

I racked the Mustang up into a steep right turn, pushing everything to the stops again. As I pulled the plane through a 4-G turn, I saw two Bf 109s behind me. We went round and round for a couple of turns without any of us getting a shot off. The 109s suddenly broke off the encounter and dived for the deck, heading home. I believe they fully expected me to do the same, especially since I was alone and a long way from home. Problem was, I was a twenty-one-year-old fighter pilot running low on fuel and without good sense, so I tore ass after them!

The 109s hit the deck and flew line abreast about two hundred yards apart from one another. This was a very good defensive position for the 109s, and only a fool would try to attack them. But you know what they say, "You can tell a fighter pilot, but you can't tell them much!" I pressed into attack and went for the one on the left. He immediately turned away from me, which caused his friend on the right to turn toward my tail, making me the mouse in the middle.

I rolled out and the two 109s mirrored me as we raced on. I began to wonder if I had made a huge mistake, not least because the two 109s were drawing me closer to the Fatherland. I couldn't think of anything better to do so I tried it again! This time the guy on the right turned too quickly and too steeply, and passed over the top of me. I figured his 109 couldn't roll out in time so I pressed in on the left and let loose with my guns. Problem was, I only had two guns firing and both of these were drawing tracer rounds, which told me I was down to my last fifty slugs!

Luckily, I was close enough to walk my hits all around him (though I never hit him). He looked back when he should have looked forward, and slammed into a small rise in the middle of a wheat field. With the 109 totally destroyed and burning, his wingman kept going. I never saw him again, which was good news for me. With my flight suit soaked with sweat and my body trembling from the effects of the adrenaline rush, I began a climbing turn for home. I just hoped I had enough gas to make it.

I recrossed the Ploesti area at twenty thousand feet, all alone. It was a very eerie feeling because just fifteen minutes earlier, so much had been going on. Pilots were yelling and screaming on the radio, and flak was bursting all around as the bombers droned on through the fires of hell. The effects were immediate as pieces of torn, twisted metal fell earth- ward from their stricken airplanes. B-24s, or what remained of them, began to spin out of control through the black clouds as the helpless crews inside tried to jump free. Most did not make it. And yet now, as I cruised overhead, the entire scene was peaceful.

It was getting very late and I was reasonably sure that no other Mustangs were behind me. As I made my approach to land at San Severo, I noted that the usually large crowds of crew chiefs and armor- ers huddled near the taxiway, waiting for their airplanes to return home, had dwindled to just four men. As I taxied off the runway, I could see my crew, Staff Sergeant Carpenter and armorer Corporal Langlois, begin to jump up and down. Two other men, realizing that their plane and pilot were down somewhere and wouldn't come back, looked crestfallen as I taxied by.

I had flown more than six hours on that mission, most of which was at maximum performance. I grayed out or blacked out countless times. I had ten rounds of ammunition left in my two working guns and only cupfuls of gas in my fuel tanks. I was physically exhausted and emo- tionally spent as I hoisted myself out of the cockpit. But I knew I had to do it all over again tomorrow. I was a fighter pilot and I wouldn't have changed any of it for the world!

Robert J. Gobel flew a total of sixty-one combat missions with the 31st Fighter Group. He is credited with eleven victories during his 303 hours of combat flying. Gobel retired from the U.S. Air Force with the rank of lieu- tenant colonel. To learn more about Robert Gobel, see his book, Mustang Ace, Memoirs of a P-51 Fighter Pilot.

5

Deeper into Germany

As the initiative in World War II indisputably shifted away from Germany in 1943–1944, long-range American fighter escorts protected ever-increasing numbers of bombers of the Eighth and Ninth air forces, on an ever-increasing number of missions. The Luftwaffe, stretched beyond its limits because of shortages of fuel, appalling losses of experienced fighter pilots, and an inability to match Allied industrial production, was overmatched. With some bomber missions getting through to Berlin and other German cities with little or no challenge by enemy fighters, U.S. fighter emphasis shifted to ground targets, particularly airfields (where parked German planes were easy meat), trains and other rolling stock, and marshaling yards. The losses taken by Mustangs from flak and other ground fire were greater than those from air-to-air combat, but the fighters persevered, punishing the enemy. Following D Day, Patton's Third Army pushed into Germany, opening up close-in airbases for Allied planes. Although German fighters reappeared to do battle in March 1945, the end game was already underway. The Mustangs had helped bring the Allies to final victory in Europe.

OFF WE GO INTO THE WILD BLUE YONDER!
Lt. James L. McCubbin
385th Fighter Squadron, 364th Fighter Group

As I sat in the cockpit of a beautiful P-51D Mustang on September 23, 1944, waiting for the "start engines" command, I could hardly believe I was finally going on my first combat mission. The first flight I ever took was in a Piper Cub on a warm June day in 1940. Now, four years later, after completing Primary, Basic, and Advanced, I was sitting in the ultimate fighter plane of the war. I was surrounded by other men, mere cookie cut-outs of me, all of us following the same path to the air and all of us fighter pilots. Unfortunately, not every one of us would return home alive.

Pilots in forty-eight Mustangs went over their own private thoughts, shivering from early morning cold and nerves. This cadre represented the entire 364th Fighter Group based at Honington Air Base, England, which consisted of three squadrons: the 383rd, the 384th, and the one I was attached to, the 385th. Each of our squadrons had four flights of four airplanes each. In addition, for this mission we also had three or four spare Mustangs ready to go in case someone couldn't get off or had to abort. Finally, the call I had been longing for: "Gentlemen, start your engines!"

The sound of those Rolls-Royce engines, each one twelve cylinders and 1,695 horsepower, coughing and struggling to catch enough fuel to start, was thrilling. As the first deep-throated roar echoed above the rest as one caught, the rest followed in unison until the whole field shook and vibrated. These feelings never diminished for me, even after forty-four missions and two hundred hours of aerial combat.

Taxiing a fully loaded P-51 is not an easy task. Because it's a tail dragger and has a very long nose, the engine cowling slopes up in front, blocking any forward view. To compensate, we had to weave, or S-turn, down the taxiway to maintain forward view through the side of the canopy. To avoid a too-rich air/fuel mix that would cause the engine to "load up" and foul the spark plugs, we needed a constant one thousand rpm, which equals about a thirty-mile-per-hour taxiing speed. With the S-turn maneuvers on a taxiway crammed with Mustangs, there was a lot of heavy brake action. When our herd approached the end of the runway for takeoff, the roar became deafening. In order to gain formation with minimum use of time and fuel, the first Mustangs off made a calculated wide-climbing turn, with each P-51 that followed making an even tighter and steeper turn. It was a difficult maneuver that often left the last man really struggling to catch the group, using full power and a vertical bank from takeoff.

As we approached the English Channel, my engine began to exhibit unusual indications and sounds. When I was over water, all sorts of things went wrong. A left magneto acted up, compromising the spark and allowing an rpm drop of one hundred revolutions more than was allowed. The oil pressure seemed low and the coolant temperatures were almost certainly climbing. But as soon as we were over land, the problems somehow disappeared. Strangely, I had the same engine problems over water on every mission. For some Mustang pilots in these sorts of tricky situations, the temptation to abort was so strong that it couldn't be resisted. And when that happened more than two times, the pilot was reduced to being a "ground pounder," the worse insult ever.

BEGINNER'S LUCK

The group had a procedure that required each new member to fly his first mission on the wing of *Outshine*, the group commander. My turn came. As we approached landfall, large black puffs of fire and smoke appeared in our midst—what a shock! We were hardly over the shoreline and they were shooting at us already? All I could think was, *If it's this bad at the beginning of the enemy territory, what must it be like farther inland?* Someone later explained to me that "ol' one-eye" had a single antiaircraft battery gun perched on a small island off the Dutch coast, and he never hit anyone—yet.

Our mission was to shepherd a box of B-17 Flying Fortresses on a maximum-effort bomber run. We were stationed on the bombers' right side and at the same altitude. The sight of an endless string of boxes of bright, shimmering B-17s was just plain incredible. Heck, I didn't know our air force had so many airplanes! They stretched out of sight in both directions and looked invincible in their tight formation, with inter-protective gun patterns. At least that was what the newspapers had told us about the Flying Forts.

The sky was so clear, and everything so peaceful, that we had failed to notice the thin cloud layer over the bomber stream. Our group had to fly in a constant *S* pattern to reduce our speed to match that of the bomber train. All was clear when I took my eyes off the B-17s as we started to weave outward. But when our noses swung back toward the bombers, the sight was indescribable. What had once been a beautiful formation was now a jagged junk pile of pieces of falling air-craft, parachutes, and burning B-17s that had wandered out of forma-tion. Looking at the carnage, I noted a lone Fw 190 firing on a crippled B-17. *Outshine* swung his nose at the 190 and opened up with his six .50-calibers. But due to his speed he was unable to concentrate his fire for more than a few seconds.

As his wingman, I was in a better position behind and to the outside of the curve toward the 190; I was able to swing farther out to kill my speed, and concentrated my fire on the 190 until I saw the pilot bail out. Whether my leader's bullets or mine had the most effect became a point of controversy. But with no time to debate the kill, we went looking for more targets. The Germans had been hiding in the thin overcast and made a pass on the bomber formation when we turned on our outward path. I lost contact with the rest of my group and I reasoned that the Germans would have made a dive for the deck after attacking the bomb-ers. I spent the remainder of the mission hunting for Fw 190s, to no avail. With fuel getting low, I turned for home.

YELLOW-NOSE CIRCUS

On November 2, 1944, more than four hundred Luftwaffe fight-ers mounted an attack against our bomber formations. Although the Eighth Air Force broke the record that day for enemy fighters shot down, my flight missed the whole shootin' match. My flight leader was a guy named Wilson, who happened to be an Oklahoma Indian and a real wild guy, in the air and on the ground. His wingman was Murphy. I was the element leader but flew without a wingman because mine had aborted with engine problems. The three of us were becoming increasingly frustrated as we milled about the clouds, listening to the exciting chatter all over the radio. "Hey I got one!" "Look out, one is on your tail!" "Bandit on your left, Charlie, are you hit?"

Suddenly, we were attacked by a lone Me 109. This was almost an insult. A single 109 against three cream-of-the crop P-51s? Trouble was, the 109 was a yellow-nose belonging to the infamous handpicked Luftwaffe fighter squadron known as the "Abbeville Boys," named for the Abbeville-Ducat region of northern France, where some of these elite Jagdgeschwader 26 (JG 26) fliers were based. The pilot was so close I could almost make out his facial features. Wilson cranked his Mustang into a hard left turn. His wingman followed and I brought up the rear. The 109 fell into the circle behind me. If everything worked out well, Wilson would catch up behind the German and end this insult. Instead, the German was getting dangerously close to gaining enough lead to hit me. Since our guns were fixed and only fired straight ahead, the airplane had to be aimed ahead of the turning target (the amount determined by speed and the rate of turn).

I called Murphy and said, "If you don't turn tighter, I'm going to pass you!" In his haste, Murphy hit a high-speed stall and spun out of the circle to somewhere below. I called Wilson next, with the same result. Nothing like two 20mm guns bearing down on your ass to motivate a guy! That left me and the 109 looking at each other across the circle. It was a stalemate; he would hit a high-speed stall, lose ninety degrees, and then I would do the same. We both knew that if either of us should spin out, the other would have him for lunch. But really: only amateurs spin out.

Wilson and Murphy had almost climbed back up to our altitude for the chance to end this circle chase when a second yellow-nose 109 came out of the clouds above. Where he had been was anybody's guess—maybe observing his friend locked in a duel and only jumping in when the odds were on our side. I very quickly found myself upside down in a mild dive. Below, up relative to the airplane, I saw a 109 diving for the clouds, followed by two P-51s, and then another 109 with guns firing at the last Mustang. I was just barely able to maneuver into firing position and fill the air with enough .50-caliber rounds in front of the trailing 109 to cause him to veer away. This turn of events undoubtedly saved Murphy. Then all four Germans disappeared into the clouds. I decided to cover the logical exit point below the clouds. When I had my position, what felt like ten thousand antiaircraft guns opened up and discouraged me. And that's how the day ended: nobody hurt, nobody hit, no wins, no losses. Frustrating? Yes, but at least we all got to sleep in our respective bunks that night!

North of Berlin

December 5, 1944. I was flying Yellow Three in the 358th Fighter "B" Squadron. As the bombers began their run, we moved away from the close escort we'd been furnishing. As we headed north, we saw a gaggle of fifty-plus enemy aircraft at ten o'clock. They were heading north at about 22,500 feet; we were at 23,000. My flight leader swung in behind the nearest enemy plane. I dropped my tanks and swung to the outside of the turn to pick out a target on the other side of the gaggle. I opened fire at about seven thousand yards dead astern. The enemy aircraft took no evasive action. I closed to 300 yards, firing several bursts. The Fw 190 blew up in flames. The gaggle continued to fly straight and level. I picked another target, and at about 400 yards dead astern I opened fire, closing to 250 yards. I fired several bursts and obtained numerous hits. The enemy pilot bailed out. I immediately pulled in behind a third Fw 190, opened fire at 300 yards, and closed to 200 yards. I observed hits all over him. He appeared to be out of control and went into a straight-down dive. I got behind a fourth Fw 190 and at 200 yards I opened fire. I closed to 100 yards and observed many hits. He split-essed and I followed him. As I fired short bursts, I saw his elevator come off. I was reaching compressibility by that time, so I pulled out at eleven thousand feet. He was still going straight down. I went down to the deck looking for more enemy aircraft but found nothing. Then I headed for home.

I claimed three Fw 190s destroyed and one Fw 190 probably destroyed in the air.

JANUARY JOLLIES

I schemed with a good friend of mine in the squadron, Robert "Mac" McKibben, that if we ever became separated from the group, we would make our own fighter sweep. We made this brilliant decision because of several frustrating missions in which the group acted on information provided by a new radar installation in liberated France. For some crazy reason, the whole group milled about France chasing radar reports, to little avail. Sometimes the bogey was a barrage balloon and other times it was an unidentified aircraft. So on January 1, 1945, we were finally able to make our escape into southern France.

According to plan, we flew line abreast some 2,500 feet apart to maximize our field of view. It wasn't long before we encountered our first victim, an Me 109. McKibben and the 109 made a head-on pass at each other and then they broke into a tight Lufbery circle to chase each other round and round. Most of our Mustangs had been equipped with the latest and greatest gun sight, the K-14, which was actually a rudimentary gyroscopic computer that was designed to compensate for lead. The sight consisted of a circle of five diamond-shaped pips that were projected onto a clear glass plate in front of the windscreen. The diameter made by the pips could be controlled by a handle on the throttle. You set the sight's lever to the wingspan of your target. Then you controlled the circle to encompass that wingspan. Holding perfect coordination, so the bullets would fly straight, you had two seconds to ensure success.

Since I never had time to practice with this new sight or use it in the prescribed way, I thought this was my best opportunity. Unfortunately, Mac was not of the same opinion and was irritated that I took my sweet time to make a perfect gunnery pass on my opponent. He began to scream at me over the radio to hurry up and shoot! I did, and the shot was beautiful; my cone of fire poured directly into the 109's cockpit. The unguarded chatter over the airways between Mac and me was full of exhilaration. I should have known my big mouth would get me into trouble sooner or later, because the Germans played the recording back to me when I became a guest of the Luftwaffe.

UNSCHEDULED STOP

I thought that February 19, 1945, would have been more relaxing. Our flight had just returned to base from a two-day leave granted after four consecutive weeks in combat. Custom dictated that we attend the mission briefing on our first day back, just in case we might be needed to fly. The previous two weeks had consisted of boring bomber escorts without fighter opposition, with little opportunity for strafing due to poor weather conditions. Most of us had been itching to see some action.

When the briefing officer announced that this mission was to be a deep-penetration strafing operation, my crew campaigned me to request that our flight be substituted for one of the scheduled ones, on the basis of our previous lack of activity. I agreed with the rest, and since we hadn't made plans or preparations to go on this mission, we ended up missing breakfast, and I went up dressed only in a base uniform: tie, insignia, and low cut shoes. I should have stayed in bed!

Because all of our missions were long range, some as long as seven hours or more, our Mustangs carried two 110-gallon drop tanks, one under each wing. As fighter pilots, we often lamented the waste in dropping these tanks indiscriminately; it would be better to drop them on a German convoy. We developed a crude plan whereby the lead plan on a strafing run would jettison his tanks over the target and the following planes would fire on them to ignite the fuel inside.

Then the second plane would add his tanks to the roaring inferno as he overflew the same target. Unfortunately, the best-laid plans seldom work as planned.

Because of heavy, thick clouds, we were almost to Berlin before we could find a break in the overcast to enable us to drop to the deck. Once we made it down, our squadron encountered three trains within a very small area. I directed Lieutenant Berry, my element leader, to hit the train first so that I could set off his tanks on my run and drop my tanks for Lieutenant Kenworth on *his* run. I observed numerous hits on the locomotive on my pass, but failed to notice any flames. (Actually, I thought the whole idea was rather juvenile, since the drop tanks wouldn't fly like bombs and were difficult to place on target.)

As I pulled up from my run, I noticed that Berry continued straight away from the target at low altitude. When I called him over the radio, he informed me that he had been hit. It was later that I noticed a flak car toward the end of the train, with an antiaircraft gun concealed under camouflage. I caught up with Berry, and after examining his Mustang, I could not detect any obvious damage. I asked him if he could make it back to base and he responded, "No!" I then asked if he planned to bail out and he said, "Yes!" I soon saw his canopy come off as he jettisoned it. His Mustang rolled and crashed into the ground. My only conclusion was that he had been badly injured and couldn't get out. The worst was yet to come.

The weather wasn't very good for this type of strafing operation, as there was a low-level, solid cloud base some 2,000- to 4,000-feet thick starting about 1,500 feet above the ground. In between that were several 1,000-foot interludes of fairly clear area before you hit the next solid layer. This pattern extended upward past twenty thousand feet. Due to the deteriorating weather and the unfortunate loss of Berry, the squadron leader instructed everyone to form up and set course for home. I disagreed with his decision for several reasons, not the least of which was that Berry could not return with us. He was a roommate of mine, and his loss hit me hard.

As the rest turned for home, I "conveniently" became lost, in order to follow the main train tracks west and look for more targets. The ceiling was gradually dropping, which further reduced my forward vision. I was able to stumble across a few good targets before entering a large railroad-yard marshaling complex. A good pilot avoids such areas because that's where the guns are. But because of the poor visibility I had little choice but to shoot and go. I reasoned that a 180-degree turn would offer too much target for the German gunners, who undoubtedly had been notified of this "nut in a Mustang" coming down the line.

The targets were so numerous that I had difficulty concentrating my fire. The other problem was that because of my low altitude, I had to "porpoise" up and down a hundred feet in order to point the aircraft at the target on the next shallow dive, and repeat. The altitude had to be limited because each gain allowed more of the gunners to shoot at me. I almost made it across. But during one of my jump-ups, a shell opened a two-foot-diameter hole in my right wing just outside of the right machine gun. As I zoomed up into the overcast, I noted that my airspeed and artificial horizon instruments weren't functioning. When I tried to compensate for this, I was struck with vertigo and literally didn't know which way was up or down!

Instead of breaking out on top of the first layer of overcast, I instead broke out on the bottom, diving for the ground. I reentered the overcast on the second try and scanned my engine instruments. All of the things a Mustang pilot never wanted to see were happening at once. The coolant temperatures were climbing, oil pressure was dropping, and the oil temperatures were quickly rising. Even as I shifted the coolant doors from auto to manual-open, I knew that the engine was going to burn up soon. I broke out of the top of the bottom overcast, and because of the wing damage, I could manage the Mustang only by holding the control stick to the extreme left side of the cockpit.

I was flying about a hundred feet above the clouds and some 3,000 feet above the ground. As the engine began to lose power, I radioed my squadron leader one last time to say, "Hasta luego" ("See you later")—I hope! Bailing out would be tricky because whenever I released back pressure on the control stick, the Mustang would start to snap roll. I elected to try and jump straight up from a crouching position on the seat instead of the normal (and recommended) procedure of diving for the right wing.

Strangely, I had always wanted to jump from an airplane, but not under these conditions. I imagined it would be a peaceful affair, with no engine noise or vibrations from my dying Mustang. By the time I finally got a grip on the ripcord, I was already in the clouds and falling fast. I lost valuable time and altitude because I couldn't get my parachute to deploy until I yanked on it a second time. I could see a small crowd gathering below, alerted by the sound of my stricken Mustang. By the time my chute blossomed, I made one complete oscillation before hitting the ground—hard! Fortunately, the ground was marshy, which saved me from breaking something. My capturers were not very impressed by the escapades involved in my shooting up their train station. And for the rest of the war, the only time I saw Mustangs was when they flew over our POW camp.

Aerial combat was the ultimate experience for a pilot. Several explanations seem called for here. Part of the allure is that in war, the situation is you or them. Each of you wants to kill the other, plain and simple. Most of the time our encounters were machine against machine; we rarely saw the bloody results of aerial combat. The rest of the flying experience depends on the aggressiveness of the individual. We were carefully selected for this job, first to be a pilot and second to be a fighter pilot, which requires both an aggressive and independent nature. As fighter pilots, we thought we could do anything because we had been programmed to be the elite of the elite. Some may call this kind of indoctrination stupid, but it was highly effective. I wouldn't have changed flying a P-51 Mustang in combat for the world.

RISKY BUSINESS
1st Lt. Frank Oiler, USAAC (Ret.)
78th Fighter Group, 84th Fighter Squadron

TURN IN YOUR JUGS, BOYS!

In early December 1944, most of the pilots in the 78th Fighter Group, especially those with over twenty-five combat missions under their belts, felt "fat and sassy" flying the reliable and hard-hitting P-47 Thunderbolt. Seasoned pilots realized early on that the "Jug" was like a flying tank that could deliver deadly punishment to the enemy and absorb most anything that might be thrown back at it.

Whether flying a bomber escort, dive bombing a bridge, or strafing an airfield, the P-47s of the 78th FG cut a destructive swath through Occupied Europe. A great affection and bond between pilot and plane soon established itself as the Eagles of Duxford tore apart the Axis. Many times the black-and-white-checked-nosed P-47s brought their pilots back from a mission with extra weight in the form of German flak and cannon shells embedded in the Jugs's fuselages!

Fighter pilots were creatures of habit, and most everyone in the 78th FG agreed they wouldn't change or give up flying the P-47 for anything in the world. In mid-December 1944, the world fell apart as the winds of change blew cold and harsh across Europe, and onto the fighter base at Duxford, England. Bad news seemed to come in threes.

First, the Germans had smashed through the thin Allied lines in Belgium and were now on the offensive. Second, some of the worst winter weather to hit England and the Continent grounded the desperately needed Allied fighters and bombers. And finally, the worst news yet for the 78th FG was an order issued by Gen. Jimmy Doolittle. It simply read, "Turn in your Jugs, boys, and transition into Mustangs!" I felt as though I just lost my best friend. After much "kicking and screaming," all of us realized that change was not really all that bad, especially at the controls of a P-51 Mustang.

We had been forewarned it was coming. All the pleading and complaining in the world didn't change a thing. By much higher authority than mine, these changes had been in the works for some time. General Doolittle's plan was to make the Eighth Air Force all P-51 Mustangs. Even though we dug in our heels, they began to pull our P-47s and ferry them to the Ninth Air Force. The war-weary ones went to air-sea rescue. We loved our P-47s, so the P-51B Mustang felt like a demotion. Our brothers in the 56th FG seemed to have all the luck because they got to keep their Jugs!

Mustang Ops

An airman's worst enemies, snow, ice, rain, and fog, had hit our base at Duxford, like all the others spread across England. We were socked in by some of the most horrendous winter weather to hit England in a long time. Even if it cleared up enough for us to take off, the weather over the target was zero-zero: no visibility. Our poor boys on the ground at the Battle of the Bulge needed our help, and all we could do was throw snowballs at each other.

I stood on the frozen ground and stared at my new mount. I was actually scared of it. The Mustang looked so fragile compared to the Jug; I thought surely this was some kind of nightmare. The Jug was like a flying tank on strafing missions and a flying truck on bombing runs. It had saved my butt countless times, and now I began to wonder if I would survive this war.

My whole attitude changed in an instant when I became airborne in the Mustang for the very first time. She was quick and nimble and very responsive on the controls. She had "longer legs" than the P-47, which enabled us to stay with the bombers as they flew deeper into Germany. The Mustang climbed like a homesick angel, and in a dogfight there was nothing that could beat it except another Mustang and a better pilot! All my fears and doubts were replaced by confidence and exuberance. This was one hot fighter!

For the next ten days we learned the tricks and traits of the Mustang, and what it took to fly this beauty. By early January our squadron became fully operational in P-51s. To make things even better, we received brand-new, bubbletop P-51Ds.

Instead of the four guns on the B model, we now carried six. Still two less than the Jug, but that was an acceptable tradeoff for the extra speed we now had. The interior heating system was much improved over the B models; not only did my big toe receive warm air, but so did the rest of my body! North American Aviation also added a relief tube for those long, long missions. You were OK as long as the tube didn't freeze up on you. If it did, you'd have a long, wet ride!

Because of my seniority in the squadron, I received my own P-51D right away. It still had that "new fighter" smell to it! Being somewhat of a joker, I decided to name my Mustang *Sherman was right!* This was in honor of General Sherman's speech to his troops right before their attack on Atlanta during the Civil War. Sherman told his men, "Don't think this is going to be a turkey shoot. There is many a boy here who looks on war as all glory, but, boys, it is all hell!" I couldn't agree more and thought Sherman was right!

INTO THE HEART OF GERMANY

I began to fly long bomber-escort missions deep into Germany. I flew to places such as Berlin, Leipzig, and Hamburg, and my Mustang never missed a beat. I attribute that fact to my ground crew. My crew chief and Mustang caretaker was Charlie Clark. His assistant was Dennis Shupe, and the armorer was Forest Terry. The very first time I met ol' Charlie was back in the spring of 1944. I was just a green second lieutenant assigned to fly Charlie's black-and-white-checked P-47 Thunderbolt. As an officer and a pilot, I outranked Charlie, but I learned right away who was running the show! When I introduced myself to him, he looked at me for what seemed an eternity and sized me up. The only thing he said was, "I've never lost a pilot or airplane. You're not going to screw my record up, are you?!"

I stammered back, "I'll do my best not to." I had the best damn crew in the air force!

My crew had the Mustang finely tuned for my mission on January 14, 1945: my first opportunity for aerial combat! The 78th was on an area bomber-support mission to the Cologne area. Microwave early warning (MEW) radar called us and told our group to check out bandits beneath us in our sector. We were at twenty-five thousand feet with Capt. Leonard Marshal leading the mission. He spotted the German fighters and called for a bounce.

I was flying Yellow Three in Turquoise Squadron when Rainbow White Three called out, "Twenty-plus bandits directly below on the deck." All four flights dropped wing tanks and raced down onto the enemy planes. Bf 109s and Fw 190s were everywhere, and they scattered in all directions, like chickens! Rainbow Squadron split up the gaggle as Turquoise Squadron attacked. The Germans quickly split into twos and threes.

Turquoise Yellow leader and his wingmen, along with my wingmen and I, went after two German fighters that were fleeing up a creek bed. An Fw 190 went between our flight of four Mustangs, firing. My wingman and I made a hard turn into him and got on his tail, but we lost him over some woods. We immediately picked up a Bf 109 and two Fw 190s that were being chased by a lone P-51.

I called to the Mustang and told him to pick one of the German fighters and let my wingman and me take care of the other two. Like a bomb burst, the 190s broke into opposite directions and the Bf 109 went straight up. I went after one of the 190s and got into a Lufbery dance with him at 1,100 feet. Had I been in the P-47, I would have just about committed suicide. At these low levels in a Jug, especially with a 190, there was no way I could turn as fast as he could. But in my Mustang, things were a whole lot different!

I dropped some flaps and got onto the 190's tail in less than two turns. I squeezed the trigger and a three-second burst of .50-caliber rounds spilled from my guns. At thirty-five degrees deflection, I observed many strikes in the cockpit, fuselage, and wing root section. Pieces flew off the 190 as he snapped into a half-roll and went into the ground upside down. We were only at four hundred feet, and it was time for me to get some altitude under my wings!

My wingman and I started climbing back upstairs when I noticed a Bf 109 above us. The 109 was circling at six thousand feet, and seemed to want no part of the fight below. As we spiraled up to try and catch him, he kept climbing, keeping his altitude advantage. We were both getting nowhere with this game. My gas gauge quickly dropped, and I was farther away from home than he was!

In desperation and at full throttle, I pulled the Mustang straight up and managed to get within two thousand feet of him. I raked his belly from below and observed hits on his tail. I stalled out and broke off my attack, rejoining the squadron as another Mustang finished off the crippled 109. As we headed for home, I was eager to put the Mustang through its paces to see how it did as a ground strafer.

It didn't take long to find a suitable target. A locomotive pulling ten freight cars appeared below us. My wingman and I gave it the once-over, looking for canvas-sided boxcars concealing antiaircraft guns. Satisfied that the train cars were all made of wood, we dived. Our .50 calibers danced across the train, blowing up the engine and setting five of the freight cars on fire.

The 78th really celebrated that night! Our group claimed five aircraft destroyed and four damaged, along with a laundry list of ground targets we had destroyed on the way home. The biggest treat for us was that no one was lost from the group. That in itself was reason to celebrate! More celebration would follow, especially after we stretched the Mustangs' legs all the way to the border of Czechoslovakia.

TARGETS OF OPPORTUNITY

This would truly be a test for us and the P-51: an extreme long-range bomber escort mission deep into Nazi territory. No bombers were lost as they dropped their load on the military target and we turned for home. After passing the bombers off to a new set of "Air Corps shepherds," we did a little strafing and then stopped in Belgium to top off our tanks.

Like good fighter pilots, we patted each other on the back for a job well done. Then someone in the group got the grand idea to dip into our escape kits and "borrow the francs" that were in them to purchase some champagne at the base PX. We took all our remaining ammo and gun belts out of our Mustangs and donated them to the Ninth Air Force. We then filled the empty gun bays with our liquid booty.

Fully loaded with gas and champagne, we flew back to Duxford on the deck in order not to "pop the corks" on our bubbly cargo. That night at the base we had a rousing party. Our intelligence officer found out about the loan we'd taken from our kits and decided that he was going to dock our pay to replace the missing money. What the hell! It was all worth it! Even the hangover!

Unfortunately, not every mission ended in celebration. More often than not, the one thing that turned a party sour was German flak, especially during our strafing attacks on enemy aerodromes. It was on these missions that I really missed the ruggedness of the Thunderbolt. With all that plumbing running through the Mustang, one small nick or round could knock you out of the fight in a heartbeat. I witnessed this firsthand on February 3, 1945.

After our usual escort mission and release from the bombers, we dropped to the deck and looked for targets of opportunity. Unfortunately for some of us, *we* were the targets. When we spotted a German airfield near Lüneburg, we found out the hard way what the Mustang's weakness was. All it took was one lucky rifle round to hit the engine's coolant and you could almost be guaranteed that this would be a one-way mission.

Aerodrome strafing turned many a pilot prematurely gray. The standard practice was to fly on as if we didn't see anything, then drop down and do a hundred-and-eighty-degree turn back into the field. At full throttle with our propeller blades mere feet off the ground, we came screaming across the aerodrome. Heavy flak erupted all around us; the Germans weren't going down without a fight. After a couple of passes, two Mustangs were hit and both pilots became guests of the Luftwaffe for the remainder of the war. Woe unto the foolhardy pilots who circled back for a second pass, as they seldom survived to register their claims. Strafing was "risky business," and I was a lucky fool many times over!

My tour was winding down in the spring of 1945, and so, too, was the Luftwaffe, which had been decimated by our air power. The

P-51 proved its worth in combat time and time again, and saved my butt more than once. But my beloved *Sherman was right!* was lost on March 4, 1945, as it entered an overcast sky over Germany with replacement pilot 2nd Lt. Louis Hereford at the controls.

1st Lt. Frank Oiler finished his tour with seventy-three missions and three hundred hours of combat flight time. Oiler spent fifty-three of those missions in the P-47 Thunderbolt. He flew an additional twenty missions in P-51s, and was credited with one aerial and three ground victories in his new favorite airplane.

BIRDS OF A FEATHER
Capt. Harrison B. Tordoff, USAAC (Ret.)
353rd Fighter Group, 352nd Fighter Squadron

In the fall of 1942 I was attending Cornell University, where I was enrolled in the ornithology program: the study of birds. I joined the Air Corps as a patriotic duty, and also because I wanted to be like the birds I studied, flying and soaring in the heavens above. I also wanted to fight and defend our freedoms while wearing my own set of wings.

By the time I made it to basic training, I knew I wanted to be a fighter pilot. I had one "small" problem that stood in my way: How was I going to cut two inches off my six-foot two-inch frame to meet the legal limit? The answer came in the form of my instructor and partner in crime, Frank "Mickey" Spillane.

It would be many years later that Mickey would become a famous author and star of beer commercials, but in 1943 he was all about flying. We conspired on a devious but very simple plan to get me into fighters: he had me bend my knees when I got measured! He later called me "Li'l Abner," because my flight suit would only reach to the top of my boots.

Mickey was a good instructor with a healthy fear of the inexperience of his students. In order to spare himself the anguish of prolonged dual-control instruction, he soloed us quickly. He kicked me out of the nest early and sent me on my way. Because of him, I eventually made it to England in June 1944 and joined the 353rd Fighter Group, 352nd Fighter Squadron, where I would fly my own "birds of prey."

At that stage of the war, our group, like most others in England, flew the P-47 Thunderbolt. The P-47 "Jug" was a mammoth airplane, with eight .50-caliber machine guns. It was a nice, stable gun platform. I named my Jug *Anne*, after a girl I had feelings for back in the States. I liked the Jug, but it was also an odd bird. During a stall, the nose became very light, but when you pushed it over into a dive, the nose was like a grand piano: very heavy! But, boy oh boy, the Jug had lots of power and could turn on a dime, a fact I appreciated whenever I met the Luftwaffe. I got a few victories in the Thunderbolt by late September 1944 before we turned the plane in for a new, sleeker bird, the P-51 Mustang.

I was a little apprehensive about this new bird until I flew her. The Mustang was everything the Jug wasn't. It was faster, had much more range, and was a better dogfighter than the Jug. For me, it flew like an AT-6 trainer but with a lot more pep. The P-51 was very maneuverable and predictable in flight. I regard it as the ultimate prop fighter. We couldn't turn as tightly as a Spitfire, but we could sure manhandle an Me 109 or FW 190 in a turning battle. Because the Mustang carried six .50-caliber machine guns instead of the Jug's eight, I thought the P-47 was indestructible. I didn't quite feel that way about the P-51, especially at low level.

The only thing that concerned me was the Mustang's coolant system, and all the thinly protected plumbing that ran from its Rolls-Royce Merlin inline engine to its belly. But the Mustang had better cruising speed and sipped fuel compared to the P-47, which meant we could fly farther with the bombers than we ever could before. As long as he didn't have to strip his tanks too soon, a good pilot could milk almost eight hours out of a Mustang.

Most pilots in the Eighth Air Force had pet names for their airplanes. Some chose to have cartoon characters painted on the planes' noses. Others used the name of their hometown or sweetheart to adorn their bird. I named my P-51 *Upupa Epops*, Latin for the hoopee, a European species that always tickled me with its bizarre appearance, weak flight, and untidy nesting habits. I had also cooled off on Anne by then! I flew twelve more missions in this Mustang, mainly bomber escorts and ground support, before I rotated home at the end of my first tour.

I returned for my second tour with the same squadron in early March 1945. I was handed a brand-new P-51D and gave it the same unique name as my first Mustang. Our black-and-yellow-checkered P-51s flew deeper and deeper into Germany as Hitler's once-vast empire shrank before his eyes. He threw his wonder weapons at us, but it was too little and way too late.

JET KILLER

March 31, 1945. "Sly Bird," our call sign for the 353rd Fighter Group, was escorting B-17s and B-24s over central Germany. I was leading the second flight in Jockey Squadron of eight P-51s. About twenty minutes before target time, six Me 262 jet fighters appeared above us. All eyes locked onto them. We were well versed on their tactics and tricks. The 262s wanted us to strip our drop tanks and leave the bombers unprotected as we gave chase. That's when their unseen buddies would swoop down and peck away at the unprotected B-17s and B-24s. The Luftwaffe jets were high-priority targets for us, but were almost impossible to catch; we stayed put with the bombers.

About fifteen minutes later, at twenty-three thousand feet, I looked down to my left and saw two more of the swept-wing 262s pass under us at nine o'clock low. Now with an altitude advantage, I called my flight and told them to strip tanks and bounce them. I rolled the Mustang over and dived nearly straight down under full power.

By the time I approached the jets' altitude (sixteen thousand feet), my P-51 was bucking like a wild horse. I was also on the verge of compressibility (wing failure). I must have been going well over five hundred miles an hour, and yet as I leveled out six hundred yards behind the 262s, I was going no faster or slower than they were.

I cranked in "Me 262" on my computing gun sight, and turned the handle on the throttle to close the ring of diamond pips down to just the wingtips of the enemy jet. The diamond rings wouldn't close down, which meant, essentially, "You're out of range, sucker!"" I was too far behind them.

I aimed at the 262 on my left and held the trigger down. I pumped the stick a little bit and kicked the rudder back and forth, using my time-tested, battle-proven theories of aerial gunnery to spray bullets all over the place! I obtained my usual fine results: one API (armor-piercing incendiary) strike on the left jet engine. And this after firing only 1,545 rounds!

I had burned my guns out in the process but decided to stay with the jets to see where they were going. For the next eight minutes, I chased them with my throttle wide open. A thin stream of vapor started coming out of the left engine of the jet I had hit. The 262s were now almost two miles ahead of me as they approached an aerodrome. That's when the one with two good engines decided to cut loose and split up from the cripple.

The rest of my flight chased the faster 262 as I stayed with the wounded one. The 262 I had hit pulled into a sixty-degree climb as the vapor trail turned into thick, black smoke. He slowed way down, and when I caught up to him, I cut him off. I thought he was going to do an Immelman, but at that moment a great glob of fire came out of his stricken engine. I was two hundred feet behind him when his canopy came off.

I was going nearly straight up behind the 262 when the pilot ejected and shot back over the top of me. The 262 stalled out and dived straight into the ground as I skidded away from it.

I claimed one Me 262 destroyed—by a single .50-caliber bullet.

I wouldn't have had a chance against these jets had it not been for the altitude advantage. Had I reacted a second or two earlier, I'd probably had a chance at both of them since the 262's only advantage over a P-51 was raw speed. The Luftwaffe pilots knew this and avoided turning fights with us at all costs. Their very limited fuel range at regular power made them vulnerable to our fighters. Our tactics were to simply wait for them to run low on gas and pounce on them as they returned to land at their bases. The Me 262 was a great technological achievement. We were lucky it came so late in the war, when fuel was scarce and the sky over Germany was alive with P-51s that could afford to be patient. I proved this theory against a Bf 109 on April 7.

ME 109 SUNDAY DRIVER

By the spring of 1945, the Germans were in pretty desperate shape. On April 7, our group was on a bomber-escort mission over northern Germany when I spotted a lone Me 109 and called it out to the flight. He was a token of German resistance and had no business being up here with the big boys. To put it bluntly, he was inept!

A flight of four other Mustangs beat me to him at and made a firing pass on him. For a little while he held the other Mustangs at bay with a seldom-used tactic, flying straight and level, so that the four P-51s missed him as they overran his slow-moving 109. The guy never flinched and continued on his merry way.

I realized what was happening and pulled off to the right and below him, instead of going around in a big circle to watch him over my shoulder. I chopped my throttle way back, dumped some flaps, and slowed down. If this guy would have had anything on the ball and been a good pilot, he would have had me for lunch! But it was my turn to pick up the check as I pushed my throttle forward. I was confident he didn't know what he was doing. I poured the coal to the Mustang, drove forward straight and level, and opened up on him at close range.

As I closed up, I covered the 109 with hits. I shredded the plane but stopped firing when his canopy came off. The pilot stepped out onto what was left of his wing and floated back to the Fatherland below. That was the last time I saw a German aircraft in the sky during the war.

I saw lots of German airplanes on the ground, and on April 17, 1945, most of them were on fire, compliments of the 353rd Fighter

Group. I destroyed a Bf 109, a Do 217, and half a Ju 88 as our group strafed the heck out of the Luftwaffe field at Bad Aibling. Although the field was packed with a variety of fighters and bombers, it was also well defended by accurate flak gunners. It was in this sort of situation that the Mustang was outclassed by the Thunderbolt. Regardless, I made it through the wall of flak as I zoomed over many burning German airplanes. This was my last flight in *Upupa Epops* and the last time I ever piloted an airplane.

My Mustang and I parted ways in the summer of 1945. I returned to the United States and continued where I left off in college. *Upupa Epops* stayed in Germany with the occupation forces before being sold to the Swedish Air Force in April 1947. In October 1952, she was sold to the Dominican Air Force, where she proudly served until her return to the United States in May 1984.

Eventually, *Upupa Epops* landed in the hands of the Seattle-based Flying Heritage Collection. In 2003 I was invited out to see my old friend. We drove across the field in a World War II jeep and pulled into a wooded glade. And there before my old, watery fighter pilot eyes she stood, just as I had left her almost sixty years before.

There was no sensation to compare with the bliss of this one. I touched her and caressed her aluminum skin. The Mustang was beautiful and looked a heck of a lot cleaner than when I flew it. It was everything a hoopee bird wasn't!

I climbed back into the cockpit and looked at the instruments, realizing I had come back home. I got a good feel for it again. Tempting as it was to crank her up and take her around the patch, I knew better. My final aerial victory had shown what happens to inept pilots. Now over eighty years old, I was content to just sit and reminisce with an old friend.

Captain Tordoff flew a total of eighty-five combat missions in both the P-47 Thunderbolt and P-51 Mustang, and received credit for five aerial victories.

PATIENCE IS A VIRTUE— BUT NOT FOR ALL FIGHTER PILOTS!

Most fighter pilots by nature were team players. Oh, sure, there may have been some who were considered "hot dogs" by their fellow pilots—but that's true in most any profession. But when it came to competing against other Eighth Air Force fighter groups during World War II, it was every group for itself, to see who would be the top dogs over the Luftwaffe. Although there were no special awards or prizes bestowed upon the fighter group with the most aerial victories or ground kills, there was one thing greater than gold in fighter pilots' minds: bragging rights!

Follow along with 1st Lt. Arthur C. Cundy as he shows his aggressive side, never allowing himself to be outflown by another fighter group, while at the controls of his P-51 Mustang, *Alabama Rammer Jammer.*

ENCOUNTER REPORT: JANUARY 14, 1945
353rd Fighter Group, 352nd Fighter Squadron
20 MILES SOUTH WEST OF DRUMMER LAKE
DECK TO 1,500 FEET

Jonah was working his box of bombers homeward from the target when in the course of an orbit I saw several scattered little bogeys south of the bomber course, flying in a confused rat race from 15,000 feet down to the deck. I headed down that way and called Jonah saying Jockey White Three and Four were going down into the mess over there, and dived from about 20,000 to 1,500 feet into the middle of the many P-51s there. Right above a couple of Airdromes there were from three to five separate Fw 190s hotly perused by many 4th FG P-51s who seemed to be spinning their wheels and not doing much in the way of aggressive action. I picked out an Fw 190 which was getting away from 3 P-51s far behind him, went into a steep pass on him overtaking rapidly. With throttle pulled back into my ribs and full flaps down, I overshot this 190. I pulled up sharply, did a big barrel roll around him, and then slid right down on his neck. Being that close to the guy a gun sight was useless equipment. I let him have it right in the fuselage and wing roots, clobbering him in a big way. The 190 did a sudden flick, burst into flame all around the cowling, and several articles flew off—one of which I recognized as the canopy. I don't know if the pilot came out with all the other debris, but the 190 rolled over and went in.

I got pretty bloodthirsty and looked around for more stuff. Right down on the deck was another 190, flaps down, prop wind milling, getting ready to belly in. Hot on his tail were five or more 4th FG P-51s firing from very long range. This irked me to no end so I went down on the 190 and cut out all the other P-51s. I opened fire at 300 yards, spraying the snow in profusion all around the jerk, getting no hits but walking the stream of bullets right along at him by kicking all kinds of rudder. Just as I was about to scoop up a snowdrift with my left wing, I overshot and pulled up into a fury of light flak from the airfield. The 190 got down untouched but the 4th FG boys must have strafed him up a little. The 190s took no evasive action but seemed to depend entirely upon the intense light flak from the airdromes to save their necks.

1 Fw 190 destroyed in the air, 539 rounds fired.

1st Lt. Arthur C. Cundy

Lieutenant Cundy was killed in action (KIA) on March 11, 1945, when his P-51 Mustang developed engine problems and he attempted to ditch in the English Channel. Neither his body nor the P-51 were recovered.

A REFLECTION FROM THE AXIS SIDE

The sky was blackened with the massive bomber stream. Unfortunately for us, they always brought fighter escorts with them. Early on it was the P-38 Lightnings and later the P-51 Mustangs that shepherded the bombers. But our orders were not to tangle with the fighters, and instead go after the bombers. Inevitably, though, we ended up dogfights because there were so many of them and so few of us.

The Mustangs pushed over as they began their attack on us. I was flying wing on my leader and good friend, Lt. Laszlo Molnar, a proven ace with the Hungarian Puma group. Our squadron was in the first row of 109s as Molnar sped ahead to warn the Luftwaffe 109s about what was coming. A pack of Mustangs latched onto him and he never made it. I tried to block the Mustangs' shots by pulling up and into them, firing wildly to scare them off, but they just kept hammering away. By the time I got turned back around, my leader and good friend was already dead. I dove away, passing through ten thousand feet. I thought I was home free until I saw another 109 being chased by two Mustangs. There was no way I could turn my back on a fellow 109 pilot. I yanked my 109 around in a hard turn and watched as the Mustang began to fill my gun sight.

I picked out the lead Mustang and began to fire. My machine gun and cannon rounds tore into him. The P-51 began to smoke, but before I could celebrate my success, my 109 was mauled by a vicious pack of Mustangs who had snuck up behind me. I felt a tremendous jerk as the bullets tore into my 109. I skidded my fighter sideways and looked back—all I saw was Mustangs on my tail. By the time I turned my head forward, my cockpit was engulfed in smoke and flame. The fuel line on my left side had taken a direct hit. My only thought was, *I got to get out of here*!

Lt. Mihaly (Michael) Karatsonyi
Royal Hungarian Air Force
101/3 Fighter Group—the Pumas

P-51D MUSTANG, *OLD CROW*
Capt. Clarence E. "Bud" Anderson, USAAC
357th Fighter Group 363rd Fighter Squadron

As fast as the battle began, it was now over. I dove for the deck, as I was low on fuel, freezing cold beyond belief, and without any means to contact the ground controllers: my antennae was attached to the top of my shot off canopy. My greatest fear was from P-51s. My head jerked from side to side, looking for them to come out of nowhere. Fighting a P-51 was hopeless, as our Fw 190s were just too heavy and I was too damn cold!

—Oscar Boesch,
Feldwebel (Flying Sgt.) Strumstaffel 1 (JG)
3 UDET Luftwaffe

On December 5, 1944, I'm flying for the Eighth Air Force, leading Cement Green Flight on a Berlin escort mission. As we approach the target, we go north and intercept about twenty Fw 190s. We cross over them and drop tanks. When they break around, I pick one out and close the K-14 gun sight around him, firing a burst and getting good hits all over. I'd clobbered a Focke Wulf right off, but he rolls into a dive too quickly for me to tell if he's had it. There are 190s all over the place, so I have to write it off as a probable. Later, my wingman, in his debriefing, will empathetically call this a kill. I go after another. I've been at high altitude a long time. My airplane is cold, and as we dive into warmer air, my canopy suddenly goes snow-white with frost! This will get your attention. If there's any one thing that will frighten the hell out of a pilot in combat, it's suddenly going blind. Cursing the lousy defroster, I throw the plane over and make a quick exit, frantically wiping the glass with my glove. My pawing clears the windscreen in a couple of seconds, and here I am, sitting pretty, right in back of four Focke Wulfs sliding in and out of a layer of haze. I close on the last one in line and open fire up close. My tracers claw at the canopy and blow it away. The stricken 190 lurches and falls, disappearing into the under-cast, the cockpit ablaze. I turn my attention to the number-three man, give him a burst at long range, and see flashes all over the cockpit area. He goes spinning down, too, out of control and trailing smoke. He went through the overcast at one thousand feet, straight down. I pull up, again looking for targets, and a Messerschmitt is suddenly right there in front of me, his landing gear down. There is no sound reason why a pilot would fly around with his landing gear down, but his reasons don't matter to me. Tough luck either way, pal. He makes a climbing turn to the right, and my sights are just full of him. He makes a right turn and pulls inside. There is no way to miss him. I trigger the guns and they quit almost instantly. They had spit out maybe ten rounds. Now the silence is deafening. Damn! I break off the attack and climb with my wingman back to the bombers, to continue my escort—out of ammo!

KILLER PHOTOS: MEMORIES OF A RENEGADE RECCE ACE
Col. Clyde B. East, USAF (Ret.)

LEARNING TO FLY AND FIGHT
In late 1943, with over two hundred hours of RCAF Mustang time and twenty-six rhubarbs (ground-harassment attacks) under my belt, I decided to apply for a spot in the U.S. Army Air Force. In the two years I had flown with the Canadians, I began to talk, walk, dress, and drink like them—all in all, a very pleasant experience. But I knew I wanted to make the military a career, so I jumped ship in hopes of getting posted with an American fighter group. My aim was to join up with the famous 4th Fighter Group led by Don Blakeslee. But as luck would have, it I applied a week too late. I was told that the Ninth Air Force was forming a brand-new reconnaissance group with P-51 Bs and Cs, and they needed experienced Mustang recce pilots.

I joined the 15th Tactical Reconnaissance Squadron (TRS) in early 1944 and was surprised to learn that I would be flying the Spitfire Mk Vb. What surprised me the most was that this British fighter not only allowed me to learn how to fly well, but it also taught me how to fight aggressively in combat. The Spitfire had tremendous maneuverability, and in all respects was a very honest fighter. I learned combat tactics, formations, and how to bounce unsuspecting aerial "victims." With so many P-38s and P-47s flying around England, it was easy pickings for us to practice our combat tactics on them.

We could outmaneuver them quickly, anytime we wanted to. Although they were faster than us, they could never seem to get their guns on our tails. For the next two months, I learned most of the aggressive fighter pilot tactics by bouncing Jugs and Lightnings. I employed those tactics later in the war.

D-Day Surprise

By mid-1944 in England, you had to be a blind man not to see the invasion buildup occurring all over the Continent. Our group finally received both the camera and noncamera version of the P-51B/C. Either model was fine with me because both carried four .50-caliber machine guns. The RAF had demonstrated the value of recce pilots traveling in pairs, so we were quite busy in the spring of 1944, flying all over France in preparation for the landings. Wave after wave of multi-purpose A-20 Havocs and B-26 medium bombers headed across the channel to bomb entrenched German positions. We would take off an hour behind them and come in low to take bomb-damage-assessment (BDA) photos for the intelligence people. The Germans knew we'd be coming but never bothered us—I guess they were overloaded with all the other Eighth and Ninth Air Force fighters and bombers that blackened the skies.

During the afternoon hours of June 6, 1944, I took off with wingman Lt. Bud Schonard and headed out across the channel into France. It would have been darn near impossible to get lost on our way there;

all we had to do was follow the endless string of ships that were in the channel to support the invasion. We entered France just south of the invasion beach Utah, made it past all the parachutes in the air and gliders on the ground, and headed toward the Laval area 125 miles inland from the beach. Everything in the rear seemed pretty quiet, as if the Germans didn't fully realize what was occurring on the coast. That's when we saw four of them.

This was the first time I saw a German fighter up close. All four were Fw 190s, circling to land. They hadn't noticed us—yet. I tacked onto the Tail-end Charlie of the bunch and gave him a quick squirt. He crashed and burned, probably never knowing what hit him. My wingman doubled my score when he hit one right away and then raked another 190 trying to get on my tail. When we looked back, we saw three distinct fires burning near the airfield. We left the area before we could locate the fourth 190. June 1944 turned out to be a good month for me. Although I didn't find any more of the Luftwaffe to tangle with, I did find plenty of targets on the ground to shoot at. July, however, was not so good. I was ordered home for thirty days R&R, which didn't sit too well with me, given all the aerial combat taking place!

MAKING UP FOR LOST TIME

The only good thing that happened while I was home in the States was that I married my sweetheart, Margaret. By the time I returned to combat in the fall of 1944, our group was supporting General Patton's Third Army area. Our fuel was our only limitation on how long and how far we could fly. There were a couple of us in the squadron who figured out that in order to get in on some action, we would have to fly deeper into Germany. I volunteered for a lot of those longer missions.

On one flight, right before the Battle of the Bulge, my wingman and I were up in the Frankfurt area, trolling over the Autobahn, looking for targets. I spotted a lone 109 nearby and quickly shot him down. Two days later, though, I was nearly paid back as I was locked in on the action below in the Ardennes Forest and was nearly taken out by a 109 that snuck in behind me; thank God for my wingman, who took care of the 109 before he took care of me! For the next several months I stayed busy, keeping up with Patton's army and finding an abundance of ground targets to shoot at. It wouldn't be until mid-March 1945 that I started to see German airplanes again—lots of them.

On March 15, the 15th Tactical Reconnaissance Squadron (TRS) was based inside of Germany, at Trier. I had been out on patrol and spotted another lone 109 over our sector near Aschaffenburg. I closed on him and began to fire when I was over three hundred yards away. My rounds found their mark. The 109 began to smoke and flame, and I saw the pilot throw off his canopy and jump.

Things really began to get interesting the farther General Patton raced into Germany. We seemed to encounter more and more of the Luftwaffe on a daily basis. By March 24, I got a couple more 109s, bringing my total victories up to five.

STUKA SURPRISE

During the mid-afternoon of March 27, I was sent out with my wingman, Lt. Henry Lacey, on a routine recce mission. Because of bad weather ahead, we had to abort on the way to the target area. As we made our way back home, we stumbled upon a half dozen Ju 87 Stuka dive bombers tearing apart some American troops below, near Hammelburg. Lieutenant Lacey and I split up the flock of Stukas, carefully selecting slower-moving targets. It didn't take long for the two of us to thin the Stuka flock: I claimed two destroyed and Lacy claimed one as well. It was good teamwork between lead and wingman, but the best was yet to come.

In early April 1945, General Patton crossed Germany's Rhine River, allowing us to leapfrog to our new base at Ober-Olm. On April 4, I was flying a recce with Lt. Lee Larson, a Scandinavian hailing from Upper Michigan. Lee was an excellent wingman who always looked around and called out trouble for me. He had a great set of eyes; I swear he could see the Luftwaffe through clouds! Near Wittenberg we found a Ju

88 wandering around, and we both took turns shooting it down. Later in the mission I bagged an Fw 190, hammering away at him from a hundred yards out. This time the devastation was unsurvivable. The 190 nosed over and slammed into the ground below. It was a good day for Lee and me, but a few days later the action in and the air and on the ground only got hotter.

On April 8, Lieutenant Larson and I were paired up again on a recce near Dresden. It didn't take us long to spot three Stukas that were looking to dive bomb our troops nearby. In a matter of seconds, Lee and I had two of the enemy smoking and spiraling downward. The third Stuka must have thought we left the area because he began to circle his fallen comrades. I held a good lead on him from a long distance and got him burning right away. He joined his burning wingman below. As we continued on our recce, we stumbled into an He 111 medium bomber; Lee and I shot out the engines on either side. With the He 111 burning on the ground, we turned for home—only to find another victim waiting for us.

This one was a twin-engine Fh 104 transport. It was no match for two P-51s, and we made short work of it. By the time the smoke cleared, I had raised my score to twelve victories, but was a little disheartened at the reception I received back at my base. For whatever reason, both Lee and I ruffled a lot of feathers on that mission. Maj. Gen. Otto Weyland, commander of Ninth Air Force Tactical, was enraged with us. He made his point quite clear: "Recce people need to forget about shooting down airplanes and concentrate on being recce pilots. We have fighter outfits that should be doing that—you people need to worry about taking photos and gathering intelligence! Your primary role is to gather info, collect it, and bring it home, not mixing it up with other airplanes and chancing getting shot down! You will not attack any more airplanes unless you are attacked first—that's an order!"

With all due respect to the general, *we* were the ones on the front lines. As recce pilots, we knew our job better than anyone else, and we certainly knew it was our business to shoot down enemy airplanes. I suspect the complaints came from some other fighter groups that were jealous, because as recces we were free roamers with more opportunities to mix it up with the Luftwaffe. I may have been young, but I was far from stupid. I made a vow that if I got into another combat, all I would say was, "He came out of the sun, guns-a-blazing!"

Final "Unofficial" Victory

I increased my score to thirteen on April 13, when I was "attacked" by a 109 and shot him down. On May 8, 1945, I flew my final mission of the war, accompanied by another P-51. We had been out on a recce, watching for German movements near Austria, just hours before Germany's surrender took effect. I looked below and saw this little Fieseler Storch observation plane kicking along. I really didn't pay too much attention to him. I made up my mind that I wasn't even going to mess with it because I certainly didn't need the added headaches that would be caused by General Weyland's wrath. Just as the Storch passed behind us, it seemed like the whole town below erupted in a heavy concentration of flak—I guess the attempt to knock us down was their last salute!

It took a lot for me to get angry, and now I was steaming mad! I whipped my Mustang around, pulled the throttle back, and dropped a notch of flaps. I lined up the Storch and gave him a half-second squirt from my six .50 calibers. He began to burn right away and folded up like a piece of paper. As I circled the wreckage, I knew that if I had tried to claim this victory I might end up on the ground developing photos instead of up here taking them. Just imagine the general's anger if he read a combat encounter report that stated, "While on a recce flight I was attacked by a light observation airplane that dove at me from out of the sun with its guns blazing!"

Shoot, everyone knew that a Storch has a gun that fired rearward!

Clyde East ended the war with thirteen confirmed victories during his 350 hours of combat flying. He continued to fly recce missions during the Korean War and during the Cuban Missile Crisis.

FOTO JOES

From the very moment that the airplane was thrust into the combat role, military commanders on the ground quickly realized they needed hard-copy evidence of future targets, troop buildups, and battle-damage assessment from bombing raids. The bottom line in warfare was whoever possessed the greater knowledge of what the other guy was doing held a distinct advantage—not only where to hit him next, but how hard. Enter the camera-equipped Allied fighters, the Foto Joes.

Probably the best known of all the Allied Foto Joes was the F-4/F-5 P-38 Lightning. With its built-in redundancy of two engines instead of one and a high-altitude capability, the "photo" Lightnings were stripped of their machine guns and cannon and fitted with a variety of vertical and oblique aerial cameras. Depending on the exact model number, the Lightnings carried a combination of cameras, including the Fairchild K-17, which produced a nine-by-nine-inch negative; the twenty-four-inch vertical K-18, producing a nine-by-eighteen-inch negative; and a K-22 oblique camera, with lens options of six-, twelve-, twenty-four-, or forty-inch focal lengths, producing a nine-by-nine-inch negative. Over 1,400 photo Lightnings were produced by Lockheed, and served in all corners of the war-torn globe.

Although the unarmed Lightnings may have carried more cameras over the battlefields than the F-6/P-51 Mustangs, the Mustang held its own advantage: it could quickly switch roles, from cameraman to street fighter. The F-6 retained its six .50-caliber machine guns, along with a K-17 camera mounted on the rear fuselage, alongside two K-24 cameras, one in the lower fuselage and one mounted under the fuselage and pointed straight down. The K-24 weighed in at a mere ten pounds, and was manufactured by the Eastman Kodak Company. It produced a five-by-five-inch negative. The F-6 Photo Mustangs were renamed RF-51D and soldiered on during the Korean War in a photo/recon role.

6

A Christmas Story

Mid-December 1944, European Theater of Operations (ETO). The German army, under the leadership of Field Marshal von Runstedt, began the "season of giving" sooner than expected. The fierce German army smashed through the American front lines protecting Belgium and Luxembourg. Ferocious ground fighting in the Ardennes Forest, keyed by coordinated attacks of German armor and troops, caught the American front lines completely by surprise. Under the cover of harsh winter weather, German troops advanced at will, pushing the horrified and overwhelmed Allied forces rearward. Thus began the Battle of the Bulge.

Allied airpower, the greatest and mightiest aerial armada the world had ever seen, was completely and utterly halted by the nemesis air crews feared most: foul weather. The Germans had received an early Christmas present: some of the worst winter weather in years. Snow, ice, fog, and thick, low clouds blanketed much of England and the Continent, effectively eliminating the possibility of assistance from the air. Allied ground forces and airmen prayed in earnest for the horrendous weather to clear. Then, in the early predawn hours of December 23, 1944, prayers were answered. Announced by a display of twinkling stars, the weather began to break.

Two days later, it was Christmas.

Aviation historians fascinated with World War II fighter combat operations in the ETO have ready answers to the question, "What happened on Christmas Day 1944?" Many will say, "That's when Major

Preddy was shot down and killed by friendly fire over Belgium." Others, who have a keen interest in the 4th Fighter Group, will proclaim, "That's the day we lost Capt. Don Emerson."

But these are only partial answers to a very complex question. The Christmas Day loss of 352nd FG, 328th FS CO, Maj. George E. Preddy, the USAAF's leading Mustang ace, was one of the most tragic, unfortunate occurrences of the entire war. Coupled with the loss of a lesser-known but equally valiant Mustang ace, 4th FG, 336th FS Capt. Donald R. Emerson, you have events that will forever overshadow all other U.S. aerial combat of that day.

But what became of the other pilots flying combat on that cold Christmas morning, especially those operating P-51 Mustangs? And why, on the day that has become synonymous with the sentiment, "Peace and good will toward men," was there so much vicious and ravenous fighting in the air and on the ground?

To begin to answer these important questions, we must rely on the firsthand accounts of the gallant men who flew in the bitterly cold, hostile skies over Europe that Christmas day. These "flying horsemen" put their lives on the line, willing to sacrifice their goals, wishes, and dreams, all in the name of freedom and a Christmas wish for Peace on Earth. Here are their stories.

REQUIEM FOR THE GREATEST MUSTANG ACE
1st Lt. Alden Rigby
352nd Fighter Group, 487th Fighter Squadron

I had arrived at Bodney, England, just after D-Day and was assigned to the 487th Fighter Squadron of the 352nd Fighter Group. I spent my first half dozen or so combat missions flying on Col. John Meyer's wing, protecting the bombers and looking for targets of opportunity. Colonel Meyer didn't have much time for the new guys. He wasn't the fatherly type, and he ruled with an iron hand, but he was the head honcho and you had to have clear discipline in order to survive in a fighter unit. After I flew some more missions with Colonel Meyer, an experienced pilot from the squadron kind of took me under his wing. His name was George Preddy. He called me "Rig" and made me feel like one of the guys. I began to fly as George's wingman on quite a few missions during the late summer of 1944. He was a great guy to fly with because he was smooth with his throttle and at the same time a real tiger. I could pretty much anticipate his maneuvering except when it came to combat. Then, I just tried to stay glued to him and protect his six o'clock. Believe you me, that was easier said than done! When George Preddy latched onto a fleeing 109 or 190, you didn't hear him talking on the radio. Some of the other guys got a little excited and kept a running log of the battle, but George kept silent and focused on the task at hand. When we returned from a mission and debriefed a flight, George was very matter of fact and to the point during the critique. He was a lot easier to deal with than some of the other "big boys." We had good leaders and a great squadron, and I felt fortunate to have flown with them. When George was sent back home in the fall of 1944 for some well-deserved R&R, I was really hoping he would come back to the squadron. When he returned, he was given command of the 328th Fighter Squadron. I had mixed feelings about it. I missed flying his wing, but I knew he was a great leader who deserved the promotion. Both George and I flew on Christmas Day, 1944, but unfortunately, we did not fly together. I was back on Colonel Meyer's wing again, flying in a new P-51D Mustang with a leaking oil seal. It was one of those missions where I had a lot of problems keeping track of Colonel Meyer's P-51. When we landed, the only thing he said to me was, "Get that thing fixed and go out again this afternoon!" I flew two missions that Christmas Day and returned to our base safely. Unfortunately, my friend, George Preddy, never made it back home; he was killed by friendly fire. It was a horrible loss of a great pilot and a great man, on a day set aside for peace.

BLUE CHRISTMAS
Capt. Donald S. Bryan
352nd Fighter Group, 328th Fighter Squadron

December 22, 1944. Our orders were straightforward and unmistakable: move your planes, pilots, and crews to an airfield called Y-29, near Asch, Belgium, as soon as practical, if not sooner!

Our role in this desperate situation called for the "Blue Nose Bastards of Bodney" to provide constant, up-to-the-minute air coverage during the Battle of the Bulge. Our P-51s were to provide aerial protection for Ninth Air Force P-47 fighter/bombers, which were heavily laden with five-hundred–pound bombs and rockets needed for their ground-attack mission in the Ardennes battle zone. Being sent to a forward air base allowed us to be over the battlefield in a matter of minutes, where a single minute could mean the difference between life and death.

On December 23, 1944, dozens of shiny, blue-nosed P-51 Mustangs began to crank up their cold Merlin engines. Major George Preddy led the first section of the 328th to Asch. Flying off the frozen ground at Bodney, England, in his blue-nosed, red-tailed P-51, appropriately named *Cripes A'Mighty*, Preddy climbed effortlessly into the frigid, English sky. As I watched, I had no idea that this was the last time George Preddy would ever touch English soil.

Captain Earl Abbott was to guide the second section. Because we had been briefed that this would be a ferry mission, not a combat one, we wore our dress "pinks and greens." After startup, we began our taxi to launch, but received a sudden shut-down order.

Like the ever-changing English weather and battle lines in the Ardennes, so, too, had our plans been altered. We were informed that this was a combat mission, and here we were, all "dressed up for nothing!" Our mission was quite simple: take care of the menacing German fighters.

With mission details in hand, Captain Abbott led our section up and away from Bodney. My P-51, *Little One III*, was flying perfectly. My crew had polished "their" bird up before they allowed me to take off, enhancing the performance. I awaited our airborne order from Captain Abbott. They never came.

Abbott had developed mechanical problems and aborted from the mission. The rest of us flew on into the unknown without the slightest idea what we were supposed to do. Making matters worse in an already tense situation, we had no call signs. Ninth Air Force radar, perhaps assuming a German ruse, refused to acknowledge our flight or our frantic calls.

Temporarily confused and flustered over our situation, we wondered what we were doing here—until we saw the Fw 190s. If there was one thing we all knew how to do, it was how to fight! I latched onto one of the 190s near Liège, Belgium, and spoiled the pilot's Christmas plans. The other 190 met the same fate at the hands a fellow blue-noser, as we began our search for airbase Y-29.

I landed on a rough field that contained Ninth Air Force P-47s. As I taxied up to the flight line, I wondered if I'd landed in a junkyard. I parked next to a P-47 that by all accounts should have been proclaimed "war weary," or scrapped for parts! Standing next to the Jug were two Ninth Air Force pilots in roughly the same shape.

I hopped out of my bright, shining Mustang, adjusting my Bancroft fighter cap on my head and checking its placement in the reflection of my P-51. I strolled up to the two pilots, my dress uniform still crisp after the three-hour combat flight. My greeting was short and to the point: "Hi, where am I?" The two looked at me in my dress pinks and greens, then stared at my shining Mustang, then at each other. After a long pause, one of them said, "God damned Eighth Air Force!" And then he walked away. Boy, was I mad! That was until I looked around and started comparing my airplane to the others around me. That's when it hit me like a sack of coal! This was frontline fighting. Merry Christmas, idiot!

I flew two missions on Christmas Day. The first lasted nearly two hours, and the second for three hours. We were all dog tired sitting in the officers club (a tent) celebrating Christmas in our own way when a figurative bombshell was dropped on us: Major Preddy was dead. I became very angry, asking the obvious question, "Why him?" We drank a "few" to him as he would have wanted, and then got back to winning the war!

ALL I WANT FOR CHRISTMAS IS TWO FW 190Ds!
1st Lt. Timothy J. Cronin
4th Fighter Group, 334th Fighter Squadron

Our Mustangs looked like pieces of tinsel thrown across the bitterly cold Christmas sky. With our red noses and three .50-caliber machine guns embedded in each wing, we were more than prepared to spoil any German fighter's holiday plans.

As we escorted B-24s on a target-penetration withdrawal just south of Bonn, Germany, the German fighters rose up to greet us. Not happy about the "gifts" left behind by the B-24s, the Fw 190Ds and Bf 109s were spoiling for a fight. The Germans attacked out of the sun. They should have had great success with this tactic, but they ran right into us on the way down.

In a matter of seconds, a savage and lengthy battle erupted. P-51s, Fw 190s, and Bf 109s were everywhere you looked. The large battle soon broke into smaller ones. Streaks of black smoke marked where someone hadn't been lucky.

My Mustang was named *Spurtz*, which is Swedish for "squirt." I formed up with another Mustang and we latched onto an Fw 190D. He was twisting and turning, rolling and reversing, but six .50-caliber machine guns shredded his 190 into pieces.

We tangled with another Fw a few seconds later, chased him from twenty-five-thousand feet down to ten thousand. Our K-14 gun sights worked perfectly. He didn't have a chance. Suddenly we were alone. It was amazing! Only seconds before, the sky had been filled with airplanes. Now, as I looked around, there was nothing; like a slate wiped clean, there was no evidence that a battle had even taken place.

Major Louis "Red Dog" Norley, CO of the 334th FS and ace with 10.33 air victories, stands by his P-51D Mustang at Debden, England, in April 1945.

Lt. Col. Ray Wetmore, top ace of the 359th FG with 21.25 kills, poses by the canopy of his P-51D during March 1945.

Major George "Ratsy" Preddy, CO of the 328th FS and top Mustang ace with 26.833 kills, was killed in action by friendly fire on December 25, 1944.

Captain Don Bryan, 352nd FG ace, was awarded the DSC for downing 5 ME-109s on Nov. 2, 1944.

With 1st Lt. Darwin Berry at the controls, this P-51D WD+A of the 4th FG's 335th FS is ready for takeoff on a bomber escort mission over Germany in July 1944.

First Lieutenant Bob Maloney of the 38th FS checks the starboard wing of his P-51D, "The Squirt," after hitting a telephone pole while strafing a train near Ulm, Germany, on February 17, 1945.

Clyde East captures a fellow photo-recon P-51 Mustang high over a target area. The photo recon pilots were considered the "eyes of the Army Air Force," as they provided valuable intelligence for mission planners. Photo courtesy Clyde East.

Buzz job! A RCAF Mk II Mustang scatters a bunch of Allied troops like chickens as it makes a high-speed, low pass over them. Many of these "hotshot" Mustang pilots considered themselves good sticks and eagerly showed off their talents whenever possible.

Colonel Don Blakeslee, CO of the 4th FG "Debden Eagles," stands by his P-51D's prop in August 1944.

Fourth FG aces Captain Duane Beeson and Captain Don Gentile pose by the latter's P-51B at Debden, England, in March 1944.

Captain Ernest "Red" Fieblekorn of the 77th FS poses with his ground crew at King's Cliffe air field after downing four German fighters near Magdeburg, Germany, on September 28, 1944.

First Lieutenant Bob Eckfeldt in P-51B "Bald Eagle" leads a flight of four 376th FS P-51s over Germany in 1944.

Colonel Thomas J. J. Christian, CO of the 361st FG, flying his famous P-51D "Lou IV" shortly before he was killed in action on August 12, 1944.

Lieutenant Araval "Robbie" Robertson relaxes on the wing of his P-51B Mustang as he chats with his ground crew before another mission. Lieutenant Robertson named all his P-51's "Passion Wagon" and on later models had a life-size naked woman painted on the nose! Lieutenant Robertson ended the war with six victories, logged while flying with the 357th Fighter Group. Photo courtesy Araval Robinson.

First Lieutenant Chuck Gumm of the 355th FS poses with his ground crew after scoring the first kill for a Merlin-powered Mustang on December 16, 1943.

Captain Herb Kolb of the 350th FS destroyed 14.5 German aircraft while strafing in P-51D "Baby Duck."

Lieutenant Colonel Bill Bailey, CO of the 352nd FS, poses with his ground crew by their P-51D "Double Trouble Two" in March 1945. Colonel Bailey named his Mustang "Double Trouble" because he was seeing two women at the same time! Photo courtesy Bill Bailey.

A ghostly voice crackled in my headset. "Hey, red nose up there. Come on down and help me!" Whoever this "phantom" pilot was, he sure sounded as if he was in a "heap of trouble," poor SOB. A second frantic call for help prompted me to jerk my stick left. I rolled over and saw a P-51 and Fw 190D at treetop level below me, locked into a tight-turning battle, each pilot trying to gain the advantage over the other.

I saw that that the distressed Mustang was a fellow red nose. As I raced down, the 190D was searching for the opportune moment to unload a combination of 20mm cannon and machine gun fire. Luck, however, was the one thing this German pilot lacked. He never saw me coming and took hits all over his plane. He took evasive action and broke away, but my newfound wingman also scored hits on him on the way down. After a half hour of almost continual aerial combat, the Germans headed for home to lick their wounds.

As my wingman and I flew back to base, I noticed the humorous caricature of a warthog, and the words *Ridge Runner* painted on his plane's nose. Numerous German crosses were also visible. My wingman was Pierce McKennon, CO of the 335th squadron. I felt pretty good at that moment, like I really accomplished something—including saving a CO's butt!

When we landed in England, McKennon and I exchanged Christmas greetings. I had also given him a gift: half credit for the 190. After all, isn't Christmas about sharing?

The 4th Fighter Group, 334th Squadron, also received a unique Christmas present that day: recognition as the first squadron in the ETO to destroy three hundred enemy aircraft.

WINTER WONDERLAND
Col. William B. Bailey
353th Fighter Group, 352th Fighter Squadron

Our group, along with many others in the Eighth Air Force Command, had an exasperating time during the Battle of the Bulge. Our base, and most of East Anglia, was socked in by freezing fog. Ice particles floated in the air, sticking to trees, wires, and our grounded aircraft. On a "good" day, ground visibility varied between zero to maybe a hundred yards.

December 23, 1944. Weather began to clear and four P51s from the 352 FS took off to escort two F-5 photo Lightnings on a recon flight over the Ardennes. Because the Germans didn't want any uninvited guests at their Bulge party, two Me 262 jets were sent up to engage the party crashers. During the aerial encounter, 352 FS pilots claimed both 262s as damaged.

On December 24, our group launched sixty-eight Mustangs with black-and-yellow-checkered noses on several different missions. I led one of them, a B-17 escort to the Biblis (Germany) Aerodrome. This was a very active German fighter base with involvement in the Bulge operations. We ran into twenty Bf 109s. They took serious offense at our ruining their Christmas season, and we argued about it for a while. The net result was that seven 109s failed to return home.

We were frustrated at not being much help to the GIs below. I took my *Double Trouble* P-51 down to look for trouble, but couldn't find any because of the damned foul weather over the battlefield!

On Christmas Day, I again was tasked to lead an escort mission, accompanying B-17s to Ahrweiler marshaling yards used in support of German Bulge operations. Fifty-two P-51s flew as "guardian angels" as the bombs fell on target. Six Bf 109s were encountered, but amazingly, only one was shot down!

With the bombers safely on their way home, we went "downstairs" to look for targets of opportunity, but there weren't any. We were completely frustrated by cloud, snow, poor visibility, and the simple fact that we didn't even know where our forces were. Hopeless and helpless, we flew back home.

We had a Christmas dinner of sorts; however, no one had any "Christmas spirit." How could we? While our fellow soldiers in the 101st Airborne were trapped at a place called Bastogne, we sat on the sidelines, wondering and praying. Christmas 1944? Bah, humbug!

ENCOUNTER REPORT: CHRISTMAS COMMOTION
55th Fighter Group, 343rd Fighter Squadron

Tudor Squadron was west of Koblenz, flying close escort for two boxes of bombers headed northeast. I was flying Red Leader. Just south of the target I observed a box of B-24s going south, or 180 degrees relative to us. We were at twenty-six thousand feet. About a minute after the bombers passed below us, bogeys were called in about five hundred to one thousand feet below us; they were following the bombers. I identified them as three 190s flying about a mile ahead of fifteen 109s. The 109s were flying flights of four, line abreast, with a trio of 109s bringing up the rear. I called Tudor Leader and received permission to engage the enemy aircraft. We broke left and attacked astern. The German fighters started a climbing turn to the left in one gaggle, flights in trail (a follow-on formation with staggered spacing). They made climbing and diving turns until broken up by my flight. I picked on Tail-end Charlie and fired a short burst, but saw no strikes. I pulled onto the next man. He took evasive action, but I got some good no-deflection and deflection shots at 300 to 250 yards. I observed many strikes on the wings and fuselage. He rolled over and started down-spinning—he never pulled out—and I saw him crash and burn fiercely in the center of a small town. I pulled back up to fifteen thousand to twenty thousand feet and tacked onto the rear of four 109s. The rear enemy aircraft broke off, and after some violent evasive action he headed straight down; I stuck on his tail. I fired several bursts at no deflection, and at very small deflection, from about two hundred to three hundred yards. Many strikes were observed on the wings and fuselage. Coolant began pouring out and small pieces of the plane began to break off. I pulled out of the dive at eight thousand feet, going 480 mph. I saw the 109 auger straight in and explode near a small woods.

I claimed two 109s destroyed during this engagement.

Lt. Robert Welch

ENCOUNTER REPORT: DECK THE HALLS WITH 190s AND 109s!
355th Fighter Group, 354th Fighter Squadron

I was Falcon White Leader, giving cover to the left side of the box of bombers. I had gone down from twenty thousand feet to five thousand to investigate some bogeys, which turned out to be friendly. I was coming back up to about ten thousand feet when I heard over the R/T that a gaggle of enemy aircraft was hitting another box of bombers. Realizing that I couldn't intercept the gaggle, I got below the bombers at thirteen thousand feet and waited for the enemy aircraft to split-ess from their attack. I saw two of the enemy at eleven o'clock, level to me, going down and east. I cut them off and got on their tails. As I closed, the Fw 190 cut throttle and fishtailed violently. I cut throttle, too, and slid up sideways above him and then dropped back on his tail. I shot from six hundred yards and five degrees deflection, scoring many hits all over him. He began a slow, diving turn to the right and I shot again, from four hundred yards and five degrees deflection, scoring many more hits. He started smoking and fell off in a left-diving turn that continued all the way to the ground, where he broke into many pieces.

I claimed this Fw 190 destroyed.

Right after that, an Me 109 tried to get on my wingman's tail, so we started a left-climbing Lufbery to keep the wingman's tail clear. Pretty soon, the enemy aircraft broke and hit the deck in a northeast direction; he led me on a wild chase and really clung close to the deck. My first burst from seven hundred yards with zero degrees of deflection (K-14 sight) scored many hits all over him. I chased the Me 109 some more and shot at him again, over a small town, from about five hundred yards and zero-degree deflection, scoring more hits on the fuselage. When the Me 109 made the mistake of turning to the right, I closed in to about 350 yards, ten degrees deflection, and clobbered him good all over. Pieces of the wreckage flew all around me. The 109 exploded just before he hit the ground, his tail flipping up and a good-sized patch of woods set ablaze.

I claimed this Me 109 destroyed.

Lt. Charles Hauver

IT'S BETTER TO GIVE THAN TO RECEIVE
Capt. Donald J. Strait
356th Fighter Group, 361st Fighter Squadron

Far from home and loved ones, we still maintained a Christmas spirit at the Martlesham Heath airfield. The ready room was decorated with traditional Christmas trees, holly wreaths, and candelabra made from empty .50-caliber shells; they gave a convincing glow in the ready room window. With only one day before Christmas 1944, we looked forward to our planned party the following day. There would be no rank at this party. Everyone from enlisted man to officer in our squadron would spend Christmas Day together, forgetting about the war.

Unfortunately, the war did not forget about us. I was awakened in the early-morning hours of December 25 and handed a teletype from Wing that read as follows:

Weather conditions for mission of December 25 may necessitate groups taking off as soon as possible to avoid fog bound and probably landing on continent. Group leader will launch aircraft an hour early if necessary. In the event that groups are forced to land on continent, they may be forced to remain there two or three days. Groups landing on continent will become freelance units. Maintenance facilities will be limited or nonexistent. Pilots will endeavor to carry spare plugs, wrenches and small parts for minor maintenance. IT'S A TOUGH DEAL GANG, BUT THIS IS WAR AND WAR IS HELL—MERRY CHRISTMAS . . .

So much for our party plans! We received our field order shortly thereafter: a fighter sweep over Bonn, Germany. It looked as if a really miserable Christmas was in the making.

Because the fog was expected to roll in rather quickly, our P-51s took off at 8:40 a.m. We arrived over the Bonn area at 10:45 a.m. and immediately began receiving reports of bandits in the Bonn-Cologne-Koblenz area. Investigating these reports was a waste of time. We found P-47s but no Germans. I was glad I had given orders to the men back at Martlesham to go on ahead with the party, because at this rate it was anyone's guess when we'd be coming home!

At last, after droning around for over four hours, we were told to investigate bandits twenty-five miles southwest of Bonn. My wing-man and I headed to the area and picked up another Mustang on the way. When the three of us arrived at the area at 19,500 feet, I spotted ten Bf 109s orbiting left below us, at 18,000 feet. As we dove to attack, three against ten, the odds were still stacked in our favor. With superior planes and pilots, along with the altitude advantage, I thought we had it made. But, then, too, I was young.

Four 109s broke into a right-diving turn as I picked out the Tail-end Charlie. I fired a few short bursts and saw hits on the tail, fuselage, and right wing. The 109 straightened out and went into a shallow dive. I closed to a very short distance and got more strikes on the tail and left wing. Smoke and coolant came pouring out of the 109, and my wind-screen was suddenly covered with radiator fluid. I was too damn close!

I had "given" and now I was "receiving!" I couldn't see a thing straight ahead. I cut the throttle and skidded the airplane from side to side, to slow down to just above stalling speed. The 109's propeller had stopped and he practically hung in mid-air. I had to "pop" my stick for-ward to avoid ramming him. I passed the smoking 109 just as it began a shallow glide for a field below. I was looking back at the 109 when I saw that my wingman was about to be bounced. I called for him to break, shoved in full throttle, and turned back to help him. My wingman took some hits as I maneuvered into position. The 109 broke and dived for the deck just as I was about to open fire. I couldn't follow him because the coolant still covered my windscreen. My wingman and I climbed back up and headed for home. Of course, thanks to the weather, just "where" home might be was anyone's guess.

Our squadron must have been "good little boys," because we received word that Martlesham was open. It seemed that Santa visited while we were gone and left four kegs of ice-cold beer under the Christmas tree. What more could a fighter pilot want?

When the weather cleared on December 24, 1944, the largest airstrike yet was launched, with almost 1,900 bombers escorted by 800 fighters. The Allies continued to pound the Germans on Christmas Day, with more than 400 bombers escorted by 400 fighters, all in support of the GIs fighting to break the German advance in the Ardennes. Momentum had now been placed into Allied hands, turning the tables on the Germans and forcing them to retreat. Allied airpower reigned supreme once again on a day set aside for peace.

7

New Year's Resolution

They had planned the surprise, large-scale offensive mission to the last and smallest detail. Even before the sun rose on New Year's Day 1945, there was much excitement and anticipation among the pilots and ground crews, as the engines of their fighters and bombers were slowly brought to life in the bitterly cold morning. The pilots, with predetermined targets, shook hands and wished each other "good hunting" as they set off to annihilate their enemy. Most of them believed that if they were successful with their strafing and bombing attacks, this would be the turning point of the long, drawn-out war. And to the victor came air superiority.

As more than eight hundred planes thundered westward, low on the deck to avoid detection, the men hoped that their counterparts on the ground would be fast asleep in their bunks, hung-over from a long night of celebrating New Year's Eve. But none of the Luftwaffe fighter pilots sent to destroy the 352nd Fighter Group airfield at Y-29 in Belgium could ever imagine what was waiting for them. Still, the Germans were confident. Operation Bodenplatte had begun.

HAWK EYE
1st Lt. Dean M. Huston
352nd Fighter Group, 487th Fighter Squadron

Less than twelve hours earlier, our commander, Lt. Col. J. C. Meyer, had told us to get to bed early and ease off on the drinking, because we were going to fly an early-morning mission on New Year's Day. Colonel Meyer had a sixth sense about the Germans and figured that the Luftwaffe had us pilots pegged to be sitting up all night, drinking and celebrating. But instead of being drunker than skunks, all eleven of us were alert, and led by a sly and sober fox who outfoxed the Germans!

I was in the second flight of four Mustangs on that mission, right behind the lead four Mustangs in White flight as we taxied into position. My call sign was "Yellow Four," and I was flying my assigned P-51D, which I called *Hawk-Eye-Owen*, named after my home state of Iowa. I watched as Colonel Meyer led White flight down the runway, and was amazed to see him shoot at incoming German fighters with his wheels still hanging down and his Mustang barely off the deck. Our Yellow flight soon chased Colonel Meyer's flight off the ground, and hell, it was a donnybrook as we were thrown into a dogfight with the Germans even before we got *our* wheels up.

It was impossible to stay with my element leader, Lt. Sanford Moats, because there were airplanes going every which way. I was barely in the air, less than a thousand feet off the ground, when I spotted a Bf 109 below me. I turned my Mustang hard and went tearing after him, and as I closed on the 109, I let him have it. My .50-caliber rounds tore into him. I was concentrating on the 109 I had shot down and didn't realize where I was or how close I was to the airfield when I suddenly got clobbered. My own antiaircraft batteries mistook me for a 109 and peppered my Mustang with Allied rounds I knew I was hit because I could sure feel the tremendous thud that the ground gunners gave my fuselage.

I didn't know how bad I was hit, though, and was surprised that the Mustang was still flying. That thought didn't last long: I glanced at my instrument panel and the oil pressure gauge, which was racing to the zero mark. No oil in a Mustang is a bad, bad thing, and I knew I had to set it down in a hurry. I was too low to bail out and there was no way I could belly it in because I was over such a heavily wooded area. My only hope was to try and make the runway, which was less than two miles away. Of course, my fear was that the few precious drops of oil I had left wouldn't be enough to get me there. I lowered my flaps and dropped my landing gear as the runway raced up toward me. I was just beginning to flare the Mustang and was only a few feet in the air when my engine froze up and the propeller stopped dead.

I'd been in the air less than ten minutes. In that time, I shot down a German airplane, got shot down by my own people, landed with a dead engine, and found one single .50-caliber bullet that had penetrated not more than three feet in front of where I was sitting. I was the luckiest guy in the world that day and have never stopped thinking about how close I came to buying the farm. I survived, but only by the skin of my teeth.

LOW-LEVEL DUEL
1st Lt. Sanford K. Moats
352nd Fighter Group, 487th Fighter Squadron

New Year's Day, 1945. I was flying Yellow Three in Major Halton's flight. As I took off, I spotted more than fifteen Fw 190s at a hundred feet coming from my three o'clock on their way to make a pass at the airstrip to the north of our field. At the same time, I noticed about fifteen Me 109s flying top cover at 3,500 feet, just below a thin cloud cover. When two 190s broke into my wingman, Lieutenant Huston, and myself, we entered a Lufberry to the left, under intense, light, friendly flak. I closed on the first 190 and looked back to see another one chasing on the tail of my wingman. I called to him to break just as the 190 started shooting his way. I fired a short burst at three hundred yards and thirty degrees deflection at the 190 ahead of me, observing strikes in the cockpit area and left wing root. He burst into flame, and I saw him crash and explode as I continued my turn. The pilot did not get out.

Approximately fifty enemy aircraft were in the vicinity, and the entire area was full of friendly flak. For my second target, I chose a 190 that was strafing. He broke left and started to climb. I fired a short burst at two hundred yards and twenty degree deflection, observing a concentration of strikes on both wing roots. His wings folded up over the canopy and the 190 dropped straight in. The pilot did not get out. I continued my left turn and rolled out slightly above and behind another 190, which broke left. I fired a short burst and observed strikes on the left side of the fuselage, canopy, and left wing root. He burst into flames, the canopy came off, and he crashed. The pilot did not get out.

I then broke into several 109s and 190s that were coming at me from the rear, heading toward Germany. They split up and I picked a 190, who broke into me. We made several head-on passes and I pulled up and came down on his tail, firing a two-second burst, observing strikes from wingtip to wingtip. He leveled off and hit the deck. I closed and fired several bursts from dead astern, observing strikes all over the tail and wing sections. As we passed over Maastricht, the Netherlands, I fired a short burst that exploded his belly tank, and my aircraft was hit by 40mm ground fire. At this time, lack of ammunition had left me with only one gun firing. As we crossed the front lines, the 190 continued to take violent evasive action on the deck. I fired a burst at him every time I had a chance and observed many strikes in the tail section. I climbed and made an attack from above and to the right. I fired and observed a few strikes around the right wing root. The enemy aircraft broke left, pulled up slightly, and dived into the ground. The pilot did not get out.

As I returned to our airdrome area, I was fired at by our ground batteries. A lone Me 109 came across the field and I made a pass at him. He broke up into me, and I tried my remaining few rounds of ammo at ninety degrees deflection and one hundred yards' range. He hit the deck and I and I chased him into Germany before returning to our airdrome to give it top cover. Another Me 109 came by, and I followed him through a couple of barrel rolls but could not shoot as I was out of ammo. He went straight up, chopped throttle, tried to get on my tail, couldn't, stalled out, recovered, and split-essed at 1,500 feet, barely pulling out above the trees. Another P-51 came into the area at this time and shot the 109 down, four miles northeast of the field. I later found out that the pilot of the P-51 was Captain Stewart. All the enemy aircraft were very aggressive, and that last 109 was absolutely hot! We were all handicapped by heavy fuel fuselage tanks and ground fire, so I feel very proud of our twelve-ship squadron that destroyed twenty-three bandits on takeoff, without loss.

HIT THE DECK!
Capt. Henry M. Stewart, II
352nd Fighter Group, 487th Fighter Squadron

I was flying Yellow Two on Major Halton's wing. Before I gave my ship the throttle on takeoff, Colonel Meyer already had a 190 spinning down in flames. I followed Major Halton on takeoff, as he started after two 190s. They were on the deck heading east toward the front lines. I stayed at two thousand feet, giving Halton cover. He got a few strikes on one 190. The ground fire got so intense I had to break.

When I broke, I ran into a 109. I made a few turns with him but couldn't get into firing position. I followed another 109 up through the clouds at about 150 miles per hour but could not close and almost spun out. I came back down and went around with another 109. I fired but did not observe any strikes. I came back toward the field and tagged onto a 109 heading my way. I closed on him and pulled the trigger—nothing happened! My knee had shut my switches off. I got them back on and fired. I got a few strikes, and we started turning over a slag pile. Captain Whisner came along and clobbered him.

I came back toward the field again and saw two P-51s chasing a 109. The 109 broke; I cut my throttle and slid in behind him at one hundred yards and a hundred feet off the deck. I fired and observed many strikes as the 109 went straight in and exploded. After I pulled up to two thousand feet and started a turn, I saw another 109 on the deck, heading east. I closed my throttle again and dived behind him. At 150 yards I opened up and got many strikes on the wing root and fuselage. The 109 went straight into the ground. All this time the ground fire was very intense, .50-caliber and 20mm.

I started back toward the field and picked up another 109 on the deck with a P-51 chasing him. The Mustang broke and I dived down on the 109 at one hundred feet. He turned and I followed him east. I closed to 150 yards and fired, getting strikes all along the right side of the plane. Coolant came out and the 109 crashed into the ground.

I claimed three 109s destroyed during this engagement.

DIAMOND IN THE ROUGH
1st Lt. Walter "Jack" G. Diamond
352nd Fighter Group, 487th Fighter Squadron

I joined the 352nd Fighter group in September 1944 and began flying combat missions in October. As a new guy, I was posted to fly wing on a more senior, experienced pilot who could show me the ropes and, we hoped, keep me alive. I was teamed with one of the leading aces of the group, Capt. William Whisner. I flew a lot of missions as Bill's wingman; my sole purpose was to protect his tail, as he did most of the shooting. New Year's Day 1945 was no different. Captain Whisner was leading Red flight as Red One. I was assigned Red Two, part of the last

ENCOUNTER REPORT: TEAMWORK
352nd Fighter Group, 487th Fighter Squadron

I was leading Red flight on January 1, 1945. As we taxied out to the strip I saw some air activity east of the field. The squadron consisted of three four-ship flights that took off singly. As I started down the strip, Colonel Meyer called the controller and inquired about bandits in the vicinity. As I pulled my wheels up, the controller said that there were bandits east of the field. We didn't take time to form up, but set course, wide open, straight for the bandits. There were a few P-47s mixing it up with the bandits as I arrived. I ran into about thirty Fw 190s at 1,500 feet, watched by many Bf 109s above them. I picked out a 190 and pressed the trigger. Nothing happened. I reached down and turned on my gun switch and gave him a couple of good bursts. As I soff sharply to the right, and up. A 190 was about fifty yards behind me, firing away.

As I was turning with him, he was attacked by another P-51 and broke off his attack on me. I then saw that I had several 20mm holes in each wing, and another hit in my oil tank. My left aileron control was also out. I was losing oil, but my pressure and temperature were steady. Because I was over friendly territory I could see no reason for landing immediately, so I turned toward a big dogfight, where I shortly had another 190 in my sights. After hitting him several times, he attempted to bail out, but I gave him a burst as he raised up, and he went in with his plane, which exploded and burned. Several 109s were still in the vicinity, so I engaged one of them.

We fought for five or ten minutes, and I finally managed to get behind him. I hit him good and the pilot bailed out a two hundred feet. I clobbered the 109 again as the pilot jumped. The plane tumbled into the ground. I saw fifteen or twenty fires from crashed planes. Bandits were reported strafing the field, so I headed for the strip. I saw a 109 strafe the strip's northeast end. I started after him, and he turned into me. We made two head-on passes, and on the second I hit him in the nose and wings. He crashed and burned east of the strip. I chased several more bandits but they evaded me in the clouds. I had oil on my windshield and canopy so I came back to the strip and landed.

> All of the enemy aircraft were very aggressive, and extremely good pilots. I am very happy that we were able to shoot down twenty-three with a loss of none. We were outnumbered five to one with full fuselage tanks. The P-47s on this field did a fine job, and helped us considerably. The cooperation among our fighters was extremely good, and we did the job as a team.
>
> Capt. William T. Whisner

group of four Mustangs scheduled to fly the mission that day from our base at Y-29 in Asch. I was assigned my P-51D, which I'd named *Twyla Sue*, after my wife. Captain Whisner was in his Mustang, *Moonbeam McSwine* (named for a pretty girl in the *Li'l Abner* comic strip).

Twelve of us were lined up in a string on the runway, waiting to launch. We were supposed to take off, join up with one another bunch, and be vectored by radar control to go look for German aircraft in the area. Unfortunately for us, the Germans didn't play by our rules; instead, they came streaking in toward our airfield. Our line of Mustangs began to roll. After takeoff, we went tearing after the incoming Germans. I was supposed to latch onto Captain Whisner's wing, but by the time I got my wheels up, he was gone. I called him several times over the R/T, but I guess he was too busy flying and fighting the Germans. By the time I got airborne, I didn't see anybody, friend or foe. I was all alone.

I started searching for other Mustangs, *any* Mustang to join up with, but I couldn't find any. What I found instead was a German fighter. As I flew closer, I saw that it was an Fw 190. I tucked in behind him, staying in his blind spot. I was inexperienced at shooting, probably because Captain Whisner had always done most of it before. I wasted a lot of ammunition on the 190. I stayed with him, though, and got some good hits as he tried to evade my guns. But it was hopeless for him. My rounds found their mark, and he crashed into a field below.

A BLOODY GOOD KITE! MEMORIES OF THE P-51 MUSTANG IN THE RAF FROM THE PILOTS WHO FLEW THEM

Sqn. Ldr. Charles E. Edmondson, RAF
249 Squadron

It was in Italy in 1945, during my third and last tour of the war, that I was privileged to fly both the Spitfire Mk IX and the P-51 Mustang, as a squadron leader with 249 Squadron.

The Mustang was a superb dive bomber and strafer that destroyed countless locomotives, rolling stock, vehicles, ammo dumps, marshaling yards, and shipping during our combat over northern Italy and into Germany. Our dive-bombing technique, whether in the Mustang or Spitfire, was pretty standard and very quick. You simply push the nose over, you dive, you bomb, you pull out, and then you black out. When you awoke a few seconds later, you got the hell out of there!

I had a wonderful time flying the Mustang, but if I would have had to tangle with the Luftwaffe in straight-out air-to-air combat, a la the Battle of Britain, I would have much rather preferred to be at the controls of the Spitfire Mk IX. To me, the Spitfire Mk IX was much more maneuverable. She was extremely sensitive on the controls. When I flew her, I felt like I was a part of the Spitfire. My inputs were like an extension of my body. As a fighter, the Mk IX proved much too good against the 109s and had a slight edge over the Fw 190s. The one drawback, however, was the Spitfire's limited range, due to its light fuel load. The Mustang had much longer legs, and because of all that extra fuel it could travel much farther. Being of British foundation, I am obliged to the RAF types such as the Hurricane and Spitfire, but in all honesty and gratitude to the Yanks, the P-51 Mustang was also a "bloody good kite" in my mind!

A FIGHT IN THE CLOUDS
FLT. LT. WARREN B. PEGLAR, RCAF

On August 3, 1944, east of Mannheim, Germany, I was flying Yellow two in Falcon Squadron. We were approximately three o'clock to a box of southbound B-17s, and a half mile to their side when about ten Me 109s came in from seven o'clock on a bounce. Several people called in "break," so I broke to the left, dropping my tanks on the turn. When I turned into about six 109s, several fired at me head on. I turned about 360 degrees left, and when I felt it was safe enough to straighten out, I could not find Yellow one. There were many aircraft turning, and I identified one about a thousand feet below me as an Me 109. He was turning left. I dived on his tail and gave a short burst, one-ring deflection, about twenty degrees, at three hundred yards. I observed no strikes and the 109 went into a very tight diving turn to the left. During this turn, from twenty thousand feet to about ten thousand feet, I fired three more short bursts, all at about three hundred yards, one ring deflection. Again, I observed no strikes. The Me 109 pilot was very good in his evasive action—until he straightened out and attempted to pull up into the sun. Then I came to dead trail two hundred yards behind and placed the gun-sight dot just above his nose. I fired a two-second burst and saw strikes from the nose to the tail. Pieces flew off the aircraft and there was a white flash at the engine cowling.

The 109 seemed to stagger, then pulled up steeply and rolled onto its back, streaming white and black smoke. When it fell into a spin, I followed it down to about four thousand feet. It was completely out of control and streaming smoke. The area was full of enemy aircraft, so I decided to leave it. In view of the number of strikes observed, the damaged caused to the aircraft, and the resulting spin unrecovered at very low altitude, I claimed this Me 109 as destroyed. On the climb back up, I saw a fire burning in a field; the blaze may have been a crashed 109.

Upon leaving the first combat, I joined with four other P-51s and climbed to twenty-two thousand feet. We positioned ourselves at three o'clock, half a mile out, from a box of B-17s that was about five miles beyond the target (Strasbourg), heading out at about twenty thousand feet. We had been with them about two minutes. I was flying on the extreme left of the "bastard" flight, nearest the B-17s, when I noticed an untidy gaggle of German fighters coming in on the rear B-17s at six o'clock. I called out and rolled over and down to catch them breaking away. The whole flight came on down. I saw one enemy plane go in on the B-17s and break up to the right. I couldn't identify his type, so I broke over to the right and followed him up, "balls out." We pulled up to about twenty-one thousand feet and I came up dead behind him. Before I came in range, I saw him fire his guns straight ahead into thin air. The puffs from his guns showed that he was using 20mm self-destroying ammo, for maximum blast effect. I came to approximately two hundred yards dead behind and identified him as an Fw 190, rusty brown camouflage with a long-range tank attachment on his belly. I fired a two-second burst from about 150 yards but observed no strikes. Because I was overhauling him, I pulled up and over to the right. He still didn't see me, and I was able to get in another burst at 150 yards, five degrees off, and saw strikes all around the wing root and engine. The 190 rolled over and started a vertical dive. I followed him, at times hanging in my straps. He headed for a large cumulus cloud at about thirteen thousand feet, and made it before I could catch him and fire another burst. I followed him through the cloud and came out slightly to his right, two hundred yards behind. I fired another burst, five degrees off, and saw strikes all around the cockpit and engine. He then went into another cumulus cloud at eight thousand feet. I followed, and while still in the cloud I saw his canopy float past me. Breaking into the clear again at about five thousand feet, I saw the 190 dive vertically below me, straight into the deck, where he exploded in a large orange fireball. I pointed my nose at the fire and fired a few rounds to take a picture of the wreck.

I claimed this Fw 190 destroyed.

PATIENCE IS A VIRTUE
FLT. LT. LIONEL SIDNEY FROST, RAF

On September 11, 1944, I was flying a Mustang Mk III as Bentley Green No. 3. The group was escorting B-24s, about thirty miles south of Kassel, Germany. At approximately 1150, I saw five aircraft attack the box of bombers on our right; one of them broke away toward us and came across the flight from about three o'clock and five hundred feet below. As it came out from under us on the other side, I saw that it was a 109. I called it in to Green leader and said I was turning left to get it. I dropped tanks and turned sharp left. I opened fire from about six hundred yards at about thirty degrees, closing to four hundred yards and twenty degrees. I saw several strikes on the wings. The 109 started to take evasive action; it split-essed and went down in wide aileron turns. I decided that because of the difficulty of hitting the 109 in these aileron turns, I'd follow it down and wait until it straightened up on the deck. When it did, I started my attack from three thousand feet above; meanwhile two other P-51s came in from eight o'clock. The leader of these two started firing. I throttled back and trailed behind the two, and eventually saw the leader shoot the 109 down. As the two P-51s began a left-hand turn, I noticed an aircraft coming in at about six o'clock relative to them. They must have seen it a moment later, and went into a sharp left turn. I came in on the aircraft from about seven o'clock and saw it was a 109. I broke away from the P-51s and started a gentle, steep-climbing turn. I started firing from about six hundred yards and twenty degrees, closing in to approximately three hundred yards and ten degrees. I saw strikes on the left wing and canopy. The left wing came off in company with other bits of the enemy aircraft, and the plane spun into the ground. The pilot did not get out. I went down and took some photographs of the small fire on the ground.

As I could not see my wingman, I joined the two P-51s and we went down on an unidentified airdrome. I saw an enemy aircraft parked on the north side and shot at it. I think it was a Do 217, a twin-engine medium/ heavy bomber. It seemed to be under repair; part of the fuselage covering was missing. I saw several strikes on it and a little smoke. As I turned away from the field, the sky became dotted with quite-accurate 20mm flak. I went down on one of the adjoining fields, where I fired on four other aircraft that I discovered were dummies. I then came home.

I claimed one Me 109 damaged, one Me 109 destroyed, and one Do 217 damaged.

NASTY LITTLE BUGGER!
FLT. LT. G. M. DAVIS, RAF
129 SQUADRON

March 23, 1945. I was piloting a Mustang Mk III, flying Fixture Three to the wing leader on a ramrod escort of 118 Lancasters to Bremen, Germany, at 1512 hours. Immediately after leaving the target area, as we turned right with the bombers, an Me 262 jet dived beneath us from starboard, then climbed from under the bombers' port side to turn toward the bombers' rear port side. He attacked a straggling bomber that was wide of the main stream on the rear port side. When I dived across the rear of the bombers, the enemy aircraft turned port and dived away to the southeast, much too fast to catch.

About twenty-five miles southwest of Bremen, as I was catching up the rear of the bombers, I saw another single Me 262 at the rear of the bomber stream, flying approximately westerly. I was flying west, and overtook the bombers a little south of them. With my number four following, I winged over and opened up at plus-twenty-five pounds of boost, at 3,000 rpm. The enemy aircraft was approximately one thousand to two thousand feet below me, five miles in front and flying very fast. I dived to engage.

As I closed the range, the 262 turned port in a wide radius. I flew across the diameter of that circle, turning with the jet to attempt a forty-five-degree head-on attack. Range was about four hundred yards when I fired a half-second burst. I pulled quickly to port and fired a second burst from dead astern; range was about seven hundred to eight hundred yards. After the first burst, the enemy aircraft's starboard motor belched white smoke, and a large piece of metal flew past my port wingtip. The 262 then began to lose height, dropping to the southeast with white smoke still pouring from the starboard motor. The range increased as the jet gathered speed, so I disengaged to rejoin my formation.

I claimed one Me 262 damaged.

As I flew over him I saw another 190 above me, so I went tearing after him. I got behind and became so transfixed that I got too close to him, way too close.

I could feel the buffeting of his prop wash on my Mustang as it threw me all over the sky. I was so close to his tail, for a second I thought about chopping it off with my propeller. I came to my senses and realized that I probably would have gone down, too. I was bouncing up and down and being thrown from side to side as I began to fire at him. I saw some strikes on his fuselage, but none of them were in any critical areas. I was really letting this guy have it when four of my six guns went dry and I thought, *Man, I better keep a little bit of ammunition in case someone attacks me.* I broke off my attack on the crippled 190 and flew around looking for other Germans. I was also waiting for things to settle back down at the airbase so I could come in and land. When I finally got back to Y-29, I found out what happened to Captain Whisner. Then it became obvious why he didn't have time to answer my radio calls.

GEORGIE BOY: INSPIRATION TO A FIGHTER PILOT
Capt. Kenneth G. Helfrecht, USAAC (Ret.)
4th Fighter Group, 334th Fighter Squadron

The "greatest generation" as a whole did not need a reason to fight. Provoked by a ferocious Axis that threatened to enslave the world, hundreds and thousands of young American men answered the call to arms. Preserving freedom, peace, and security for future generations were the primary reasons men signed up for service. They saw service as a patriotic duty to their country, and some saw glamour in war. Each man had his own source of inspiration. For one young flier, it took the unselfish act of a six-year-old boy to help him realize what he was fighting for.

JUST A KID IN COMBAT

Shortly before turning eighteen, I enlisted in the Army Air Corps. I came down with an illness that sidelined me for a couple of months. My original class went on ahead without me, and when I recovered I was placed with a group of experienced servicemen. They were a grizzled bunch and filled me with a lot of baloney. Training with these rogues forced me to grow up fast, but because of them, I learned things that saved my butt!

After earning my wings, I was selected to go into fighters. Here I was, not even old enough to drink and barely old enough to shave, yet trained to fly in combat. The closest thing to any real horsepower I touched before the war was when I tinkered on used cars. And now, blindfolded with minimal flight time under my belt, they put me into a real hot rod called the P-40 Warhawk.

I really enjoyed checking out in the P-40. I found landings to be real simple, even with the narrow gear. Not only did they give me horsepower, but they gave me guns, too! Learning to shoot from a fixed sight, with a trigger on the stick and a tit on top for dropping bombs, became second nature to me. Unfortunately, I had to unlearn these skills when I arrived in Europe.

The pipeline of replacement pilots was starting to build when I was deemed combat ready. I arrived in Goxhill, England, on September 12, 1944, and was introduced to the P-51B Mustang. I had never been close to one before. With all the glass and bars over the canopy, it looked like it was dressed with French windows; I just hoped I could see out of it. After completing my checkout and orientation of the English coast, I was placed into a fighter group.

I found my name and assignment posted under "Fourth Fighter Group." I rejoiced at the prospect of being a member of the oldest fighter group in the ETO. There was heritage to the 4th, a group that had been formed around the original three Eagle Squadrons established in September 1940, with American volunteers flying Hurricanes and Spitfires against the Germans. That knowledge caused me to break out in a beaming, proud smile. Men next to me, though, had other thoughts about the 4th. "They kill them left and right there!" "You'll never survive." These were the words of "encouragement" from the nonbelievers gathered around me. It didn't bother me a bit. Besides, I was young and dumb.

JOINING THE FAMED FOURTH

I arrived at Debden Airfield as a member of the 334th Fighter Squadron. I began flying combat operations in late October 1944, but there was something different about my P-51B. It was still hard to see out of (the bubbletop canopy didn't appear until the P-51D) and colder than an icebox inside. But up front on the dash was a brand spankin' new gyro gun sight. Because all my gunnery training had been with fixed gun sights, this was completely new to me; I'd never seen one in my short life as a fighter pilot. I guess during wartime, some things are less formal. I was shown my airplane, and given words of encouragement by my crew: "Good luck, and don't get your ass shot off!" And off I went into the unknown world of aerial combat.

November 6, 1944. I had survived my first mission and was now cruising along at twenty thousand feet on mission number two. I couldn't take my eyes off the fancy gun sight in front of me, trying to figure out how it worked. Shortly after 11:00 a.m., an Fw 190 came roaring at our group from behind and shot down 2nd Lt. John Childs, who was up ahead in his Mustang. I was flying wing on my flight leader Bob Dickmeyer as we poured on the coals to catch this fleeing bandit. R/T chatter became unintelligible as people began talking and screaming when they shouldn't have. Dickmeyer was trying his darndest to get hits on the fleeing 190 when he unloaded his guns and began to draw tracers. Although the R/T chatter was garbled at times, I could clearly hear Dickmeyer yell at me, "Come up here and get that German SOB!"

The adrenaline was really flowing inside of me. The chase of the 190 started up high and now we were below the clouds as I pulled behind the 190 for my shot. Sensing that I was near, the German pilot jinked his stick back and climbed to reach the scud layer above. From instinct bred by training, I pulled the trigger. No recoil, no tracers, no hits, no nothing. I pulled the trigger again as we both entered the cloudbank. Were my guns even loaded? Jammed, maybe?

Although I was in a cloud, the cloudiness in my brain cleared, and I figured out what I was doing wrong. The 4th Fighter Group was a descendant of the Eagle Squadrons, which had flown Spitfires before America's entry into the war. The group didn't use a trigger to fire the guns. They used the button on top of the stick. The trigger on *my* stick was for dropping bombs. As I exited the clouds, I was ready to shoot anything that moved, including the bogey in front of me! There he was, dead ahead. My finger resting on the tit, I lined up the enemy airplane using my "super duper gyro sight" and fired at him. The "enemy" turned out to be a fellow 4th Fighter Group red-nosed P-51! Untrained on the gyro sight, I missed him, of course—thank God!

IN THE SHADOW OF LEGENDS

Here I was, part of the elite group that produced so many noteworthy pilots, such as Don Blakeslee, Dominic "Don" Gentile, Howard "Deacon" Hively, Pierce "Mac" McKennon, Louis "Red Dog" Norley, James Goodson, and countless others. And yet, the way I had flown in combat that day made me worry that the rest of the fellows would think the Germans sent me here—especially after shooting at one of our own! I was told it was natural and that with a few more missions under my belt, the "jitters" would go away.

And for the most part they did, except on one mission when things went spiraling out of control. Most of our missions were bomber escort. Loaded up with heavy fuel and ammo, the Mustang could be a real handful until you burned some of the internal gas off. I learned this the hard way during my fighter-pilot schooling, when I formed up with my wingman on another bomber escort to Germany. I was fully loaded with paper drop tanks under each wing. (These tanks were made of glued and laminated paper painted with silver dope. They were designed for short-term use only.) During climb-out, my engine was acting up and began to cut in and out. I tried to stay with the other Mustangs beside me, but my engine wouldn't respond to my inputs. Suddenly, the engine just up and quit. For a second, I felt as if the P-51 just hung there in the sky, as I helplessly watched my fellow Mustangs accelerate away.

I got the Mustang restarted and applied boost to catch up. Problem was, I put way too much boost in, so my closure rate on the bomber formation was faster than I wanted it to be. I began turning the Mustang from side to side in attempts to slow down. With all that extra weight from the drop tanks and my internal fuel, the Mustang became hard to control. I tried S-turns back and forth and went into a high-speed stall. I was behind the curve again and didn't expect it. As I lost my lift, I immediately started to spin with my drop tank still attached.

The golden rule was that if you were in a spin with drop tanks, you were to release them before you over-stressed the airframe. As the ground rushed up at me and I fought to control my spinning mount, I forgot all about the rule. There was no way I was going to abort this mission. If I punched the tanks off now, I would have to head back home. I was not a quitter! I somehow managed to break out of the spin with my tanks still attached and rejoined the formation. If I was going to survive this war, I needed to focus on the tasks at hand, or I needed one helluva good luck charm!

LETTERS FROM HOME

My good luck came in the form of a letter from home. I came from a family of patriotic beliefs and moral obligations. My brother Don was stationed in the Philippines, and my sister Rose was a WAC in Michigan. My mother, who was widowed when I was still a young boy, was left home alone while her children fought abroad. Enclosed in the letter from my mother was a picture of a little six-year-old neighbor boy named Georgie Armstrong. Georgie used to tag along with me and the older boys in the neighborhood back in Madison, Wisconsin. Although he was quite a bit younger than we were, we tolerated his presence. My mother informed me that since last spring, when I, along with most of the guys from the block were in the service, Georgie would help her around the house, doing the dishes, raking leaves, sweeping the front porch, and other odd jobs. After months of constant help from Georgie, my mother finally asked him why he was helping her. Georgie answered very matter-of-factly: "Somebody's got to take care of you now that the big boys are gone." That practically tore my heart out. I also became focused on the task at hand.

Due to combat losses and men finishing their tours, the turnover rate was quite rapid in the 4th FG. Because of this, I was issued my own P-51D. With its prominent red nose and its bubbletop canopy, it was an impressive piece of machinery. It just seemed to be missing something. Some of the other fellows had bathing beauties and pin-up girls painted on their aircraft, while others had cartoon characters, the names of wives or girlfriends, and an assortment of other artwork. Not wanting to be left out, I begged our "ace painter," Staff Sgt. Don Allen, the best in the ETO, to paint the nose of my plane. I showed Don the picture of Georgie and indicated where I wanted his name and face to be.

After it was all said and done, I stood back and marveled at the sight before me. The face looked just like the photo and was accompanied by his name in large red letters. *Georgie* and I were destined to do great things. There was a lot of snickering and laughter from some of the other pilots. "A little boy's face on a fighter plane!" "Don't you have a girl back home?" The laughter stopped after they read my letter. Then I was given pats on the back.

The only person who had some concerns over the nose art was my crew chief, Sgt. Robert Lewis. Not because he didn't like it. Actually, he thought it brought good luck to "his" plane. His concern was that because the face was painted too close to the exhaust stacks, keeping Georgie's face clean was no easy job! He even made me write a letter to Georgie's mom, explaining that "Sgt. Lewis has more trouble keeping Georgie's face clean than you do!" I also wrote a letter to Georgie, and in it I said, "Your gift to my mother is just another reminder of all the good deeds you have done for me. You can't realize how much strength your little heart gives my mother and I."

DOWN AND DIRTY

As the war progressed into 1945, Georgie's face became a lot dirtier. Less and less German opposition was encountered on our bomber-escort missions. With or ammo bays stuffed full of rounds, we were released from our escort duties to go down and sweep the area for targets of opportunity. *Georgie* and I shot up trucks, trains, canal barges, and anything else that moved. We also shot up German airfields that were heavily defended by antiaircraft fire. When I saw flak, it scared the daylights out of me, especially when it came spiraling up at us. I really liked flying the P-51D, but I never liked using it as a strafer. With those coolant lines running two-thirds of the way down the fuselage, pumping the Mustang's life-blood of glycol, even the smallest damage could put you out of the game. There were airfields I overflew that had the German wonder weapon, the Me 262 jet, parked wingtip to wingtip, but the flak was so intense we never got close to them. It didn't matter, though, because by that time the Germans were out of fuel and pilots.

April 16, 1945. One airfield I really became "close" with was Gablingen Aerodrome in Germany. Our group that day was led by Maj. Lewis "Red Dog" Norley on a penetration target withdraw support/strafing mission. After we were released from the bombers, Major Norley led us down on the deck looking for targets. Gablingen airfield was packed full of German aircraft. As we made our first pass, flak was light and quickly suppressed. A racetrack pattern was set up as Mustang after Mustang made gun runs across the aerodrome, shooting and annihilating everything in sight.

My "trusty old" gun sight worked flawlessly as I made repeated runs over the airfield. Burning German aircraft were everywhere as my .50-caliber rounds found their mark. My gun sight was filled with targets that day as I helped to beat up Gablingen. My tally for the day: five German aircraft set on fire, and five destroyed: two Me 410 heavy fighters, two Fw 190s, and one He 177 long-range bomber. All told for that day, our flight of sixteen Mustangs destroyed forty-four German aircraft without a single loss to our squadron.

Back at Debden, I received the DFC from Major Norley for my actions that day. *Georgie* and I really made a good team and helped shorten the war in our own little way.

Later, with the war finally over in Europe and abroad, I eventually rotated home. After all, the real-life Georgie was entitled to some well-deserved R&R now that the big boys were back home!

8

Double-Nickel Killers:
Late-War Aerial Combat
with the 55th Fighter Group

The early strategy of the Eighth Air Force fighter groups was to stay with the bombers, escort them, save them; do not leave them and go chasing after the Luftwaffe. That all changed when Gen. Jimmy Doolittle took over in the summer of 1942. The motto quickly changed to, "Get rid of the Luftwaffe!" We were turned loose to go down on the deck and strafe our way back home. We went looking for everything—boats, trucks, troops, flak towers, and airfields—especially airfields.

—Maj. General Edward B. Giller,
USAF (Ret.)

MISTELS IN THE MIST
2nd Lt. Richard G. Gibbs
343rd Fighter Squadron, 55th Fighter Group

On February 3, 1945, I was on my third combat mission of the war as Tudor White 2 on a bomber-escort mission near Boizenburg, Germany. I was flying a P-51 Mustang on the right wing of Group Commander Lt. Col. Elwyn Righetti, with two other Mustangs flying on his left wing. Our squadron was released from the bombers and we began to let down through the overcast, breaking out at around two thousand feet to look for targets of opportunity. Our section was about to go after some locomotives when Lieutenant Colonel Righetti called out a gaggle of three Fw 190/Ju 88 bomber combos. We called them *mistels* or *pick-a-backs*: an Fw 190 perched atop a pilotless, explosives-packed Ju 88 flying bomb. Viewed from a distance, they looked to me like swollen bombers.

The three of them were in a sloppy V formation, flying through the mist at about six hundred feet. Righetti and I broke away and went after them while the other two Mustangs went after the trains. Righetti went after the middle combo of the three *mistels* and told me to take the third one. I put the proper wingspan in my ranging K-14 gun sight and cranked the handle around to get the correct pipper size around the Ju 88. I began to fire and observed hits dancing around the left engine and wing root as the Ju 88 began to burn. As soon as my rounds impacted the Ju 88, the Fw 190 turned himself loose and pulled up fairly steeply. He went into a left-hand turn, and for a moment I thought he stalled out.

I was really moving and was closing on him pretty fast as I began to fire. I observed hits along the right rear and right wing root area, and observed parts of the cowling and canopy fly off. I quit shooting at about a hundred yards away and went zipping by him as I ducked under his right wing, missing him by twenty-five feet. My concern was that because this guy was now behind me, he'd start shooting at me at any second. I reefed the Mustang's nose up hard and pulled into the overcast. I rolled over and came back down inverted, making a hard turn, and saw the two ground fires from the Ju 88 and 190. It was only after I saw my combat film later that I saw that the German 190 pilot was in the process of bailing out when I went zooming past him. Lieutenant Colonel Righetti claimed two Ju 88s and an Fw 190 destroyed. Unbeknownst to us at the time, another wave of *Mistels* was behind us; these were attacked by the other Tudor White Mustang element.

ENCOUNTER REPORT: TUDOR WHITE 3
55th Fighter Group, 343rd Fighter Squadron

At about 1230 we dropped to the deck to strafe. As I pulled up from the first pass on a locomotive, I sighted a formation of three pick-a-backs, Fw 190s strapped on top of Ju 88s, in string formation at about 400 feet. I turned into the second combo with my wingman, Lieutenant Moore, behind me. I fired a short burst from ninety degrees at about 350 yards, and observed a few strikes on the 190. As I fired on this one, the 190 on the third unit was released. The prop was windmilling, and on release the 190 seemed to nose up for a minute and then, apparently out of control, the nose went down and the plane headed for the ground. I claim this Fw 190 as destroyed.

As soon as the 190 was released, the 88 turned sharply left. I followed, firing a short burst, but observed no strikes. I fell outside the turn and lost sight of the 88 momentarily. My wingman behind me was in position and shot the 88 down. When I looked back, I saw it crash into the ground. I pulled up and saw the first unit I had fired at; now it was about three hundred yards in front of me. There were flames coming out of the 190, so I went after it again. I fired another large burst and saw more flames. When I made a second pass, the right engine of the 88 burst into flame, and I saw them both crash into the ground.

From this entire encounter I claimed two Fw 190s and one Ju 88.

1st Lt. Bernard H. Howes

APRIL SHOWERS JET JOB
Maj. Edward B. Giller
343rd Fighter Squadron, 55th Fighter Group

I was leading Tudor White flight on April 9, 1945. We had just been turned loose from the bombers somewhere south of Munich at about twenty thousand feet. I looked down and observed an Me 262 jet being chased by a pack of Mustangs. By this time in the war, we had been well versed on the 262's tactics of drawing the Mustangs away from the bombers. We dropped our tanks to give chase, but the 262s zoomed away from us. After we turned for home, low on fuel, the German jet fighters had free reign with the bombers. The great weakness of the 262, though, was its lack of fuel capacity. I knew this guy below me would run out of gas. Sooner or later, they had to go in and land, and that was the only time to catch them (unless, of course, they were asleep at the wheel while airborne).

Our bombers were being escorted by another group, so I thought, *Okay, let's just see what we can do with this guy.*

My wingman and I dropped our tanks, pushed our noses over, and pushed our throttles forward in our Mustangs. The 262 was now at just five thousand feet, so we certainly had the height advantage. As I went zooming down, I looked at my airspeed indicator and saw that I was doing five hundred miles per hour as I overtook the pursuing P-51s. I kept going and finally caught up to the 262 as he was on final to land at the Munich-Riem airfield, with his flaps down and wheels hanging out. He was still in the air when I gave him a pretty strong burst from my six .50-caliber machine guns. I stayed on the deck as I zipped past him while every German on the ground with a gun began to fire at me. I was moving way too fast and the gunners couldn't compensate; their rounds stayed ten feet behind me. I looked back and saw the 262 belly-in hard at about two hundred miles per hour. I stayed low and fast for the next thirty miles and then rejoined my flight.

After the war, I had the opportunity to speak with Luftwaffe Gen. Adolf Galland while he was a POW on our airbase. Through an interpreter at dinner one night, I told Galland about my jet encounter. He said he remembered the incident. Galland told me the 262 pilot survived the crash, but he disappeared the very next day, hightailing into Switzerland. Galland never saw him again. I kind of felt sorry for the 262 guys, who were always outnumbered and always low on fuel. They knew that when it was time to land they'd have six to eight Mustangs circling overhead, ready to pounce on them.

Having dispensed with the "blow job" (pilot jargon for the Me 262, which was fast but not particularly maneuverable), on Munich-Riem and discovering heavy flak, White and Red flights of our squadron flew to three thousand feet, south of Munich, to wait for the bombers to knock out some of the airfield's antiaircraft. While I was down low, I observed a tug towing an He 111 south along the autobahn. He was heading for the woods, which lined both sides of the road. I saw seventy-five to a hundred enemy aircraft of all types dispersed in the woods off both shoulders of the highway. After receiving permission to shoot up a few, I called my Red flight, led by Captain Welch, to set up a pattern from west to east. Then I started down.

The first aircraft was at the south end of the woods. I got some good strikes but could start no fire. I made a total of four passes from east to west, hitting a different target each time. My second pass was made on an Me 262; I observed a good concentration of hits, and the jet burst into flame. My next pass was against an Me 410 heavy fighter; I got strikes all over it, igniting another fire. On the last pass, I hit another 410 and observed many strikes and a large plume of heavy, black smoke. As I pulled up from my last pass, I saw an He 111, with the tug still attached, sitting on the north side of the woods. I put a short burst into it and got a nice explosion in the right wing root and engine nacelle area. Since I was now out of ammunition, I called the flight together and we started out for home.

FLAK TRAP ON THE AUTOBAHN
Maj. Edward B. Giller
343rd Fighter Squadron, 55th Fighter Group

There was an old saying written on the wall behind our squadron bar. It read, "Just One More Pass." Those were the last words of many fighter pilots who thought they could fool the German gunners just one more time. Our fighter losses were much higher during strafing attacks than they were during air-to-air combat. While strafing, you often flew through a gauntlet of German guns. And on this mission it seemed as if every gunner in Germany was waiting for us. My trouble was that I thought I could get away with it. Boy, was I wrong!

During those deep-penetration missions, we would tour Germany at two hundred feet, cruising along at 250 miles per hour and pulling our noses up only to avoid trees and church steeples. And we always hoped to catch a German airplane flying along. On April 16, 1945, we were south of Munich on a big fighter sweep, looking for airfields to shoot up. The Germans must have got wise to our tactics because they began to disperse their aircraft elsewhere. I separated my section into elements, to tool along above the autobahn. We hit pay dirt when we spotted all kinds of airplanes parked along the roadway. I called the others and told them to set up a racetrack pattern as I dived down and started shooting up airplanes. I hit an He 111 and an Fw 109 on my first pass, and returned for a second, where I bagged a Ju 52 transport. Feeling lucky, I made a third pass and sprayed a Ju 88—and that's when my luck ran out.

I was only at four hundred feet when a 20mm shell came through my canopy and detonated above my left shoulder. I felt as though I'd been hit by a sledgehammer! I pushed the throttle forward and jerked my stick back as I zoomed out of there. Metal fragments that were embedded everywhere made a fan shape throughout my cockpit, and some were embedded in my arm and shoulder, too. Most of the shell's energy came from a single piece that slammed into the top of my parachute harness. Thankfully, there was a lot of nylon to absorb the brunt of it; by the time it entered my shoulder, skidded across the front of my rib cage, and exited, most of its energy was gone. With my cockpit covered in blood, I called my wingman and said, "We're going home." I pointed the Mustang's nose west. I eventually made it back to England, but my combat flying was kaput—the war ended before I could get back into it.

Although strafing was a dangerous and often deadly thing, it was the bomber boys I felt most sorry for. It was said that you could plop a complete stranger down in a bar at any Allied base and within thirty seconds or less they could tell the difference between a fighter base and a bomber base. One bunch of pilots was lively and full of excitement, smiling and slapping each other on the back, saying, "We're going to fly again tomorrow!" The other group was less than enthusiastic and said, "Good God, I have to go back through that flak again tomorrow?" At least we fighter pilots could shoot back, zig and zag, and zoom away. The bomber guys just had to grin and bear it.

On April 16, 1945, over 750 German aircraft were destroyed on the ground by Eighth Air Force Fighter Groups, in the largest single-day total of the war.

ONE PASS TOO MANY
1st Lt. Richard G. Gibbs
343rd Fighter Squadron, 55th Fighter Group

I was flying Tudor White 3 above Germany on April 17, 1945. We had left the bomber stream in the target area as planned, and set out to hunt targets of opportunity. We headed about 160 degrees for ten to fifteen minutes when we sighted Kamenz airfield. We were at nine thousand feet and headed to the south side of the field. When we saw two enemy aircraft take off, Tudor Leader, Captain Welch, and his wingman, Lieutenant Erby, started down after them. I started down, too, but when I found only the two enemy aircraft and lots of flak, I pulled back up to about 4,500 feet and started to circle around the south and east sides of the field. My wingman had gotten separated from me in the flak that was thrown up from the field. As I got to the north side, I saw more enemy aircraft taking off into the west. I picked one, an Fw 190, and waited until he had gotten beyond the perimeter of flak. I dived on him from three thousand feet, closed to about five hundred yards, and started firing. The 190 burst into flames and did a half-roll into the trees. We were only at about one hundred to two hundred feet high when he rolled in.

My Mustang had become covered in oil so I pulled up to check it. I decided it was oil from the 190 I had just shot down, so I started a few climbing turns, looking around for something else to latch onto. I spotted another 190 above me at about four thousand feet. He was coming in about ninety degrees to me, so I pulled my nose up and fired a burst into him from two hundred yards away. As I passed underneath him and turned hard to the starboard, I saw quite a few strikes on his wing. The 190 also did ninety-degree starboard turn and was now in a slight diving turn. I came in behind him and fired again, getting strikes along the fuselage. The 190 continued in his dive. I passed him up at about a thousand feet. He had holes in his tail and his canopy had been jettisoned. The pilot was still inside, looking at me. When he hit the ground, the 190 caught fire immediately.

With my windscreen covered in oil and the rest of my squadron God knows where, I turned for home all alone. At fifteen thousand feet, I kept an eye out for enemy fighters that might be lurking above me. I glanced out the side of the clear-top canopy and noticed these "funny-looking" things below me. I looked up and was stunned to see a box of B-17s above me, with their bomb bay doors open. I was flying right over their target—Dresden! (This was two months after a well-known Allied bombing raid had flattened the city.) As I pushed the nose over, I realized that the funny-looking things I saw were bombs bursting below. After all I had been through I certainly didn't want to become a victim of friendly fire!

That mission was bittersweet for me that day. Although I bagged a pair of Fw 190s, our 55th Fighter Group lost Lieutenant Colonel Righetti to ground fire. He ended the war with 27 strafing victories and 7½ aerial victories. Although he had successfully bellied his Mustang in on that last flight, his final words over the radio to us were, "I broke my nose, but I'm okay. I got nine today. Tell my family I'm okay. It's been swell working with you, gang. See you shortly."

That was the last time any of us heard from him. He had made multiple passes on that airfield and paid the ultimate price for it, making "just one more pass" before his death.

ENCOUNTER REPORT: ST. VALENTINE'S DAY MASSACRE
479th Fighter Group, 434th Fighter Squadron

On February 14, 1945, I was twenty miles southwest of Berlin, leading Newcross Green Section on an Eighth Air Force escort mission to Magdeburg. Our squadron was between the two German cities, at an altitude of twenty-seven thousand feet. As we began a 360-degree turn to the left, two bogeys were called in at six o'clock low, passing from north to south. I glanced back and saw not two but four. As we made our turn, we lost altitude, going down to approximately 24,500 feet. In the meantime, the four bogeys made a 360-degree left turn also, but they gained altitude during their turn. As we rolled out of our turn and headed approximately ninety degrees again, the bogeys were an estimated three thousand feet above and behind our formation. I thought they were enemy, but could not identify them positively. Then more bogeys were called in at twelve o'clock high, passing twenty degrees across our front. We turned right and started climbing after them. They split into three small groups, one continuing southwest, one heading west, and the other north. The squadron split up to go after them. I was closest to the six bogeys going southwest; they flew in one flight of four, as in a regular P-51 formation, with two Tail-end-Charlies lagging behind. As we climbed, I indentified them as Me 109s.

Before I drew into range of the last two, the larger flight of four, well out in front, split-essed. The two bandits I was after continued at the same level. After reaching thirty thousand feet, I closed to extreme range. One of the bandits dropped his belly tank and headed down, and Lieutenant Golden, Newcross Blue Four, took out after him. Fearing that the other Me 109 would do the same, I ranged him carefully with the K-14 gun sight, and allowed a small amount of deflection above to take care of the sizeable distance between us, which was about 450 yards. I squeezed off a very short burst and got hits, much to my surprise! The Jerry started a slow break to the right. Taking my time, I ranged him again, still allowing a little for distance. Another short burst produced more hits. Having closed in by this time to a better range, I put the pipper right on his cockpit, let up a trifle on the graticules (an optical array of lines used in aiming and measuring), and gave him another burst. He took more strikes, this time right where my pipper rested. Black smoke poured out of his engine cowling and he snapped into a spin, recovered drunkenly, and then went into a violent, uncontrolled spin from which he didn't recover. I started to follow, but realized that he had had it, and broke off.

I straightened up and saw two more Me 109s ahead at thirty-three thousand feet, and below them, sixteen to eighteen Fw 190s. The whole bunch headed southwest, toward the B-17s attacking Chemnitz. I climbed again, figuring to bounce the top cover first, and then the main force. The same thing happened as before: one Jerry split-essed with Lieutenant Crieghton hot after him, and the other went straight. I fired at this one from slightly below and dead astern from about 450 yards. As soon as I could see strikes, the 109 started right, and then with that beautiful K-14 sight, I got hits all over the right side of his fuselage. I obtained a few more hits as he rolled over into the inside of his turn, yawing and skidding. He must have been out of control, because this yawing and skidding continued—sometimes he was upside down, sometimes falling sideways, other moments straight down.

This last bounce left me in perfect position to hit the Fw 190s. I dropped my nose and started down after them as they made gentle left and right turns in no apparent formation. I tacked into the tail-end man on the right side of the gaggle and closed into good range before firing. Just as I entered his contrail, I saw the flash of many strikes, and continued to fire for the next few seconds, placing my pipper midway between his wingtips, which were all I could see. The 190 fell gently to the right, and I realized too late that my closing speed was excessive. Even though I momentarily chopped throttle, I glided on past him and looked over and saw the German pilot slumped forward in the cockpit. His canopy was shattered, and I went by slowly enough to note jagged holes in the left side of the fuselage.

I blandly glided right on through the edge of the Jerry gaggle and out in front. As I had not the slightest intention to lead these Jerrys anywhere, I did a half-roll, followed by a wing low vertical three-sixty, or loop. By the time I got three-fourths around in this maneuver, I could look through the top of my canopy and see the 190s disappear into the thick cirrus formation that was between them and the bombers. I could still see my 190, because he remained in that steep diving turn to the right, while the rest of his buddies turned left into the clouds. He disappeared momentarily, and then reappeared underneath the cloud going straight down. I watched him until he disappeared into a cumulus formation at six thousand feet. He never could have recovered from a dive like that at that altitude, even if he'd been intact.

I circled and looked for the rest of the Fw 190s, but they had eluded me, and I was all alone. I flew over to the last box of B-17s that hit Dresden, and escorted a straggler halfway home.

I claimed two Me 109s and one Fw 190 destroyed while expending 407 rounds of ammunition.

Maj. Robin Olds

9

Yak Attack

The Yakovlev Yak-9 was the most prolific Soviet fighter of World War II. Designed for short-range work, it appeared in 1942 and quickly flew rings around the Luftwaffe. Although not terrifically fast (the earlier Yak-3 was faster), the Yak-9 was extraordinarily maneuverable, with a pinched turning diameter that allowed it to get inside enemy aircraft in sustained turns. Armed with a 20mm nose cannon and .50-caliber machine guns in the wings, the plane could also carry bombs underwing and was well suited to ground-attack work.

And in a happenstance that had a bearing on the nature of the accounts that follow, the Yak had an unfortunate resemblance to the German Bf 109 and Fw 190, the Mustang's most familiar adversaries.

The bomber escort mission of March 18, 1945, should have been like any other for the pilots in the 359th Fighter Group. Unfortunately, it wasn't because of confusion, bad weather, and aircraft misidentification by the Allied fighters. For all involved, this was by far the most bizarre mission they had ever flown. The disastrous events that unfolded that day not only came quickly, but also set the stage between two powerhouse nations, becoming a prelude to the Cold War. The group, which consisted of three squadrons that day, was the 368th (code name "Jigger"), the 369th ("Tinplate"), and the 370th (call sign "Redcross"). All were flying P-51 Mustangs deep into Germany while shepherding a group of B-17s.

The fighter group was split into two flights that day, "A" group and "B" group. "A" group was led by Capt. Ralph Cox and was made up solely of members of the 369th Fighter Squadron. "B" group, led by Capt. Ray Wetmore, contained a joint force of P-51s from the other two squadrons. By the time the aerial armada reached the Berlin area, "A" group split off from the rest and went looking for targets of opportunity, while on a freelance mission. Of the four flights of Mustangs that day in "A" group, it was the pilots from Red and Yellow flight that found more than they had bargained for. Utilizing official declassified reports and in-depth interviews with six of the 359th FG pilots involved, we can observe green-nosed P-51 Mustangs tangle with Russian Yak-9s, as the two allies slug it out high over Nazi Germany.

REPORT ON RUSSIAN AIRCRAFT ENCOUNTERS
ON 18 MARCH
TO LIEUTENANT GENERAL SPAATZ
CONFIDENTIAL

After leaving the Berlin area, 12 P-51s of 359th "A" fighter group proceeded down the Oder River toward Konigsberg (south of Schwedt) where they saw two unidentified aircraft (later ID as Yak 9s). P-51s pursued Yaks to Zackerick [Poland] airfield, north of Kustrin, where they found 4 Fw 190s strafing. The Fws had already started a fire at west end of the field. One Fw 190, seen by two pilots to bear white cross, was shot down in the combat. 15–20 Russian aircraft were seen milling around when one crashed in the middle of the airfield. At once the ground gunners shot up intense and accurate light flak to 5,000 feet. Captain Cox withdrew the P-51s and instructed "B" group leader not to bring in his force. The Russian aircraft were ID as Yak 9s and LaGG 3 [fighters], painted blue exactly like identified Germans. In the melee over Zackerick airfield, P-51 pilots waved hand and American flags at Russians. One of them waved back, but another Yak fired without effect.

In the dogfight a P-51 closed on a bogie, identified it as a Yak 9 and did not fire. His wing man was coming closer, identified it as an Me 109G and attacked the enemy aircraft, getting some strikes before breaking off. Recognition signals were ineffective and haze and patchy cloud complicated recognition.

F. L. Anderson
Major General, USA
Deputy Commander, Operations

Selected excerpts from letter authored by
Russian General Antonov to General Deane
USSTAF HQ
March 20, 1945
CONFIDENTIAL

This is to inform you that on 18 March 1945 between 1315 and 1330 hours, over positions of Soviet troops on the east bank of the Oder River, north of the town of Kustrin, 8 groups of American bombers type Flying Fortresses went across in a northerly direction, escorted by Mustang fighters. The American planes were being pursued by German fighters (Me 109) and (Fw 190). When the group of American planes reached Morin, at the same time over Morin region there were 6 Soviet (Yak 3) fighters. The Soviet fliers, having noticed the German fighters which were chasing the Americans, attacked the Germans, but they themselves, in turn, were attacked by the American fighters. The Soviet pilots, having clearly distinguished the American planes, avoided air battle with them, but in spite of that the American fighters continued to pursue the Soviet planes. As a result of the attack by American fighters, 6 Soviet planes were shot down. 2 Soviet fliers were killed and 1 seriously wounded. The incident indicated gives rise to justified indignation among the Soviet troops, particularly those who witnessed this exceptional occurrence. Punish those to blame for the attack on Soviet airplanes, and require the

Allied Air Force in the future to strictly carry out the agreement on this limited zone.

Antonov
General of the Army
Chief of the Red Army General Staff

RED FLIGHT LEADER
Lt. Rene Burtner

I led my flight on a freelance mission on March 18, 1945, after leaving the B-17s that were above us. I wasn't keeping close tabs on them so I guess that's how we got into trouble. We suddenly found ourselves right smack dab in the middle of both sides as the bombs from the B-17s rained down on us and the German flak came up at us. We split up pretty quickly, and except for seeing Berlin in the distance, I had no idea where we were. As my wingman and I dodged flak bursts and falling bombs, I began to hear all kinds of chatter on the radio. My fellow pilots said they had 109s over here and 109s over there, and that there was enough for everybody. Problem was, I couldn't see a thing with all the puffy clouds and thick haze draped across the sky.

I decided to drop below the haze line, and as we broke out, I saw an airplane below coming up straight at us. I could see that this airplane was blue; it looked like a German fighter to me. The odd thing was he had no markings on his wings. I rolled the Mustang over and came straight down on the fighter as I began to fire. I saw that I was hitting him as I went by, my incendiaries flickering around his cockpit. I didn't see him crash because I was moving pretty fast, but I knew he was a goner, for sure. When I pulled back around and leveled out, I saw another one out in front of me, headed toward an airfield with his wheels down. I gave him a short burst and he immediately went sideways. I was pretty sure he wasn't going to land very well in that condition.

I went low and came screaming over the airfield. A plane off to my right was attempting to taxi. I skidded the Mustang, and when I fired he blew up right in front of me. As I passed over the perimeter of the field, I saw bright red stars painted on the sides of a bunch of parked Yaks. I immediately got on the radio and told the rest of my squadron that this was a Russian airfield. Unfortunately, I wasn't quick enough as another Mustang behind me—this was Red 4, flown by 2nd Lt. Robert W. McIntosh, and already beating up the field.

RED 3
Lt. Robert J. Guggemos

My wingman and I were east of Berlin, passing over Templehoff airport at thirteen thousand feet. I looked down and saw an Fw 190 on its back ten thousand feet below, just completing a looping maneuver. There isn't another thing in the world that looks like a radial-engine Fw 190, so I dropped my tanks and began to let down and follow him. It took me a while to catch him—mainly because I didn't want to point the Mustang's nose straight down and risk ripping my wings off. I must have blinked or turned my head during my descent because I lost the 190 and picked up a Yak 9; trouble was, I still thought I was chasing the 190. The Yak saw me closing and pulled into a very hard turn. I knew I could never hit him because I couldn't pull that much deflection in the Mustang; my long nose was in the way.

As I pursued him, heavy exhaust smoke poured from his engine. I was gaining on him, and as he came into range I thought, *I'll just stick my gun barrels right up his ass, so when I pull the trigger there'll be no doubt about it.* But I noticed something odd about the "190" as I got closer to it: he had a coolant radiator under his belly. This was no 190! I swung out to the side and went sailing by him seventy-five miles an hour faster than he was going. I just about stopped in my tracks when I saw that big red star on his fuselage. I goosed the Mustang, pulled back hard on the stick, and went straight up. The problem was, the Russian dummy followed me!

Why he swung in back of me, into a firing position, I will never know. He saw my green nose and my white American star. He surely knew I was in a Mustang. I guess he was just plain stupid. My wingman did his job, and the last time I saw that Yak, great big pieces were coming off of him. I looked around and saw another Yak smoking, going straight down into a lake. I was in shock and became a little scared. We had just shot down a Russian airplane—I knew there was going to be hell to pay!

RED 4
Lt. Robert McCormack

I was the number-four man in a flight of four Mustangs. We were apparently over Russian territory, but none of us knew that at the time. Someone called over the radio and said there was a Russian airfield below, with German fighters beating up the place. I didn't see any of this because I was too busy flying off the wing of another Mustang, with one eye on my element leader, Lieutenant Guggemos, and the other eye looking for the enemy. An airplane that looked to me like a German fighter suddenly came out of nowhere. Guggemos took a shot at him but was too far out of range.

For whatever reason, Guggemos veered off to the right and passed the airplane he had just fired at. Then this guy got into a firing position right behind Guggemos. The airplane had no markings. Well, it looked like an Me 109 to me, so I slid in behind him. I had all the time in the world to line this guy up in my sights. He pulled off to the left, directly in front of me. All I saw was this guy's tail as Guggemos evaded and turned hard right. I pulled the trigger and watched my concentrated rounds hit the plane's right wing root, just below the cockpit. It was hard to miss, and my rounds continued to light up along his right wing. It was then that

Captain Cox, who was leading "A" flight, broke radio silence and said, "All American fighters cease fire, there are friendly airplanes overhead."

I stopped firing and pulled off my prey, racking the Mustang around hard to rejoin Guggemos. Everything happened so fast, and I still get the shakes when I think about it. But at the time, I didn't give it a thought when Guggemos pulled away from that guy. I had been trained to cover my wingman and that's exactly what I did that day.

YELLOW FLIGHT LEADER
Lt. Robert S. Gaines Jr.

When our squadron broke away from the bombers, each of our flights, Red, Yellow, and so on, split up to look for targets of opportunity. I had been leading Yellow flight and thought there might be more activity up near Berlin. I didn't know where all the other flights went, but I could sure hear the chatter on the radio about all the bogeys that were in the area. I began a descent from twenty thousand feet and headed in the general direction of all the commotion. It turned out that the Russians had recently captured a German airfield that was on a bend along the Oder River. When I heard that some German airplanes were strafing the field, I led my flight in that direction.

As I got closer to the field, an airplane that looked like an Me 109 went zooming by, making an aggressive pass at our flight. I didn't know if he had fired at us or not because I didn't see any tracers, but I wasn't about to sit around and wait for a second pass. I didn't have the luxury of great visibility either, because of all the cloud cover and haze. I didn't see any markings on this guy either. All I knew was that the plane looked like a 109 to me.

I turned and went after him, but I was having a lot of trouble with my K-14 gun sight because I wasn't used to firing it. I was putting way to much lead on him as my bullets spit out and missed him by a country mile. Then I woke up and remembered that the gun sight would composite for my maneuvering if I just put the pipper on him. Well, that's what I did, as this guy pulled some hard Gs to try and shake me. The gun sight was flawless, and, oh, boy, did he blossom out—my hits were all over that guy. I was pretty close to him by now, just behind his tail, as my rounds shredded him and he began to burn. I think the first couple of rounds must have killed him because he immediately went into a downward spiral, trailing a lot of smoke.

I watched him spiral down all the way until he crashed into a lake. I looked at my map and saw that it was Werbellin Lake, near Joachimsthal. After the dust settled, with other members of my flight getting some shooting in, too, we returned home. I later found out, much to my chagrin, that the plane I had shot down was a Russian Yak. When I looked at my gun-camera film, I sure couldn't tell it was a Yak—it still looked like an Me 109.

Lieutenant Gaines was later promoted to captain.

YELLOW 3
Lt. Bryce H. Thomson

It started out as just another escort mission into the area around Berlin, Germany. When I saw some airplanes below that weren't ours, I went back to how I was trained: "Anything that isn't yours is the enemy." They were heading right for us as we dived onto them. None of us, on either side, stayed in formation. We were fighter pilots ready to mix it up with one another. The guy that was flying my wing hollered at me and said, "There's a Yak on your tail!" I broke sharply to the right and laid the Mustang over on its wingtip, just as the Yak started to shoot at me.

I pulled hard and in an instant I was on this guy's tail. The Yaks were painted in a bluish-colored camouflage with red stars on the fuselage but no wing markings. The Yaks had been built for ground support; they were heavy and had lots of firepower and armament. But they were no match for a Mustang; we could turn circles around them all day long. I'm not going to tell you what happened next but I will tell you what *didn't* happen.

A while after the encounter with the Yaks, the newspapers wrote a story saying that I had flown alongside the Yak and waved to the Russian pilot as he waved back. Some accounts even say I waved an American flag as we smiled at each another. When somebody's behind you shooting at your tail, and you break away and then get on *his* tail, the last thing a fighter pilot is going to do is pull up next to his adversary and wave; at least not with all five fingers! At the time it was good PR and it sure read well. It gave the idea that there was a good, natural relationship between the Americans and the Russians. It served its purpose, but none of it was true.

YELLOW 4
Flight Officer Harley E. Berndt

I was flying on the wing of Lieutenant Gaines, who was leading Yellow flight that day. We were around ten thousand feet, heading east when Gaines saw three or four aircraft below. These aircraft were making a diving, 180-degree turn to port, with one of the aircraft lagging behind. Gaines identified these aircraft as Me 109s and made a firing pass at them. He selected one and fired a long burst; the plane burst into flames. It dived straight in from two thousand feet into a lake below and exploded. I attacked the formation's number-two aircraft and started to open fire at two thousand feet, closing to seven hundred feet.

I saw strikes and flashes on the wing root and cockpit area, as the enemy broke down and to the right. The plane just snapped right over and that was the last time I saw it. The fighter was blue and looked like an Me 109. That was my one and only aerial encounter with the enemy. Lieutenant Gaines yelled at me over the radio to "Join up!" so I banked the Mustang hard right and slid back in position to cover my leader.

AFTERMATH
EXCERPTS FROM INVESTIGATIVE REPORT,
MAY 28, 1945

> 8. *Report of investigation indicates that as soon as Russian planes were identified such information was radioed, and in each instance U.S. Army pilots withdrew, which negatives any possibility of willful shooting upon Russian planes by U.S. personnel.*

> 10. a. *It is the opinion of this section, trial by court-martial of the personnel mentioned in paragraphs 2,4,5,6 and-, will probably not result in convictions because of insufficient evidence. That no charges be preferred against Lt. McCormack, Lt. Guggemos, Capt. Gaines Jr. or F/O Harley Berndt.*

> b. *It is believed however that a prima facie case may be made against Lt. McIntosh. The report of investigation indicates that Lt. McIntosh fired at a Russian Yak plane when he observed it over a Russian airfield with its wheels down attempting to land. It appears that he was advised prior to shooting at the plane that a Russian airfield was involved and that he observed the plane landing rather than strafing. It is the opinion of this headquarters that his conduct was negligent, and disciplinary action should be taken.*

> > F.A. Bodivitz
> > Lt.Col, JAGD
> > Asst. Judge Advocate

THE COURT-MARTIAL
Capt. Robert S. Gaines Jr.

The trial of Lieutenant McIntosh took place in August, and the Russians wanted someone to literally hang for what had happened. We heard that Stalin had ordered that all of his pilots that were involved with that mission be shot—whether he did or not, I will never know. So because of politics, McIntosh was used as a scapegoat, and offered as a token gesture to show the Russians that the Americans were serious about these offenders. McIntosh was one of the only guys who still had his gun-camera film; some of us found that our "butter-fingered" ground crews took the film cans out of the Mustangs and accidentally dropped them, exposing them in the afternoon sun.

McIntosh had good film, but all it showed was his shots at a taxiing or taking-off airplane; his bullets kicked up the dirt around the guy but never hit him. The Russian must have seen the bullets because he wheeled his fighter around and ground-looped it. Every one of us had to testify, and hell, it was so long after the mission that most of us couldn't remember the events clearly. We had flown so many missions over Germany that it was hard to remember one from the next. The whole gist of the court-martial was that because there was no direct damage to the Russian airfield, McIntosh was acquitted. We celebrated with American whiskey, not Russian vodka!

10

Wonder Weapon Assassins: Rocket and Jet Killers of the ETO

For Great Britain and her people, there was nothing wondrous about the new and deadly terror weapons that Hitler and his henchmen unleashed upon the island nation in the summer of 1944. The stoic Brits had already endured the Blitz—the nightly, eight-month German bomber campaign against London and other cities that began in late summer 1940, following the Battle of Britain. Conventional German bombers were destructive and intimidating, but combined attacks by unmanned V-1 pulse-jet flying bombs and high-explosive V-2 ballistic missiles challenged Britain's air defenses and unnerved the British people. (The rocket-bomb campaign against London was halted when the Allies overran German rocket bases in the fall of 1944. But the Germans regrouped and began V-1 and V-2 attacks on Antwerp, Belgium.)

Even as the dreadfully noisy German rockets rained down at will upon England, the Nazis threw yet another trump card at the Allied airmen in the form of jet fighters and bombers. There was nothing in the Air Corps arsenal that could keep up with these propeller-less, high-speed airplanes. New strategies had to be developed while on the job, as Allied airmen quickly adapted to their adversary's tactics and exploited their weaknesses. Fly along with a handful of American fighter pilots as they become Assassins of the Wonder Weapons.

APPLE BLOSSOMS AND DOODLEBUGS
Capt. William Y. Anderson, USAAC (Ret.)
354th Fighter Group, Pioneer Mustang Group,
353rd Fighter Squadron

On June 17, 1944, I was working for the Ninth Air Force. Our squadron had just completed a dive-bombing mission near Bayeux, France, where we unloaded our five-hundred–pound bombs onto railroad embankments and train tracks. Kinsley, our controller, called us over the R/T and said there was a bandit crossing the channel near our position. I split-essed and went after it. When I made visual contact, I saw it was a V-1 buzz bomb flying at between three thousand and four thousand feet. We called these flying rockets "doodlebugs" because of the ear-piercing racket they made.

As we crossed the coast inbound near the Isle of Wight, I dived down on the V-1 and began to fire at it with my .50-caliber machine guns. I saw flashes on the doodlebug and I knew I was making strikes. But you had to look out for two things while chasing and firing at a V-1. One was the friendly fire from the antiaircraft gunners on the ground, who put up a wall of lead to knock these little rockets down. The other thing was, you didn't want to get too close to the tail of the V-1 while you were shooting at it because if that thing blew up in front of you, it was sure to take you down with it.

Fortunately, my strikes hit the V-1's rocket tube, blowing it completely off. The powerless doodlebug nosed over and went straight down into a beautiful, flowering apple orchard, where it exploded. A great shower of pink and white apple blossoms was thrown skyward amidst the smoke and flame from the explosion. After I landed, I asked my CO how many doodlebugs I'd have to shoot down to make ace. He never gave me an answer.

I was credited with over seven additional aerial victories, eight if you include my V-1 kill, but I never paid much attention to victories or damages. I just went up and did my job.

TOLL BRIDGE
Lt. Col. Donald S. Bryan, USAF (Ret.)
352nd Fighter Group, 328th Fighter Squadron

March 14, 1945. I had assumed command of the Eighth Air Force's
328th Fighter Squadron when Maj. Earl Abbot failed to return from a
mission in late January 1945. We had encountered German jets in the
past, and I remember two times I had seen the Arado Ar 234 "Blitz" jet
bomber in the air before today's mission. The first time was when I was
on a bomber escort and saw some "big friends" overhead. I called them
out to the other pilots. I heard my number-four man yell something,
but I couldn't understand what he said. After we landed, I asked him
what the "Sam Hill" he was ringing sirens about. He said, "Didn't you
see the (American) A-26s that crossed over the top of us?" I told him I
had, and that they were what I'd called out as "big friends." My number
four said, "Well, those big friends had German crosses on their wings!"

To me, the Arados looked like our A-26 Invader light bombers,
except they didn't have any propellers—and flew a helluva lot faster than
a Mustang. The next time I saw one I tried to knock it down by attacking in my normal fashion. But by the time I got into a firing position,
this guy was almost out of sight. Most of us had heard that the Arado
had guns in the nose, so we were concerned that anything that flew that
fast could shoot us down. Buster, let me tell you, that really bugged the
hell out of me! (I later learned that Arado armament was optional, and
varied from plane to plane; sometimes 20mm cannons were located in
the nose, other times 20mm cannons were in the tail. And some of these
jet bombers went up with no armament at all.)

On today's mission, our squadron had just completed escorting
some A-26 and B-26 bombers over Germany. As we dropped down to
a lower altitude, I saw an Arado underneath me making a bombing run
on the Remagen Bridge that spanned the Rhine River. I poured the coal
to the Mustang and swung in behind him. The Arado took a couple of
right turns and was walking away from me as he made his run in on the

bridge. There was no way I could catch this guy so I made a 180-degree turn and kept watching him over my shoulder. There was a flight of P-47s near the bridge as well, and after the Arado made his bomb run he turned away from the Thunderbolts and right toward me. There was no way I was going to let this guy get away!

The Arado was a hundred yards away when he passed over the top of me. If he would have so much as twitched, he probably would be alive today; I was going to break away because I still thought he carried guns in his nose. I had the Mustang vertical to the ground at a perfect ninety degrees as I swooped around into a firing position. I gave him a short burst from my machine guns and was able to slow him down by knocking out his right engine. After that, I was able to play with him as I continued to pour machine gun rounds into him. I knew my squadron was behind me, and behind *them* was a flight of P-47s, but I'll be damned if I was going to let anybody else get hits on him! I had chased this guy too long to give up now. When I knocked out his left engine, the Arado began to smoke badly. The bomber rolled over and dived straight down. Just before it crashed and exploded, the pilot jettisoned the canopy, but, unfortunately, he was unable to get out in time. The Arado was my thirteenth and final victory of the war.

GERMANY'S WONDER WEAPONS

V-1 FLYING-BOMB ROCKET

Colloquially known to hardened Britons as the buzz bomb or doodlebug, this pilotless, early cruise missile was officially called the Fieseler Fi 103. The V-1 (for *vergeltungswaffe einz*; vengeance weapon) was developed by the Luftwaffe and was operational by June 1944. Top speed was a shade under four hundred miles per hour. Its pulse-jet engine was designed to run out of fuel and quit *somewhere* over the target. Because precisely where and when was a built-in mystery, the V-1 was a particularly unnerving weapon; you never knew when the engine would go silent and allow the rocket bomb to fall. The V-1 packed a deadly punch and was the scourge of England and the Low Countries.

Me 163 KOMET

Built by the Messerschmitt aircraft company, the Me 163 Komet was designed as a single-seat, rocket-powered bomber interceptor. By the end of 1944, more than 225 had been built. Capable of reaching forty thousand feet in less than three minutes, the Komet (maximum speed: 596 miles per hour) was untouchable by any Allied fighter—until it ran out of its scarce and unstable propellant and had to glide back down to earth. And every Komet had to land just that way, because the jet burned through fuel rapidly and could stay aloft for only a few minutes.

Me 262 SWALLOW

Known as the Schwalbe (Swallow), the Messerschmitt Me 262 was the first operational jet fighter to see combat. With its swept-wing design and twin, under-wing jet engines, the 262 topped out at better than 540 miles per hour, and could easily turn the tables on any Allied fighter in a dogfight. Unfortunately for the Luftwaffe, the Swallow came too late (spring 1944) and flew too little to have any measurable effect against the vast numbers of Allied bombers and fighters that roamed the skies of Germany at will. Hitler's decision to utilize many 262s as fighter-bombers, rather than as pure fighters, also undercut the jet's success.

ARADO Ar 234

Affectionately called the "Blitz-bomber" by the Luftwaffe, the Arado Ar 234 differed from many contemporary Allied and Axis bombers due to its lack of an internal bomb bay. Instead, it carried its bomb load on external racks. The Arado bombed Allied positions during the Battle of the Bulge, but suffered—like all the German jets— because of a shortage of fuel. Although fast at a top speed of 459 miles per hour, it wasn't very maneuverable. Of the more than 210

Arados built during the war, only one remains. It is on public display at the National Air and Space Museum's Steven F. Udvar-Hazy Center, near Washington, D.C.

V-2 BALLISTIC MISSILE
This sophisticated ballistic missile was designed, like the V-1, to be a "vengeance weapon." High-speed pumps quickly fed great volumes of air into the rocket engine's thrust chamber and helped propel the V-2 as high as fifty to sixty miles into the upper mesosphere/lower thermosphere, at supersonic speeds up to 3,400 miles per hour. Maximum range was 220 miles, with average accuracy ratings of twelve kilometers from target. Operational during 1944 and 1945, V-2s made violent strikes against London, Antwerp, and other Allied cities. The V-2's speed and high-altitude capability prevented Allied planes from engaging, though one was apparently fired on by an RAF Spitfire early in 1945, at liftoff. Another tale, of a V-2 shot down at ten thousand feet by the waist gunner of a B-24, is probably apocryphal. V-2s were captured in significant numbers by American forces at war's end and led directly to the quick success of America's postwar rocket program.

ENCOUNTER REPORT: CAT AND MOUSE
339th Fighter Group, 370th Fighter Squadron

I was leading Red Section escorting bombers in the vicinity of Wittenberg, south of Berlin, on March 25, 1945, when I saw two Me 163 Komet rocket fighters circling at about twenty thousand feet. I flew toward them, and when I'd reached twenty-five thousand feet, I started after one a little below me. He saw me when I got within three thousand yards, and turned on his jet. He went up into a seventy-degree climb, but his plane quit at about twenty-five thousand feet, so he split-essed. I dived with him and leveled off at two thousand feet, on him at six o'clock. During the dive, my indicated airspeed (IAS) was between five hundred and six hundred miles per hour. I opened fire at two hundred yards. Pieces flew off all over. He made a sharp turn to the right, and I gave him another short burst. Half his left wing fell off and the plane caught fire. The pilot bailed out and I saw the Me 163 crash to the ground.

I claimed one Me 163 destroyed in the air.

Capt. Ray S. Wetmore

ENCOUNTER REPORT: SWALLOW CATCHER
78th Fighter Group, 82nd Fighter Squadron

March 31, 1945. I was leading Surtax Red Flight on an escort mission to Derben, Germany. Shortly after rendezvous, we began to sweep the target area at fifteen thousand feet. The R/T reported that jets had been spotted in the area. The early tactics of the Me 262 "Swallow" was to position a single 262 above the fighter group and then swoop down through the formation of Mustangs. The P-51s would shed their drop tanks and dive after the fleeing jet fighter. Of course, the 262 was a lot faster than a Mustang and could walk away from us. Some of the Mustangs burned out their Rolls-Royce Merlin engines in the chase, but the real damage happened when the squadron dropped their wing tanks.

Without enough fuel to complete the bomber escort, the Mustangs had no choice but to turn for home, or risk running their tanks dry over the occupied Continent. With the Allied fighters heading in the opposite direction, the remaining 262s took advantage of the situation and made slashing attacks at the unprotected bombers. It took us a while to figure out this 262 tactic. Hard as it was to avoid tangling with a Luftwaffe jet, we stayed put to protect the bomber boys—most of the time.

As we neared the Stendal area, I spotted two Me 262s off to our right, flying parallel to us and going in the same direction. When I first saw them, they looked like tiny dots off in the distance, but they quickly came into view, moving faster than we were. The duo pulled away and was out of sight before we even had a chance to get near them. We knew their tricks and stayed put until we saw another bogey nearby. We made a bounce on him and found it to be a lone

P-51 Mustang. As we pulled off the Mustang, we saw another nearby bogey and made a bounce on him.

This guy turned out to be a 262. Several flights gave chase, taking long-range shots at him until we lost him way out in the distance in a cloud of smoke. About fifteen minutes later, our flight had dropped down below the cloud layer, looking for targets of opportunity at between four thousand and five thousand feet. I looked left over the leading edge of my wing and saw a 262 flying from right to left on a ninety-degree angle, right underneath me. I hauled the Mustang over into a semi-split-ess and when I recovered I found myself right behind the 262. I closed on him rapidly and began to shoot, observing a great many strikes on the canopy and right jet unit.

The 262 pulled up slightly and broke to the left as it keeled over. He did a roll to the right and then went straight into the ground and exploded. That was my one and only encounter with the jets during the war.

I claimed one Me 262 destroyed.

Capt. Wayne L. Coleman, USAAC (Ret.)

ENCOUNTER REPORT: ARADO, TWELVE O'CLOCK HIGH!
356th Fighter Group, 359th Fighter Squadron

I was flying Farmhouse Green Three. Our squadron had spent the first part of April 18, 1945, escorting one box of B-26s over the target north of Augsburg. About five or ten minutes after the bombing we were at ten thousand feet, a little above and to the south of the bombers, and heading about three hundred degrees when a bogey was called in to us, at twelve o'clock high. The bogey was heading north. Green flight received permission to investigate and started climbing after him. He was at about twelve thousand feet when we first saw him, but when we started after him he turned to the left in a shallow dive. After Green leader announced it was a jet, he and his wingman started to attack. My wingman and I were behind Green One and Two. After firing a burst or two without results, Green Leader suddenly broke off his attack and said something over the radio I didn't understand as his transmission was garbled. Apparently, he was telling us not to continue the attack unless we made positive identification. However, I was already certain that it was an enemy aircraft.

After Green leader broke off his attack, the enemy aircraft pulled out of his dive and started to climb, flying to the southeast. I passed through the first element and pulled up behind what I recognized as an Arado 234 jet bomber. I figured he'd pull away in the climb, so I started to fire at him from seven hundred to nine hundred yards, dead astern. I scored no hits on the first two or three bursts. As I was closing, I decided to hold fire until in good range. I gave him another burst from three hundred to four hundred yards, without deflection, but again saw no hits. The enemy aircraft then leveled off and I gave him another burst, seeing strikes on the left wingtip. My sight and range seemed to be okay, so I really let him have it, scoring hits on his left wing and left jet unit. By this time, I could see the holes in the rear of his jet units, and could smell burning low-grade fuel.

When the jet started a shallow turn to the left, I continued to close and kept firing, seeing strikes move across the left wing into the fuselage and right wing. I pulled my sight back to the left and kept working on his left jet, which was smoking profusely from a visible small fire. I put the sight on the middle of the smoke and let him have it. Only the dim outline of the Arado was visible in the smoke, but I could see the flashes of my strikes.

As I overran the jet, it snapped into a spin. When I was at thirteen thousand to fourteen thousand feet, I saw him spin into the ground. He hit between two houses, and exploded and burned. I believe that the pilot did not get out.

As to the characteristics of the Arado, the cockpit was well forward in a Plexiglas-covered nose. The top of the fuselage was a straight line back to the tail; the wings were very high mid-wing; and the tail was characteristically German, the leading edge of the fin slanting back to an almost square upper edge. The trailing edge of the rudder was nearly vertical.

I claimed one Arado 234 destroyed.

Lt. Leon Oliver

ENCOUNTER REPORT: TORCH BEARER
357th Fighter Group, 363rd Fighter Squadron

I was leading Cement Blue flight on April 18, 1945, when we arrived in our target area at fifteen thousand feet. Cement White flight called in a bogey low at eleven o'clock. I recognized it as an Me 262 jet. I dropped my tanks and dived from fifteen thousand feet to thirteen thousand feet, pulling up behind the jet. I let him have a burst from four hundred yards and got very good hits on his right jet unit and canopy. He broke right in a very tight diving turn, pulling streamers from his wingtips. My "G" meter read nine Gs! As he straightened out at seven thousand feet, I was 250 yards behind him going about 475 miles per hour. I let him have another burst, getting more very good hits on his right jet unit. He popped his canopy as I let him have another burst. Large pieces came off his ship and it caught fire. I pulled off to avoid the pieces and watched the Me 262 fall apart. His tail came off and he rolled over and went in like a torch, crashing into some woods next to a river. The pilot never got out.

I claimed one Me 262 destroyed.

Maj. Donald Bochkay

NORBERT HANNIG, LUFTWAFFE
JG54, THE GREEN HEARTS

By June 1944, it had been decided that the Luftwaffe could no longer afford to let seasoned fighter pilots simply fly along with pupils on training flights. Instead, most of the fledgling students would receive "on the job training" as we led them in missions to intercept the American bomber streams. When our radar picked up a large formation of bombers and escorts crossing the Baltic island of Rügen, we scrambled—the "Indians" were on their way. We climbed to the same altitude as the bombers with hopes of making a head-on pass at them. Unfortunately, it didn't work out that way.

Because we arrived too late, we found ourselves *below* the B-17s. I piloted an Fw 190, and had a 190 on each side. We climbed into the vertical and began to fire at the bellies of the bombers. As soon as the shooting began, I looked up and saw contrails arching down toward us. I saw four sets of lines, then eight, and finally twelve, and I knew what was dragging those condensation trails down— Mustangs. Very quickly, I had twelve shiny P-51s parked on my tail. They held their fire for fear of hitting one of their own bombers and waited for me to clear the stream. When I did, I threw the 190 into some "Russian aerobatics," yo-yo-ing the 190 around the sky. The Mustangs tried to hang onto my evasive maneuvers, but their shots went either high or low with every move of my stick.

I spotted some cumulus clouds up ahead and made a dash for them. I began to fly a tight circle around the cloud bank as the Mustangs gave chase. I flew over the top of a large cloud and pulled my stick back hard, then tromped down on my rudder and threw the 190 into a quick spin down into the center of the cloud. When I felt safe, I let go of the stick, and the 190 righted itself as I shot through the bottom of the cloud deck. I looked up and all I saw were those Mustangs buzzing around like a bunch of angry bees on the outside of the cloud, waiting for me to emerge. As I raced out of there, I listened on the radio to reports of other dogfights around me. I recognized one of the voices of that of a fellow 190 pilot who had been part of my initial flight; he was reporting that he was on the deck with a Mustang on his tail. I knew he couldn't be far away so I pushed the 190 over and raced for the deck.

It was easy to spot my wingman: not only did he have a Mustang on his tail, but he had three others right behind the first, ready to jump in at a minute's notice. The 190 was fishtailing wildly as the Mustang's shots missed their mark—most of the time. When I finally caught up to the group, I let go with a burst of cannon and machine gun rounds at the three trailing Mustangs, which scattered when they saw the cannon rounds exploding right under them. As I drew closer to the lone pursuing Mustang, I yelled for my wingman to stomp down on his left rudder. By the time the Mustang pilot figured out what had happened, all he had in front of him was empty sky. My rounds tore into the P-51. With no altitude to evade, he nosed over and cartwheeled into the ground. My wingman's 190 was riddled with bullet holes; I fared much better: only seventeen holes. We learned later that we twelve 190s went up against 250 bombers and dozens of P-51s. Only one Luftwaffe fighter landed undamaged that day; the majority of the others were shot down. It was the beginning of the end for us, even with the introduction of "wonder weapons."

11

Courage, Combat, and Legacies

As World War II in Europe wound down, the level of combat remained fierce. The Luftwaffe was almost literally running on fumes. It was desperately short of aircraft, and by now had very few experienced pilots. Regardless, the prideful German fliers that threw themselves at Allied planes were desperate to prevail. Mustangs continued to escort bombers into Germany, and men continued to die. Throughout this final phase of the air war in the ETO, the Mustang burnished its reputation as the best Allied fighter plane by making the Luftwaffe pay dearly for its pilots' reckless courage. That level of U.S. excellence inspired some American pilots to ponder another, earlier war, and to consider special bonds between fathers and sons.

ENCOUNTER REPORT: JANUARY 14, 1945
356th Fighter Group, 361st Fighter Squadron

I was Lampshade Leader on the mission of January 14, 1945. While escorting the lead box of B-24s on withdrawal, Nuthouse called and said there were bandits in the Dümmer Lake area. I was then a little southwest of Hanover, so I called Chinwag Squadron to boost power. We arrived over the big lake a few minutes later. Unable to pick up anything, I started an orbit to the left. Chinwag Green

Leader called and said there were fifteen to twenty bogeys in a large Lufberry about ten thousand feet below us. Because I was unable to see them, I called and asked him to investigate. Just as he started down I picked them up, and immediately led the rest of the squadron down. Drawing into range, I called them out as Fw 190s and started a bounce, singling out a lone 190 flying on the outside of the Lufberry.

As I closed into a good shooting range, I fired a small burst but observed no hits. The 190 was still in a left-hand turn when I opened fire again, this time getting many hits on the fuselage and cockpit. Still closing, I fired another good burst, and saw many hits along the left side of the fuselage and in the cockpit. The 190 did a violent snap and went into a dive. I pulled up off to the right and followed him down. The pilot bailed out at around three thousand feet; the plane went straight into the ground. I switched my gun selector over to camera only and took a short picture of the opened chute.

As I pulled out on the deck to start a slow climbing orbit to the right, I observed a P-51 chasing a 190 on the deck. I turned to give the Mustang cover if he needed it, but the 190 did a sudden snap, dove into the ground, and exploded. I pulled alongside the P-51 and identified it as Chinwag White 3: Lieutenant Burdick. The fight was just about over so I climbed back up in the combat area and called the Chinwag Squadron to re-form and set course for base.

Maj. Donald J. Strait

FATHERLY ADVICE
Confessions of a Second-Generation Fighter Pilot
Capt. Clinton D. Burdick, USAAC (Ret.)

FOLLOWING IN HIS FOOTSTEPS

There were two things that got me interested in aviation while I was a kid growing up in the 1930s: model airplanes and my father, Howard. My dad was the bigger influence, of course, and not because of his job in the banking business. It was what he accomplished years before I was even born. Although he rarely spoke of his exploits, my father flew Sopwith Camels with the 17th Aero Squadron during "the war to end all wars"—World War I. After the conflict ended, he closed that chapter of his life and walked away from flying. He believed he was simply a young man doing his job for his country. He'd done what the military had asked him to do, then got out of the service, met my mother, and started a family. The trouble was, there was one historic issue he couldn't change or hide: from mid-September 1918 through late October of that year, my father shot down eight enemy airplanes and achieved ace status under the command of the Royal Air Force.

He kept his aerial combat memories hidden from most of us, and it wasn't until World War II was just beginning to rear its ugly head when he gave me some "fatherly advice."

He said, "Clinton, now that you've reached the age known as 'draft bait,' you really need to think about volunteering. They have an obligation to make available your choice of service if you're qualified. My advice for you is to join the Air Corps and become a pilot, before you end up in the infantry slinging a rifle and slogging through mud up to your knees." I listened to his words of wisdom, and before long I earned my wings and wound up in fighters.

TRICKS OF THE TRADE

By the time I turned nineteen, Uncle Sam thought I was ready to fly a fighter— personally, I think I needed a little more practice. I started out in the P-40 Warhawk. During my first flight I thought, *Oh dear, this small airplane has way too much power*! The P-40 had twice the go of the AT-6s I had been used to, but it was also much more maneuverable. It had very good control responses; heck, all the fighters did. When you pull back on the stick, you go like hell straight up. But when you push the nose over, you go downhill even faster! Make no mistake, flying a fighter was a very physically demanding experience, especially with the amount of Gs we pulled during evasive maneuvers. All in all, the P-40 was a good airplane, but its design was getting tired, and the plane was short on range and ran out of breath above twenty thousand feet. The P-47 Thunderbolt, on the other hand was, a whole 'nother animal.

I was sent to the East Coast to become acquainted with my new front office. The P-47 was a behemoth; there was almost enough room inside the cockpit to rent out the other half! Our training focused on gunnery and formation work, along with low-level navigation, which would really come in handy later on in Europe. We had heard stories about the ruggedness of the Jug—and, unfortunately, I proved that point during one of my training flights.

We were sent out to a point a considerable distance away from our base and told to drop to the deck and find our way back home. I came zooming across a big cornfield and must have been daydreaming because I failed to notice the line of big high trees in front of me. I was a little late pulling back on the stick and took a full six feet off the treetops. When I landed, the entire belly was covered in the remains of the trees I killed. My crew chief came out, scratched his head, and said, "Don't worry about it, lieutenant, I'll get it cleaned up before the CO sees it." That crew chief was like all the others I had, a bunch of great guys!

When I was deemed combat ready, I was sent over to England as a replacement pilot with the 356th Fighter Group, 361st Fighter Squadron. Our main job was to protect the bombers. One way to do that was to shoot down the enemy fighters that showed up when the bomber stream was over Europe. Finding the Luftwaffe wasn't hard. The hard part was shooting them down! Because I was a new wingman, my leader was always the shooter. My job was to put my head on a swivel and protect him from enemy fighters. In combat, I quickly found that the enemy appears very quickly, and disappears even quicker! The P-47 was a great gun platform, not only in the aerial sense but also for use against ground targets. I fell in love with the Jug and felt a sense of betrayal when we had to trade them in.

Mustang Follies

When our group switched over to the P-51 Mustang in mid-November 1944, most of us thought we had just lost our best friend. When I first laid eyes on the Mustang, all I could think was, *This airplane is too small for a human being to fly, let alone fight with*! The P-47 had acres of metal all round it and carried two more guns than the Mustang did. The Jug's cockpit was comfortable and roomy, compared to the tight confines of the Mustang. With all our gear, including an attached parachute, we had to wiggle our way into the cockpit, and practically had to use a shoehorn to get completely inside.

The P-47 had big radial engine out ahead of it and could punch through a brick wall and keep on ticking. I was concerned that the Mustang, although faster than the Jug, had a liquid-cooled engine that had little to no tolerance for damage. It was easy for your mission to become a one-way trip. But once I got some time in the Mustang, I began to develop a great relationship with it and found out what a truly harmonized fighter it was. The Mustang definitely topped the Jug as an air-to-air fighter—a fact that became clear as our group began to prove its worth against the Luftwaffe.

I named my Mustang *DoDo*, after my fiancée back home. Unfortunately, her father was a doctor and wanted her to marry a doctor, not "a fighter pilot." Unbeknownst to me at the time, I lost out to her father's wishes. But I had no regrets about being a fighter pilot and was glad I followed my own father's wishes.

On November 25, 1944, I destroyed an Fw 190 on the ground but didn't get my first aerial victory until December 5. We had been escorting bombers near Berlin, and when we came off the target, we made our turn for home and spotted over forty Luftwaffe fighters nearby. We broke into them and I slugged it out with a 190. I was able to get some good strikes on him before he crashed below. I turned and latched on to another 190, but was only able to claim that one as damaged. He got away during the melee and was able to lick his wounds and fight another day. And there were plenty of those days to come, especially in 1945.

Fw 190 Frenzy

It was January 14, 1945, and I was flying Chinwag White 3 southwest of Dümmer Lake on a bomber withdrawal, escorting B-24s that had just hit their target near Braunschweig. We were at twenty-seven thousand feet and on the way out when Nuthouse called that there were bandits in the area. Our group spotted fifteen to twenty Fw 190s in a left-Lufberry, below us at between ten thousand and fourteen thousand feet. Because White 2 had to abort with engine problems, White 4 escorted him back to France, and I ended up flying wing to White Leader, Lieutenant Ashby. White Leader singled out one Fw 190 and went in to attack. I observed White Leader get many hits on the left side of the 190, and saw the pilot bail out. His chute didn't open and I saw both pilot and plane hit the ground. White Leader then flew on my wing as I took after another Fw 190. At an altitude of one thousand feet, I fired a short burst from about three hundred yards with a thirty-degree deflection, and scored many strikes on the fuselage and cockpit area. The pilot of the damaged 190 jettisoned his canopy and bailed out, at about three hundred feet. He was so low that his chute never opened.

I claimed one Fw 190 destroyed.

I made a right turn to protect the tail of White Leader, who was firing at an Fw 190 that had attempted a head-on pass at me. I saw White Leader get many strikes on the 190. The 190 rolled over, split-essed from three thousand feet, and went straight into the ground. I then was able to position myself on the tail of another Fw 190, and stayed at range less than one hundred feet for about a minute. Firing with zero deflection, I scored hits several times, although I had only one gun still with ammo. After I hit the 190 several times, he broke away.

I claimed one Fw 190 damaged.

When I saw another 190 chasing a P-51, I made a pass on him. I opened fire head on, at a range of five hundred yards, and closed to about a hundred yards. I observed some strikes, but when I pulled up, the 190 followed, firing at me. Thankfully, he couldn't draw any deflection and didn't hit me.

I claimed one Fw 190 damaged.

My combat with these last two Fw 190s was at just three thousand feet; I knew I had to get some altitude and a wingman under my wings.

I sighted White Leader flying above me to the right, still giving me protection, so I started after another 190 that was on the deck. I closed to a very close range, about one hundred feet, and fired a short burst, about twenty degrees deflection, with only the single gun still firing. The 190 did a half-snap to the right and went straight into the ground from about twenty feet.

I claimed one Fw 190 destroyed [confirmed by Lampshade Leader; see personal combat report of Maj. Donald J. Strait]. Then I made a steep right climbing turn and rejoined my flight leader, Lieutenant Ashby.

We went to bounce another 190 that was stooging alone in the area when Chinwag Purple 2, Lieutenant Baskin, came out of nowhere and got between and in front of us, and began to fire at the 190. I observed him get many hits on the 190s left wing. He overshot the 190 and the German went after him. White Leader fired a short burst and got hits on the engine and cockpit area. The 190 climbed to the left and lowered his flaps to make an emergency landing. I came in next and gave him a short burst, observing hits but not enough to make a claim on this 190. The 190 tried to belly land in a field but overshot, hit a fence, and cartwheeled. He lost his left wing and broke into many pieces. I confirm the joint destruction of this Fw 190 by lieutenants Ashby and Baskin. We remained on the deck because of intense flak, and being low on gas we headed back to base. I fired a total of 882 rounds that day and was thankful I had others looking out for me, including the squadron leader, Major Strait.

LIKE FATHER, LIKE SON

Although my father and I had both survived the horrors of aerial combat, our training and combat experience were quite different because of the twenty-five years that separated our involvement. I had well over 250 hours of training alone, in a wide variety of aircraft, before I entered the combat arena. My father, on the other hand, had less than fifty hours total time before he was sent to the front lines. He had trained in a fabric covered biplane, with engines that were hit and miss— mainly miss.

HOWARD BURDICK VICTORIES

Date	Aircraft Flown	Enemy Type Shot Down
September 18, 1918	Sopwith Camel	LVG C
September 24	Sopwith Camel	Fokker D.VII
September 28	Sopwith Camel	LVG C
September 28	Sopwith Camel	Fokker D.VII
October 2	Sopwith Camel	DFW C
October 14	Sopwith Camel	Halberstadt C
October 14	Sopwith Camel	Fokker D.VII
October 25	Sopwith Camel	Fokker D.VII

Distinguished Service Cross (DSC)
The Distinguished Service Cross is presented to Howard Burdick, Second Lieutenant (Air Service), U.S. Army, for extraordinary heroism in action northwest of Cambrai, France, September 28, 1918. Attacked by two Fokker biplanes, Lieutenant Burdick outmaneuvered both machines, shot one into flames and routed the other one. Later, seeing three Fokkers attacking an American aviator, he at once dove into the combat to his assistance, shooting down one and driving off the other two. His quick and unhesitating attack, single-handed, on the three Fokkers save the life of his fellow pilot.
    General Orders No. 38, W.D., 1921

Distinguished Flying Cross (DFC)
"For skill and gallantry. On 25 October, while on an offensive patrol, this officer attacked a formation of five Fokker biplanes over the forest of Mormal [France] and succeeded in shooting down one in flames. On another occasion he dived on an enemy two-seater but was in turn attacked by two Fokkers, one of which he succeeded in shooting down in flames. Later he attacked three enemy aircraft who were attacking one of our machines and shot down one, which dived straight into the ground and crashed. This officer has now destroyed five EA (three in flames) and has at all times displayed the greatest gallantry, skill and disregard of danger." DFC citation

CLINTON BURDICK VICTORIES

November 25, 1944	Fw 190 destroyed (ground)
December 5, 1944	Fw 190 destroyed
	Fw 190 damaged
January 14, 1945	2 Fw 190s destroyed
	2 Fw 190s damaged

Although the airplanes he flew were a lot slower, they were in some aspects more stable and easier to fly than the complex airplanes I piloted.

I typically flew on missions lasting seven hours or more, flying from our base in England to the heartland of Germany and back. Our living quarters on our base at Martlesham Heath, England, were heated brick buildings. We ate at the officers mess hall and relaxed in our group's officers club. My father routinely flew less than two hours on his missions, due in part to the limited range imposed by the small amount of fuel he carried. That's why his squadron was posted near the front lines. Every time the line moved—frontwards or backwards—so did he and his airfield. He slept in a tent and rarely enjoyed a hot meal, let alone a hot shower.

Our aerial combat tactics were quite different as well. We had been trained to fly in a "finger four" formation with two elements of two. One was the leader, whose main task was to attack the enemy, and the other was the wingman, whose main job was to protect the leader, period. During World War I, my father flew in a semi-loose formation that really didn't abide to the theory of "shooter/protector." When they spotted the enemy, it was kind of like everybody for themselves, as each side tried to out-maneuver the other. That's how the term "dogfight" originated—everyone doing their own thing at close range.

I ended the war with 5½ victories. Like my father, I walked away from flying, got married, and had a family. I, too, was just doing my part for my country, to help secure our nation's freedoms.

12

Mustangs vs. Japan

The bombing campaigns over Europe and Japan were as different as tea and sake, with one exception. The B-17 and B-24 reigned supreme over Fortress Europe, and finally brought Germany to its knees. In the Pacific, the distances to the target, especially to the Japanese mainland, were much greater, thus the need for the big B-29 Superfortress. One thing common to both front, however, was the P-51 Mustang. Because of its long legs and other attributes, it became the escort of choice for the bombers to and from the target areas.

ARE WE THERE YET?
Long-Range Pacific Mustang Missions
Lt. Jerry Yellin, USAAC (Ret.)

ITCHING TO FIGHT

I had been interested in aviation ever since Lindbergh crossed the Atlantic. As a kid growing up in Newark, New Jersey, during the Great Depression, all pilots were my heroes. I always looked to the sky to watch military aircraft fly overhead, smiling and convincing myself that someday I was going to be a fighter pilot. The beginning of that journey began on December 7, 1941, when the Japanese bombed Pearl Harbor. After I joined the Army Air Force, it took me over two years to finally get my hands on a fighter. I barely survived ten hours at the controls of a P-40 and thought, *What have I gotten myself into?*

The P-40 Warhawk was a small airplane with a tremendous amount of torque; you had to be both right-leg- and right-arm-strong to keep it going straight. Shortly after my P-40 checkout, I was assigned to the 78th Fighter Squadron (The Bushmasters), 15th Fighter Group of the Seventh Air Force, where I joined a P-47 unit that was preparing to participate in a large-scale invasion of Truk Atoll, so that General MacArthur could return to the Philippines. I found the Jug to be a really nice airplane and an even nicer gun platform. We were told that most of our combat over Truk would be to strafe Japanese positions on the ground. I think we would have fared pretty good, especially with that big radial engine protecting us up front. By the time I had a couple of hundred hours in the P-47, the Truk invasion was called off and I was sent to get checked out in the P-51 Mustang. To me, transferring out of Thunderbolts into the Mustang was like riding on the back of a gazelle instead of being strapped to the back of an elephant!

When I first got into the Mustang in November 1944, I was astounded by the plane's responsiveness—you thought "turn" and it quickly turned. The Mustang was an incredible flying machine, the best one ever built. With a 1,650-horsepower Packard-built Rolls-Royce Merlin engine, the Mustang was one of the fastest piston airplanes of its time. The guys in Europe were tearing the Luftwaffe apart with them on a daily basis, while escorting bombers all the way to Germany. It was an amazing fighter, and as its reputation rose, the brass in the Pacific Theater of Operations took notice of its long-range capabilities. This was the fighter needed to take the B-29s all the way to Japan and back. Of course, one thing a Mustang pilot always worried about was getting that little "nick" in the engine; any loss of coolant and you were pretty much guaranteed a swim in the ocean. We got our orders to ship out from Hawaii. Our P-51s were loaded on a ship, and it wasn't until we were out at sea that we were told our final destination: the island of Iwo Jima.

BETWEEN A ROCK AND A HARD PLACE

During our sixteen-day voyage across the Pacific, we were briefed that the marines were going to invade Iwo Jima. As soon as they took control of the first airstrip, we would fly in and begin aerial combat operations. The taking of Iwo would serve many important purposes, and the top two in my mind were these: it was a place where crippled B-29s or those running low on fuel could safely land at while returning from bombing missions over Japan; and, more importantly, it was a jumping-off place for our fighters to escort the B-29s to the emperor's front door. It took sixteen days from the initial marine landings before it was "safe enough" for our squadron to land on March 7, 1945. When I circled to land there for the first time, I finally realized what hell really looked like.

I had been used to the lush green vegetation of Hawaii; now, over Iwo Jima, everything I observed on the postage stamp-sized island (six miles long, two miles wide) resembled the surface of the moon; dark, uneven ground with bomb craters everywhere. We landed on a dirt strip, which caused a lot of problems for our carburetors and flaps. With small rocks everywhere, we had to get the flaps up quickly for fear of damaging them. As I landed that first time and tried to focus on the "Follow Me" jeep, I was overwhelmed with the unbearable stench of death as the jeep escorted us past mounds and mounds of dead Japanese soldiers. And if that wasn't bad enough, we shut down our Mustangs right next to the Marine Corps mortuary, where hundreds of brave marines were being readied for burial. It didn't take long to realize that Iwo Jima was not a nice place to be.

But each of us in the squadron knew we had jobs to do as fighter pilots. The very next day, we lined our Mustangs on the dirt strip and prepared for our baptism of combat. The Seabees had just finished patching the runway damage caused by dozens of Japanese mortar rounds that fell the night before. Distance would not be an issue on this first mission. We lifted off, sucked our gear up, and looked for the yellow smoke to indicate the target below. We dropped down to strafe the Japanese positions and then made another run on the target with either five-hundred–pound bombs or napalm canisters. We did what we could for the next two weeks to help the marines on the ground, where their gains were measured in feet and yards. Our missions changed when we were sent on some-short range trips to the island of Chichi Jima, to attack the Japanese airfield there. All of that was part of our preparation for the very long-range missions (VLR) to Japan and back.

A LONG HAUL FOR LITTLE FRIENDS

The B-29s had been pounding Japan at night and had been doing a pretty good job. The problem was, General Lemay wanted greater accuracy of the targets, and the only way to get that was to fly at lower levels during daylight. The B-29s needed escorts of "little friends" to protect them over Japan. Flying our Mustangs from Iwo Jima to Tokyo was a 660-mile trip one way, which meant that most of our missions would exceed eight hours of flying. In order to achieve this, we had to run our Merlins at between 1,750 and 1,950 rpm, and make sure we burned the fuselage tanks first, then the 110-gallon drop tanks. That would leave us with the wing tanks for the return trip home. I had my own P-51 assigned to me, and I named it after a girl I met as a cadet. Her name was Dorris Rose so I named my Mustang *Dorrie R.* Although we never married, she kept me alive with her letters from home.

The very first long-range Mustang mission to Japan occurred on April 7, 1945. More than one hundred P-51s lifted off from Iwo Jima that morning to begin the long, slow ride to rally with over a hundred B-29 Superfortresses on the way to Japan. My anxiety was high, and I wondered aloud, "Will I make it there and back?"

Due to the lack of landmarks on the way to the target area, we had a B-29 that acted as both a "mother hen" and our seeing-eye dog; we followed it in loose formation toward Japan. There were also a bunch of "Dumbos"—PBY Catalinas—and B-17s, with lifeboats strapped to their wings or bellies, staggered every hundred miles or so, just in case we had to bail out. Closer to Japan, our destroyers would act as our lifeboats, followed by our submarines, which were even closer to the mainland. Thankfully, I never had to use any of these services. About thirty miles off Tokyo Bay, our B-29 mother ship broke off and began to orbit, waiting for us on the return home. The rest of us overflew the B-29 armada, which was at fifteen thousand feet for the bombing run. There were Japanese fighters around that came up to tangle; unfortunately, I drew the short straw and rode shotgun with the B-29s as part of the bombers' top cover.

The thing that struck me the most was how the initial flight of B-29s dropped a string of bombs in almost a perfect square on the target below. Once they exploded, there was a square of fire that made a perfect aiming point for the rest of the B-29s that followed. The fires below became so intense that the smoke rose past us, up to twenty-five thousand feet. With the smoke, came the smells and debris of the carnage below. I saw a couple of B-29s get hit: one went in with all crew aboard, and I observed three chutes from the other. I felt helpless, as if I was on a sightseeing tour and could do nothing to assist my fellow airmen. My turn would come soon enough, though, for this was the beginning of the end for the Empire of Japan.

Having survived that first long-range mission, we were now members of the "Tokyo Club." We returned to Iwo Jima to prepare for the next round. When we landed, we had to be physically removed from our cockpits by our ground crews, as if we were small children being lifted from a high chair. Sitting for eight hours in one position was a killer. To remedy that problem, we were placed into a belly tank that had been sliced down the middle and filled with 130-degree sulfur water that had been pumped from the ground. To keep us from overheating, the crews filled us with cold beer. The Iwo Jima Spa was about the only place you could relax on that island.

Nowhere to Hide

The rule of thumb for VLR missions said that you flew one, and if you survived, you got a day off, followed by a short-range mission and then another VLR, which repeated the cycle. During the war, my longest

VLR mission occurred on May 30, 1945, and lasted eight hours and twenty-three minutes. It was also the day I bagged a Zero.

Our squadron was on a B-29 escort to Japan. I was a flight leader, and had my wingman, Lt. Danny Mathis, right beside me. The B-29s were strung out at fifteen thousand feet and nearing the target area when a group of Zeros showed up. The trick for the Japanese at that late date was to send the rookie pilots after the B-29s, while the experienced "old hands" stayed just outside the bomber box to direct the younger pilots to particular B-29s. Remember, the Japanese had been fighting for over seven years and didn't have a lot of experienced fighter pilots left.

A Zero cut right in front of me to make a run on a B-29. I let him have it with my six .50-caliber machine guns and hit him hard. My rounds began to shred his airplane. As I closed in on him, his Zero was falling apart, and I saw his canopy come off. He bailed out and came within a few feet of hitting my wing. It was as if time slowed way down: I could plainly see the startled expression on his face and the disbelief that this was happening to him. For a split second, he floated by me, just above my wing, hanging in mid-air with his Zero breaking apart in flames in the background. I was going too fast to see his chute open, and really wasn't concerned. His plane was on fire and that was all that mattered. I didn't realize until after we'd landed that my wingman, Danny, was right there next to me the whole time, firing away. Danny's gun-camera film showed his hits as well, so I gladly shared a half victory with him. My jubilation was short-lived, however, because Danny was killed on June 1, 1945, while flying my Mustang. He was one of 170 P-51s that went out that day, only to get caught by a huge Pacific storm that tossed their Mustangs around like toys. Twenty-seven Mustangs went down, and Danny was one of twenty-five pilots who died.

DOWN ON THE DECK

As the war progressed into July and August, there was less and less Japanese aerial opposition to contend with. We occasionally encountered trainers, seaplanes, and floatplanes—none of which were any match for our Mustangs. When the B-29s turned for home, we were released to drop down and strafe targets of opportunity—and there were plenty of them. On one mission, I spotted a train up ahead. He must have spotted me as well, because I saw a great plume of smoke come from his stack as he shoved the throttle forward on his engine. But there was no way he could outrun a Mustang! As I lined him up in my gun sight, I was just about to pull the trigger when the train came up on a curve in the track. He was moving so fast, he jumped the rails and smashed into an embankment!

Our Mustangs went after everything and anything: buildings, railroad stations, boats, parade grounds, and airfields. We wanted to inflict as much damage as we could before the invasion of Japan. We strafed, dive, and used rockets on most of our missions, and only stopped when the first guy in the flight radioed, "Ninety gallons." That reminder about fuel was our cue to break off our attacks and turn for the B-29 navigational escort back home. I fear the war would have continued on for some time had it not been abruptly stopped by the two atomic bombs. From April until mid-August 1945, I flew my Mustang in nineteen VLR missions over Japan. Of the sixteen fellow pilots I joined the squadron with, five were killed in Hawaii during training, and eleven others were killed in combat. Although it was a long, costly war, I felt I was able to survive it because of the P-51 Mustang.

POSTWAR HORSE OF A DIFFERENT COLOR
Flying the P-51H Mustang
Capt. Darrell R. Larkin, USAF (Ret.)

I had one thing in common with the North American P-51H Mustang: neither one of us saw combat during World War II. I shared the same unique frustrations with my father George as well. During 1917, he had gone all the way through flight training in JN-4D Jennys and was deemed combat ready, but the war to end all wars ended just as he was about to board a ship on the East Coast and head over to Europe. Flying a fighter was definitely in my bloodline, so it was with great frustration in late August 1945 that I had to ferry P-38 Lightnings to Arizona, just as World War II was ending. I didn't want to give up on flying fighters, so I joined the Ohio Air National Guard, where I became acquainted with the P-51 Mustang.

When I arrived, I was interviewed by a Captain King, who initially had little faith in my flying abilities.

"Well, I see Lieutenant Larkin, you flew P-38s. Do you think you can handle this Mustang and all its torque?"

I held my tongue and smiled, then leaned forward and replied, "Did you ever fly a P-38 on one engine?"

That summer, I was checked out in the Mustang. I thought the P-51 was a fine-flying airplane. I really enjoyed my time in it. The Mustang could be a real handful for some guys, as one pilot quickly found out during summer camp, when he pulled the wings off of one while doing aerobatics. I only had a little over a hundred hours in the D model when they were suddenly pulled from our unit and sent over to Korea. As a replacement, we received the latest and greatest Mustang, the P-51H— but first we had to get them out of storage and learn all the differences between it and the D model.

When we went to get the H-model Mustangs out of storage, many of them had only thirty to thirty-five hours of total flight time. The air force called our task "Inspect and Repair as Necessary," or IRAN. We simply called it "Inspect and Repaint as Necessary"; they still had that new airplane smell inside of them!

The P-51H was a definite lightweight compared to the P-51D. Weighing in almost six hundred pounds lighter, the plane spooked some of the older guys, who thought they'd break it in two if they tried to pull even a small G load. Standing back and looking at the two Mustangs side by side, you could see a lot of obvious differences. We used to joke that the only similarity between both fighters were the hose clamps— everything else was completely different. The H had a more slender set of gear legs, with smaller wheels and disc brakes, and a much thinner cross-section to the wing, which eliminated the indent found on the D's wing. The H fuselage was stretched by almost two feet, and the hump of the bubble canopy was moved forward, right over the pilot's head. The well-known belly scoop had a much larger opening, while the chin scoop below the propeller was smaller and less pronounced. The propeller itself was also new: an eleven-foot one-inch cuffless Aeroproducts unit comprising four widened blades with rounded tips.

The H-model's oil cooler was in front of the oil tank, just ahead of the firewall, instead of in the belly scoop, as on the D. The engine was the new Rolls-Royce Merlin V-1650-9, which utilized water/ alcohol injection that could really wind up and give the Mustang its get up and go. Maximum capacity of the fuselage tank was lowered to fifty-five gallons. The pilot's seat was raised and the control panel layout was simplified. I always thought the panel on the D model was more like the AT-6's, with instruments scattered every which way. But the H-model panel was more of a half-moon shape, with the instruments located in just the right spots. I always considered the D model a mechanic's airplane and the H model a pilot's airplane. It was much nicer to fly and seemed more balanced, no matter what the stick forces were. There was one unique thing about starting up the H, though, that we quickly had to learn. But some guys learned the hard way.

The H model had what was called a Simmons Automatic Boost Control, by which the throttle wasn't connected directly to the carburetor via linkage, but with oil pressure. This meant that the engine had to be turning over in order for the throttle to be connected. It was standard procedure to move the throttle all the way forward on the D model when we shut the engine down, to clear the Merlin's bottom cylinders and avoid a damaging oil lock on the next startup. It was a hard habit to break, and H-model pilots continued to jam the throttle forward while shutting down. What this meant was that at the outset of the next day's flight, another pilot would start the engine, and when it caught, it went right to full throttle, jumping the chocks and scaring the daylights out of both the pilot and the ground crews!

When we switched over to the H, I was selected to be the flight-test maintenance officer and wound up with over one thousand hours in them. I loved to conduct the stall series followed by a spin because the H always reminded me of the docile characteristics of the Piper Cub. You would pull that long nose up, wait for the stall, and then kick into a spin. On the second time around, the nose would want to come back up toward the horizon and then drop back down again. Each time around, the turn would become tighter. My limit was five turns—boy, did that bird spin beautifully!

I only had a couple or three scares while test-flying them. The one that stands out the most is the time I thought the Mustang was going to shake itself apart. I had been assigned to conduct a normal flight test on an H model and thought everything was going okay as I took off to begin my test sequence. Thankfully, I had gained safe altitude when I heard this godawful bang, followed by three more—and then complete silence. I did a quick three-sixty over the field and was able to dead-stick the Mustang in. When they pulled the cowling off, they found that one of the mechanics had put "a little too much" carbon pumice on the spark plugs (to keep them from rusting). As I'd climbed out at full power, the pumice melted and snuffed the engine out.

All in all, the P-51H Mustang was a damn fine fighter. Although it was never able to prove itself in combat, the only reason we stopped flying them was because of the introduction of the jet fighter.

What I wouldn't give to have one more flight in the P-51H Mustang.

Epilogue

THERE I WAS ...
Maj. Roy Ihde, USAF (Ret.)

There I was . . . about to graduate from Aviation Cadets in June 1948, flying as part of a four-ship flight of P-51 Mustangs. I was in the number four (Tail-end Charlie) position and everything was going great; we had just completed a "buzz job" down deep in the Grand Canyon, way below the rim. Because I was somewhat new to this type of flying, I figured I just needed to follow the three P-51s ahead of me and mimic what they did. We followed the canyon for miles before climbing up out of the mile-deep gorge to level off at fifteen thousand feet. We began to do some cloud busting up there, making the tops of the clouds swirl as we sliced through them.

I thought the P-51 handled like a high-performance sports car, one you had to handle with the utmost respect if you didn't want to find yourself in deep trouble before you knew it. I wasn't an experienced fighter pilot yet, just a very young cadet learning the ropes of piloting a steed such as the Mustang. We had been told by our instructors not to have any fear or qualm about flying this famous World War II fighter; they said it was "just another airplane." The magnificent twelve-cylinder, 1,651-horsepower, Packard-built Rolls-Royce Merlin engine was as smooth and dependable as a Swiss watch, as long as it was operated within the limitations spelled out in the operations manual.

The cloud busting seemed rather tame to me, and because this would be one of the last missions the four of us would ever fly together, I decided to get a little more aggressive, like a "good" fighter pilot should be. Just after our four Mustangs pulled up and over a relatively tall cumulus cloud, I decided to perform a lone aileron roll as a coup de grace, before heading for home base. I noted that my airspeed was about 110 miles per hour a little slow, but in my mind I was an accomplished P-51 pilot now, and this roll would be a piece of cake. As I went upside down, I pushed the control stick forward in order to keep the number-three ship in my sight—and that's when all hell broke loose!

My Mustang shook and gyrated, causing my feet to fly off the rudder pedals and strike the underside of the instrument panel. I found myself in an inverted spin. At this point, I was thinking that I was still in complete control, and that I'd just convert this inverted spin into an upright one and then recover. I wrestled the Mustang into the upright position and applied a "normal" upright-spin recovery technique. I was able to stop the spin to the right, but only for a moment, because the Mustang shuddered and quickly broke into an uncontrolled spin to the left. I again applied normal spin-recovery techniques and stopped the spin to the left. The P-51 shuddered again and went into another spin to the right. I was becoming frustrated because the recovery techniques that I'd been taught in the AT-6 Texan were not working for me.

I couldn't stop the Mustang from spinning and had already lost three thousand feet of altitude in the process. I contemplated bailing out, because I felt as though I had lost control of the plane. If I didn't "hit the silk" soon, I would literally bore a hole into the earth below. But I was also concerned with striking the tail if I chose to jump, so I found myself almost literally between a rock and a hard place. With about eight thousand feet of altitude remaining, I heard a voice on the radio: "Roy, take your hands and feet off the controls!" I didn't know or care if it was God or one of my fellow pilots talking; I did what I was told! Without my feet or hand inputs, the P-51 slowly stopped rotating and eventually went into a steep dive—a maneuver any cadet could recover from. I leveled off at six thousand feet above the Arizona landscape and breathed a sigh of relief.

Just before I graduated, a Major George Crist gave me a piece of advice I would never forget.

"Cadet Ihde, any aircraft can be mastered with proper training and with proper respect for it. Treat a P-51 like a lady and treat a lady like a P-51!"

"Yes, sir!" I replied, "I surely will!"

Index